RESORT MANAGEMENT IN EUROPE

Also available from Continuum:

Aronsson: *The Development of Sustainable Tourism*
Godfrey and Clarke: *The Tourism Development Handbook*
Hudson: *Snow Business*
Law: *Urban Tourism*
Anna Leask and Ian Yeoman (eds): *Heritage Visitor Attractions: An Operations Management Perspective*
Ryan (ed.): *The Tourist Experience*
Tribe *et al.*: *Environmental Management for Rural Tourism and Recreation*

Resort Management in Europe

Case Studies and Learning Materials

European Tourism University Partnership

Continuum
London and New York

Continuum

The Tower Building
11 York Road
London SE1 7NX

370 Lexington Avenue
New York
NY 10017-6503

First published in 2000

British Library Cataloguing-in-Publication Data
A catalogue record for this book is available from the British Library.

ISBN 0–8264–4711–2 (hb)
ISBN 0–8264–4712–0 (pb)

Typeset by Paston PrePress, Beccles, Suffolk
Printed and bound in Great Britain by the Cromwell Press, Trowbridge, Wiltshire

Contents

CONTENTS

Illustrations

FIGURES

TABLES

ILLUSTRATIONS

Foreword

AIMS

As tourism studies have become a major university subject over the past dozen years, so teachers and students have recognized a certain number of weaknesses in the learning materials available. These are often of the wrong level, or more oriented towards research than learning. They ignore language acquisition skills, and do not compare the tourism experience in different countries.

Nowhere was this more evident than to the tourism and hospitality departments of the twenty establishments which had built up a network of student exchanges under the European Union's ERASMUS Scheme. As ERASMUS gave way to SOCRATES, with its provision for the production of 'European Modules', the chance was eagerly seized by the twenty partners of what was to become ETUP (European Tourism University Partnership) to strengthen their links still further by using their pan-European expertise to produce the learning materials they all felt were lacking.

Over the three-year duration of SOCRATES I, it was decided to target four major topic areas:

- resort management (publication summer 2000);
- the European legislative framework for tourism (publication spring 2001);
- rural tourism (publication autumn 2000);
- tourism as a force for urban regeneration (publication spring 2001).

These were felt to be areas of major importance in European tourism, while evolving round very different national approaches. As such, they seemed ideal material for drawing out comparisons and contrasts in European practice, which was another of the main aims behind this project.

From the start, it was felt that emphasis should be on the learning objective although in fact each case study is an originally researched piece of work. This in itself illustrates one of ETUP's underlying characteristics, i.e. linking research to teaching. In this respect the following aims have been targeted:

1. Illustrate as fully as possible different European practices, by taking case studies from countries ranging from Scandinavia to the Mediterranean, in order to give future tourism managers a truly European dimension.
2. Concentrate not just on content, but also on pedagogy, by building into each case study a series of exercises to help the student achieve maximum assimilation of the content presented.
3. Integrate language learning exercises, which would both help in the content assimilation aim shown above, and widen the student's knowledge of technical tourism vocabulary in several languages.
4. Make the learning process available to as many publics as possible from traditional teacher-led classroom work to private study or open and distance learning.
5. Include, through the style of exercises proposed, the development of those communication skills which are an essential asset for a tourism professional.
6. Target university students in particular, for whom little learning material is available, whether it be in the field of tourism-applied management concepts or specialized foreign languages.

Following these aims, this work is a collection of case studies meeting a list of criteria decided in common by the group, under the direction of a general coordinator and, for each volume, an editorial board. As such, responsibility for each case study lies in all respects with its author. This excludes all responsibility for ETUP as a whole, the SOCRATES office of the European Union, or any other individual member.

LAYOUT OF THE BOOK

The book is divided into two parts: Part 1 contains the case studies from different countries of the European Union, while Part 2 presents language exercises for students. In Part 1, two of the case studies are presented in parallel translation form: Chapter 7 in French and English, and Chapter 10 in German and English.

ACKNOWLEDGEMENTS

The general coordinator wishes to express his warmest thanks to all contributors.

Further thanks must go to the EU's SOCRATES office, without whose initiative and funding this project would have been impossible, and whose help has provided a constant stimulus.

A final vote of thanks goes in particular to Michel Bauer (Université de Savoie, France) for getting the ball rolling and to the editorial board for this first volume; Tim Bahaire (University of Lincolnshire and Humberside, UK) for the very complete introduction; Jan Bergsma (NHTV, Breda, Holland) and Hans-Dieter Ganter (Fachhochschule Heilbronn, Germany) for their work in editing the material and developing the cross-European perspectives; and Mike Morgan (Bournemouth University, UK) for liaising with the publisher to prepare the text for the book.

Paul Constable

Université de Savoie, France
General Coordinator

The European Tourism University Partnership (ETUP) Members

MEMBERS	CONTACTS
Bournemouth University, UK	Mike Morgan
Christelijke Hogeschool Noord-Nederland, Leewuarden, Holland	Christine Pratley
Dalarna University, Sweden	Solveig Böhn
Dublin Institute of Technology, Ireland	Marc McDonald
E.O.T. Madrid, Spain	Blanca Kraljevic
ESGHT, Universidade do Algarve, Portugal	Cidalia Correia, Paulo Aguas
Fachhochschule für Technik und Wirtschaft, Munich, Germany	Irmela Neu
Haaga Institute, Helsinki, Finland	Nina Vesterinen, Anu Poukka
Heilbronn Fachhochschule, Germany	Hans-Dieter Ganter
Helia Porvoo Polytechnic, Finland	Kaija Lindroth
Nationale Hogeschool voor Toerism en Verker, Breda, Holland	Jan Bergsma, Ariane Portegies, Theo de Haan
Norwegian School of Management, Oslo, Norway	Georg Kamfjord
Technological Educational Institute of Athens, Greece	Antonia Efthymiatou-Poulakou
Technological Educational Institute of Thessalonika, Greece	Thomas Mavrodontis
Universidad de Deusto, Bilbao, Spain	Arantza Arruti
Università degli Studi di Bologna, Rimini, Italy	Giuseppe Vino
Université de Savoie, France	Paul Constable
University of Lincolnshire and Humberside, UK	Tim Bahaire
University of North London, UK	Andrew Holden

Notes on the Contributors

Claudia Almeida is a lecturer in the Tourism Department at the Higher School of Tourism, Hospitality and Business Studies of the University of the Algarve, Portugal. Her research interests are in quality in tourism.

Tim Bahaire is a Senior Lecturer in the Department of Tourism, at the University of Lincolnshire and Humberside, with teaching and research interests in tourism planning and development and cultural and heritage tourism.

Jan Bergsma obtained his first degree in geography at the University of Groningen, The Netherlands. As a lecturer at that university and later at The Netherlands Institute of Tourism and Transport Studies, he taught a number of tourism courses and published several articles on tourism planning issues. Currently he is director of international programmes at the NHTV in Breda.

Solveig Böhn is a member of staff at the School of Transportation and Society, Dalarna University, Sweden. She holds a BA from the University of Lund in Social Sciences. As well as her academic qualifications she has fifteen years' experience of practical tourism development both in Sweden and abroad, both as Director of Tourism at the municipal level of government and as Managing Director of a tourism business in Sweden. She has also worked for tour operators and travel agencies. Solveig is now involved in projects focusing on destination development and environmental issues. She is also Executive Director and Treasurer of the European Chapter of the Travel and Tourism Research Association.

Antonia Efthymiatou-Poulakou, *docteur d'État* of the Law Faculty of the University Paris I, is Professor and Head of Department of Tourist Enterprises of the TEI of Athens. She also practises law in Athens.

Martin Elliott-White is presently a Senior Lecturer in the Department of Tourism, the University of Lincolnshire and Humberside, with teaching and research interests in urban tourism policy planning and development and the application of information technology in tourism.

Ana Ferreira is an Assistant Professor in the Tourism Department at the Higher School of Tourism, Hospitality and Business Studies of the University of the Algarve, Portugal. Her main interests are in urban tourism.

Hans-Dieter Ganter has been a Professor of International Tourism Management at Fachhochschule, Heilbronn since 1995. His major publications in English are *Managing in Britain and Germany* (London, 1993) and *Information Technology in the Service Sector* (Oxford, 1987).

Manuela Guerreiro is a lecturer in the Marketing Department at the Higher School of Tourism, Hospitality and Business Studies of the University of the Algarve, Portugal. Her main research interests are in promotional policy.

Theo de Haan is head of the Department of International Tourism Management and Consultancy of the NHTV (Netherlands Institute of Tourism and Transport Studies) in Breda, The Netherlands. He has published on tourist-historic cities, resorts and resort regions as well as on trends in tourism developments. His main interests lie in the field of tourism planning and development, especially development and change in mass tourism destinations in Southern Europe and South East Asia.

Andrew Holden is a member of the Centre for Leisure and Tourism Studies (CELTS) at the University of North London. He specializes in issues connected with the interaction between tourism and the environment. He is co-author of *Tourism: A New Perspective* (Prentice Hall, 1996) and has a new book *Tourism and the Environment* to be published by Routledge in 2000.

Evangelos P. Karavangelis is an Associate Professor at the Technological Educational Institute of Thessaloniki, Greece.

Fotis Kilipiris is an Associate Professor at the Technological Educational Institute of Thessaloniki, Greece.

Kaija Lindroth is a lecturer in Tourism at Helsinki Business Polytechnic in Porvoo. Her interests include impact studies and heritage tourism.

Thomas Mavrodontis is a Professor at the Technological Educational Institute of Thessaloniki, Greece.

Michael Morgan is Senior Lecturer in Tourism and Leisure Marketing in the School of Service Industries at Bournemouth University and course leader of the MA European Tourism Management programme. His publications include *Marketing for Leisure and Tourism* (Prentice Hall, 1996).

Alexandra Rodrigues is a lecturer in the Tourism Department at the Higher School of Tourism, Hospitality and Business Studies of the University of the Algarve, Portugal. Her research interests are in cultural tourism.

Celia Veiga is an Assistant Professor in the Marketing Department at the Higher School of Tourism, Hospitality and Business Studies of the University of the Algarve, Portugal. Her main interests are in consumer behaviour.

Nina Vesterinen is the Programme Director and a lecturer in tourism management at Haaga Institute, Helsinki, Finland. Her research interests are in the socio-cultural aspects of tourism development.

CONTRIBUTORS TO THE LANGUAGE EXERCISES

Paul Constable is currently Director of the Faculty of Tourism and Hospitality Management Studies at the Université de Savoie, Chambéry, France. He is the general co-ordinator of the SOCRATES-funded European Module which has brought together twenty universities from twelve countries to produce the series Learning Materials for Tourism Management in Europe, of which the present volume is an example. He specializes in teaching English as a foreign language in the tourism and leisure fields.

Cidalia Correia is Vice-President of the Higher School of Tourism, Hospitality and Business Studies of the University of the Algarve, Portugal, and Assistant Professor in the Language Department teaching English as a foreign language to leisure and tourism students.

Blanca Kraljevic is head of the Department of Computing applied to Tourism at the Escuela Oficiale de Turismo, Madrid, and course leader of the MA European Tourism Management.

Irmela Neu is Professor of Spanish and co-ordinator of an international exchange programme at the Fachhochschule Munich. She is a member of the German Commission for UNESCO and an expert on intercultural tourism.

Christine Pratley is a French teacher at the Leisure Management School of CHNN Leeuwarden in The Netherlands. Her specialism is the use of communications skills in the learning of French applied to the leisure and tourism industries.

Kate Torkington is Assistant Professor in the Language Department and Socrates Exchange Programme Co-ordinator at the Higher School of Tourism, Hospitality and Business Studies of the University of the Algarve, Portugal.

Introduction

This collection of case studies of tourism resorts and/or destinations throughout Europe, from Scandinavia to Greece, focuses upon management issues. The management focus may be either public or private sector and may include examples of co-operation between the public and private sectors. It is important to emphasize at the outset that besides being located in different European countries, the resort case studies are often very different in tourism context. Because of these differences the resorts include a wide variety of management styles and perspectives.

RATIONALE

Europe represents a diversity of approaches to the problems and solutions of resort and/or destination management. This collection of case studies is representative of those that exist within higher education in different European countries with regard to resort and/or destination management.

The definition of the case studies is intentionally wide to accommodate the different definitions of case study in the contributing European countries. A resort therefore, for the purposes of this collection, means an open system from a village to a region and from a hotel to a skiing centre. The case studies are intentionally short, focused and presented in a standard way so as to provide the student with clear learning outcomes. This format actively encourages the students to develop further their research of individual case studies.

WHY UNDERTAKE COMPARATIVE TOURISM STUDY?

In this Introduction we wish to explore how the tourism case studies contained in this volume might offer another way of understanding tourism resort management by using the comparative method. We will first define the comparative method and then suggest ways such a methodology might be a valuable tool for the study of tourism.

We then describe a methodology for comparative studies. Finally we point up a few of the major problems of the comparative method in tourism study.

Aristotle was the first recorded person to use the comparative method. He gathered data on the political constitutions of over 100 city states of the ancient world before developing his own political philosophy. In modern times the comparative method as a systematic study has developed over the past 35 years and it still possesses many of the characteristics first identified by the ancient Greeks. Modern comparative work is the study of how, why and to what effect different countries pursue particular courses of action or inaction.

When we look at how governments in different European countries – the United Kingdom, Sweden and France – are essentially centralized unitary states, we see that the regions have little power apart from central government. Other countries such as Germany and Spain have various degrees of federalism; their regions have real power over some areas of policy, and are to that extent independent of central government.

A comparative study might pose the question of how a country's different policy-making structures can affect public policy decisions. For example, comparative tourism studies might focus upon an investigation of different human resource management styles. Who are the the actors involved in tourism human resource management and whose interests do they represent? Who gains and who loses from their activities? And, finally, what are the results or outcomes, both intended and unintended, of different human resource management styles in different countries? However, the reasons why different countries follow different courses of action is much more complex and will depend upon a range of factors unique to that country (historical, social, economic etc.).

It is important, therefore, when conducting comparative studies, to start with an examination of the historical roots of tourism development in the countries being compared. Factors may be observed which promote convergence in resort management styles in European countries, i.e. the drive for sustainability through the adoption of Agenda 21. On the other hand, while similarities may be observed in resort management styles in different European countries, there are also great differences (or divergence). For example, in Scandinavia the tradition of social democracy has led to the development of somewhat unique resort management styles, represented in attitudes to the environment, promoting both access and care and the development of co-operative business structures.

From ancient philosophers such as Aristotle comes the idea that knowledge of the self is gained through knowledge of others. Thus comparative study will potentially enable us to acquire deeper knowledge and understanding of our own country. We are able to find plenty of information on resort management, within our own country but this will inevitably be culture-bound. For example, a study of management styles in the UK may reveal styles which do not allow for much consultation with the workforce or other actors. On the other hand, in Denmark, more co-operative management styles may be part of their business culture.

Comparative studies may also be of interest to those involved in tourism policy formulation. Studying other countries offers insights into the advantages and disadvantages of different policy options. For example, the public ownership of development land in Sweden takes land speculation out of the tourism resort development process.

It has been suggested that comparative study involves, as its basic objective, the identification of the extent to which countries differ or are similar and why this should be so. In the past, the chief objective of comparative studies was upon convergence and similarity between countries. Certainly, in tourism research the search for best practice has led to comparative study stressing convergence. However, alternative approaches to comparative work which stress divergence have also been developed and are proving of no less value than those produced by studies of convergence. Summing up the three reasons for doing comparative study in tourism following Heidenheimer:

- To achieve understanding that will lead to the design of better policies. Particularly by isolating those factors which are unique to a country from those which may be of general relevance to other countries, we can adopt strategies from other countries to develop better practice in our own country. So one of the first objectives of comparative tourism study is to improve tourism resort management policy and practice.
- A second objective of comparative tourism study is to advance tourism theory.
- Finally, because we live in a Europe where convergence particularly by members of the European Union seems set to continue, management systems in one country will interact with management systems in our country.

Other concerns such as the environment cannot make much progress without international co-operation.

A final objective of comparative study will be to bring about harmonization in European resort management policy and practice while retaining the uniqueness of individual resorts.

In conclusion, we might note that, instead of speculating on what might improve tourism management in our country, by investigating other countries we can study 'real-life' examples and evaluate best practice.

At present there is much discussion of terms such as globalization and harmonization, especially within the European Union. Comparative studies are central to understanding these international changes. Comparatives studies are of undoubted value. However, one major difficulty is the paucity of comparable data. It is one of the aims of this book to remedy this in some small way.

HOW THE COLLECTION OF MATERIALS IS TO BE USED

What is a case study? Because of the wide variety of possible definitions of case study the intention here is to formulate a wide definition that can encompass practice in the various countries and at the same time encapsulate the contributions contained within this collection. Accordingly, for the purposes of this collection, my definition is as follows:

> a case study is a focused examination of tourism management and related issues at locations in Europe that have been developed for tourist visitation or are in receipt of tourist visitation.

The case studies may be used to do the following:

- to promote discussion of 'what', 'how' and 'why' and maybe 'so what' questions;
- to focus one or two teaching sessions;
- for comparative research, aiming to bring out convergence or divergence in practice;
- to test theoretical perspectives: for example, the tourist area life-cycle; the tourist beach model, Jung's model of village transformation; Miossec's theory of how tourist areas may develop; and
- to provide a student resource book for independent study; the short bibliographies attached to most of the case studies will assist students in further research.

Tourism perspectives found in the case studies include:

- human resource management;
- product development;
- responses to regional comparative decline or peripherality;
- environmental/ecological sustainability issues;
- economic resource management; and
- community action and participation.

EXERCISES

1. (a) Outline the different approaches to regeneration/renewal/rehabilitation of at least three of the resorts identified in the book of case studies.
    (b) Give reasons for the different approaches identified.
2. Analyse the approach taken in ONE of the case studies to either
    (a) marketing, or (b) product development.
3. (a) What problems does management face in multifunctional resorts, e.g. Faro?

(b) What techniques have management developed to deal with the problems of multifunctional resorts?

(c) Using a named example of a multifunctional resort from your own country, identify how far the management techniques are transferable.

4. (a) How far do the relationships you have identified contribute to successful resort management, and how far could they contribute to successful resort management where public–private sector partnerships do not exist?

5. (a) Outline the different interpretations of the built heritage by analysing the following case studies: Plaka, Faro.

(b) What problems and solutions have management of these built heritage resorts developed for their different visitor markets?

ACKNOWLEDGEMENTS

I would like to recognize the assistance of my colleagues at the University of Lincolnshire and Humberside for helpful criticism and ideas on earlier drafts of this Introduction.

REFERENCES

Heidenheimer, A. J. (1990 3rd edn) *Comparative Public Policy.*

Miossec, J. M. (1976) 'Elements pour une theorie de l'espace touristique'. *Les Cahiers du Tourisme*, C-36, CHET: Aix-en-Provence.

Miossec, J. M. (1977) 'Une modele de l'espace geographique', **6**(1), 41–8.

Tim Bahaire
University of Lincolnshire and Humberside

PART 1

CASE STUDIES

CHAPTER 1

Downhill Skiing, Cairngorm Mountains, Scotland

Issues in development and management of high impact tourism in environmentally vulnerable areas

Andrew Holden

Aim
The main aim of this case study is to make students aware of the development and management issues of tourism in environments.

Keywords
mountain environments; economic opportunities; physical impacts; skiing activities; development; ethics

Summary
The development of activity tourism such as downhill skiing in physically vulnerable areas raises questions about its suitability to mountain environments. Yet the development of skiing in the Cairngorm area in the Highlands of Scotland provides economic opportunities for local people to improve their standard of living in an area where alternative development opportunities are limited. Unfortunately the development of skiing at Cairngorm and other mountainous areas is now known to have negative consequences for the physical environment. Therefore, the development of downhill skiing raises ethical questions about how humans interact with the environment and also questions the role of skiing in a sustainable future for the Cairngorms or other mountainous areas.

The student target groups are students of planning and development within the areas of tourism, geography, and environmental studies.

Learning outcomes
To make students do the following:

- understand the economic and social dependency of rural areas with few other development options upon tourism;
- be aware of the environmental impacts that can be introduced into an ecosystem by tourism development;

- consider different interpretations of the meaning of 'sustainable development';
- consider the ethics of development issues.

Exercise
One student group should take on the role of a company favouring ski development and explain the benefits of ski development to rural areas. Another group should represent opposition to any proposed scheme explaining why they are opposed to ski development. A third group should be neutral judges, listening to the arguments of both sides, and deciding whether ski development should be permitted or not.

Discussions topics
- What are the economic and social benefits that development of an activity such as skiing could bring to a rural area that has few other economic development options?
- Is it ethically acceptable to develop downhill skiing in an area which has unique flora and fauna and is environmentally sensitive? For instance, if people enjoy downhill skiing and the area benefits economically, is it important if a plant or bird species becomes extinct as a result of the development of skiing?
- How could downhill skiing be made more ecologically sustainable (i.e. how could the negative environmental impacts of skiing be reduced)? Thought should be given to aspects such as codes of behaviour and marketing as well as technical solutions.
- Is it right to use large amounts of money to support very marginal industries? To what extent can downhill skiing be categorized as an 'industry'? Should the money be used instead towards the employment of local people in conservation projects, for example?
- Thinking of new sectors of the tourism market, are there other kinds of tourism that should be developed to replace skiing? If so, why?

THE CAIRNGORM SKI AREA

Situation: the ski area is one of five ski areas in Scotland as shown in Table 1.1. Cairngorm was the first ski area to be developed in Scotland as part of a regional development policy aimed at securing economic and social benefits for the political region of Badenoch and Strathspey. Today tourism (of which skiing is a key component) is estimated to provide 70 per cent of the region's employment. Winter tourism also counteracts the problem of seasonal employment endemic in the tourism industry.

The area is a very marginal ski area. It is regularly affected by high winds (which close the chairlifts) and has unpredictable snowfall. These factors influence the number of skiers that arrive at the ski area at Cairngorm. The number of arrivals between 1980–81 and 1997–98 is shown in Table 1.2. Peak visitation was reached at the end of the 1980s. Since then there has been a decline in skiers and this is

Table 1.1: History and characteristics of the ski areas in Scotland.

Name	Location	Established (First lift)	Uplift capacity/hour (Numbers of skiers)	Maximum vertical descent in metres
Cairngorm	9 miles east of Aviemore	1961	12,043	620
Lecht	4 miles east of Tomintoul	1975	8,500	230
Glencoe	12 miles east of Ballacluish	1956	4,300	860
Nevis Range	4 miles east of Fort William	1989	9,600	620
Glenshee	8 miles south of Braemar	1950	18,500	500

Table 1.2: Number of skier arrivals at Cairngorm 1980–81 to 1997–98.

Year	Winter visitors	Days skiing	Ratio of no. of winter visitors: no. of days skiing
1980–81	189,000	120	1,575
1981–82	277,000	151	1,503
1982–83	289,000	176	1,642
1983–84	292,000	133	2,195
1984–85	319,000	145	2,200
1985–86	348,000	157	2,216
1986–87	363,000	156	2,326
1987–88	391,000	147	2,659
1988–89	237,000	84	2,821
1989–90	225,000	122	1,844
1990–91	299,000	174	1,718
1991–92	65,000	84	773
1992–93	195,000	126	1,547
1993–94	214,000	168	1,274
1994–95	211,000	132	1,598
1995–96	187,000	119	1,571
1996–97	96,500	101	955
1997–98	75,067	60	1,252

Source: Cairngorm Chairlift Company

attributed to the economic recession at the beginning of the 1990s, poor snow conditions during the decade, and lack of 'product development' e.g. a new lift system.

CONTROVERSY OVER SKI DEVELOPMENT

Although important to the economy of the region (by providing direct employment and expenditure on local services), the development of skiing at Cairngorm is controversial because of the environmental impacts that it has caused. The area is

Table 1.3 Environmental impacts of ski development at Cairngorm.

Activity	Consequence
Piste preparation – removal of vegetation and boulders to allow for snow accumulation	Ecosystem damage; loss of arctic–alpine vegetation Loss of aesthetic quality Less water retention because of reduced vegetation – increased flash flooding Fewer insects because of vegetation removal, subsequently less food for birds
Lift installation	Destruction of the natural vegetation and fauna Native birds such as the ptarmigan and grouse killed by flying into cable wires Visual intrusion onto the landscape which because of the height and lack of tree cover makes them very visually intrusive
Littering left by skiers and other visitors who use the lifts in the summer time	Attracts predatory animals such as foxes and crows which has led to a decline in native bird species Aesthetic pollution of a remote wilderness area
Activity of skiing	Skiing off-piste disturbs animals and birds Skiing on low snow levels means protruding vegetation is damaged
Infrastructure – road to car parks for chairlifts; cafes and ski hire shops on the mountainside	Previous wilderness area had a road built through it to bring skiers to the mountainside Aesthetic pollution of a transformed mountainside

characterized by an Arctic–Alpine fauna and flora, containing many species of birds and vegetation (such as the ptarmigan and dotterel) that are unique in the United Kingdom. The environmental impacts that have resulted from the development of skiing at Cairngorm are summarized in Table 1.3. Owing to these environmental impacts any plans to extend the ski area are highly controversial and meet with opposition from conservation-based non-governmental organizations (NGOs) such as the World Wildlife Fund for Nature (WWF) and the Royal Society for the Protection of Birds (RSPB).

However, the Cairngorm Chairlift Company believe they need to make the ski area facilities competitive with other ski areas, including ones in mainland Europe. Hence, there is a need for 'product development'. The latest proposal is the development of a funicular up the mountainside to replace the main chairlifts at a cost of approximately £16 million. Approximately £12 million will come from public sources, £9.4 million from Highlands and Islands Enterprise and £2.7 million has been applied for from the European Commission.

The scheme has been opposed from conservation groups on the basis of incurring extra environmental damage and the use of public resources or money to support an 'industry' whose success is highly dependent on weather conditions. However, the majority of local people are in favour of the scheme because of the employment opportunites and extra expenditure it will bring to the area. Many regard the WWF and RSPB as outsiders who are trying to stop economic development to protect the environment.

SUGGESTED READING

Key article on the concept of sustainable tourism

Hunter, C. (1996) 'Sustainable tourism as an adaptive paradigm'. *Annals of Tourism Research*, **24**(4), 850–67.

Key reading on the environmental impacts of tourism

Jenner, P. and Smith, C. (1992) *The Tourism Industry and the Environment*. Special Report no. 2453. London: Economist Intelligence Unit.

Key readings on environmental management

Kaltenborn, B. P. (1996) 'Tourism in Svalbard: planned management or the art of stumbling through?', in M. F. Price (ed.) *People and Tourism in Fragile Environments*. Chichester: John Wiley & Sons, Chapter 6, pp. 89–108.

Todd, E. S. and Williams, E. P. (1996) 'Environmental management system framework for ski areas'. *Journal of Sustainable Tourism*, **4**(3), 147–73.

World Tourism Organization (1993) *Sustainable Tourism Development: Guide for Local Planners*. Madrid: World Tourism Organization.

CHAPTER 2

The Restoration of Plaka

Antonia Efthymiatou–Poulakou

Aim

The aim of this case study is to analyse the management of an ancient but popular tourist part of a city in a traffic-bedevilled capital.

Keywords

capital's historic centre; monumental interest; traditional urban pattern; building boom; transformation; traffic; pollution; financial interest; public reaction to the destruction; area protection and preservation as living city quarter; pedestrianization; monuments to be conserved; active participation of the inhabitants

Summary

Plaka is the oldest and best-known quarter of Athens. It has always been inhabited and there have been periods in the city's history when Plaka constituted Athens itself. By reason of its particular position Plaka forms an extensive monumental record of the civilization and history of the people who lived there during each historical period. Monuments reflecting all epochs in Greek history can be found there. This district continues to be inhabited and forms a lively and much frequented section of modern Athens.

Around 1950 some serious pressures on the district appeared, due to many factors such as the building boom of Athens, the sharp increase in the number of motor cars, etc. Thus Plaka has been gradually transformed functionally, architecturally and as far as town planning is concerned, but to its detriment. The conditions that caused this transformation reached their climax in the mid-1970s when a wave of public reaction rose and pressed the government to take measures in order to solve the problems and save Plaka.

This case study provides some information on the measures and interventions that have been proposed by study groups and subsequently realized to a great extent, in order to restore the historic character of the area, to prevent any further deterioration and transform it into a tourist attraction for Athenians and visitors.

Learning outcomes

Strictly speaking, Athens cannot be considered a resort. Nevertheless, it is a city where a form of tourism, cultural tourism, could be highly developed under certain circumstances. During the last decades, fewer and fewer tourists have visited Athens, preferring other Greek destinations, mainly the islands. This is partly due to some relatively recent problems of the city, such as air pollution and the chaotic traffic, which makes it more difficult to reach the cultural attractions. Among the measures taken in order to render the city more appealing to its inhabitants as well as the tourists are some projects destined to 'connect' the present to the past. Hence our choice of a case study for the management of places, that might attract a considerable number of tourists.

After working through this case study students will have looked at a clear example of the following:

- the possibility of management of places which are rich in history but smothered by the mushroom development of cities (urbanization) by time and development;
- how tourism can actually upgrade an urban area as well as the environment instead of degrading and causing environmental problems;
- how this is only possible by thorough reorganization, careful management with respect for the environment, the permanent inhabitants as well as the cultural heritage;
- how careful planning of similar areas (ramps, bridges, etc.) can facilitate the guides, provide access for viewing by pedestrians and motorized traffic without hindering the day-to-day activities of the permanent inhabitants

When examining this case study, students will be fascinated by the way organization, management and planning can offer the opportunity to visitors to see a mixture of different areas in a limited space of a very densely populated city, i.e. they can imagine visitors walking from one area to the other without any disruptions and imagine the work of a guide or tour leader during this sightseeing visit.

Discussion topics
- What, if anything, does the name 'Plaka' mean to you?
- Do you think that the traditional elements of an area should be maintained?
- In your opinion, are the pressures that appeared in Plaka after 1950 common?
- Give an example of similar effects on the evolution of an area in the last decade.
- Do you think that an archaeological site should be preserved as such or transformed into a living city?
- Are you in favour of the pedestrianization of some areas within a city or not? Why?
- Do you think that the inhabitants of an area should be asked for their opinion when a transformation of this area is planned?

INTRODUCTION

The Plaka area, the oldest and best-known quarter of Athens, now forms what could be described as the inner core of the capital's historic centre. It is, in any case, a district very closely associated with the history of Athens since it has continually been inhabited from Neolithic times to the present day and, in the darkest moments of the city's history, the area known today as Plaka constituted Athens itself.[1]

The Plaka area embraces the northern and the eastern sides of the rock of the Acropolis in a semi-circular belt approximately one kilometre long by an average breadth of 350 metres. To the north and to the east its boundaries touch the commercial and administrative centre of Athens while, to the west, it stretches as far as the limits of the site of the ancient Athenian Agora, an area which also formed part of the historic centre of Athens but was sacrificed for the sake of evacuations undertaken from 1931 onwards by the American School of Classical Studies. The Plaka district, by reason of the particular position it occupies in the Athens area, obviously forms an extensive monumental record of the civilization and history of the people who lived there during each historical period. It therefore presents exceptional monumental interest because one can find in it monuments reflecting all epochs in Greek history.

Indeed, it is in Plaka that the form and the scale of the traditional urban pattern have been preserved. These are factors directly related to the topography of the district and are consequently capable, on their own, of giving the area its peculiar atmosphere of an historic core and of justifying its major importance. Also, it has been ascertained that the present streets of Plaka such as Adrianou Street and Tripodon Street, are located exactly on the tracks of the ancient streets.[2] Finally, it has to be stressed that all this occurs in a district which continues to be inhabited and forms a lively and much frequented section of modern Athens, a district much beloved of all Athenians.

THE PROBLEM OF PLAKA

Plaka developed and assumed its present form during the hundred years between Athens being proclaimed the capital of the modern Greek State and the eve of the outbreak of the Second World War. The slow growth rate of those years and the resulting gradual assimilation of the new elements helped to produce an aesthetic entity which was fairly uniform and homogeneous, especially as regards the town planning form and the architectural scale.

On the other hand, the survival of traditional elements in the house types, such as the inner courtyard and the glazed corridors as well as the presence of stylistic elements of Neo-classical architecture, blended with the monuments of various periods which remained embodied in this newer aesthetic entity. All this endowed Plaka with its unique atmosphere and the character of an historic core of Athens and of a distinctive central residential and light industrial area, coupled with handicrafts and traditional form of entertainment in its small taverns.

The first serious pressures from without appeared after 1950 and these were due mainly to the following:

- the building boom in Athens which came as the result of a sharp increase in the population of the capital;

- the increasing needs of the commercial and administrative centre of Athens which touches on the boundaries of Plaka, in combination with the post-war building boom;
- the sharp increase in the number of motor cars and the resulting traffic intensification; and
- the equally brisk increase in tourism and the number of visitors for whom Plaka is in itself one of the main attractions of Athens and also a quarter which offers pedestrian access to the Acropolis.

TRANSFORMATION OF PLAKA

Under these combined pressures, Plaka gradually began to be transformed in three main ways:

1. Functional transformation.
2. Town planning transformation.
3. Architectural transformation.

Functional transformation

The home, the artisan's workshop, handicrafts and the traditional form of entertainment, began to give way to mass, organized tourist entertainment, and trade in tourist gift shops and services. These new conditions forced a large proportion of the residents to move out and this resulted in the dissolution of the social structure of the district. Suffice it to say that, of the 17,000 inhabitants of Plaka in 1961, only 4500 remained in 1974, while, by contrast, 200 places for entertaining 20,000 customers were found there! During the same period, 7,800 persons were employed in Plaka.[3] Thus, the old historic quarter lost its traditional and functional composition and the individuality which stemmed from it and it was transformed into a section of the centre of Athens which came to life only at night while remaining almost dead in the daytime.

Town planning transformation

Plaka's urban pattern, adapted to the particular natural surroundings through the processes already described and destined mainly to serve the needs of pedestrians, was forced under the new conditions to accept the traffic caused by thousands of motor vehicles and to provide parking spaces for many of them. This meant that pedestrians in the area were at a disadvantage while, at the same time, noise and atmospheric pollution increased. These factors downgraded the environment and increased the tendency of the inhabitants to move out.

On the other hand, the need for additional parking spaces had accelerated the demolition of old houses whose sites were used as open-air car parks, and it also caused many other available spaces to serve as legal or illegal parking lots. What was even worse, motor cars required the nature of the streets to be changed in order to render their movement easier.

Architectural transformation

Changes in the functions of the Plaka district, the modest and sometimes poor quality of the buildings themselves, natural wear and tear through ageing and lack of proper maintenance and also the fact of their having been put to uses incompatible with their original layout and scale, have been the principal factors in the transformation of the architectural form of Plaka. To these factors must be added the replacement of a considerable number of buildings during the years between the two World Wars and even more so during the post-war building boom throughout Greece but especially in Athens. Encroachment on the architectural form of Plaka is evident in the section which borders onto the commercial and administrative centre of Athens which, as stated above, is the one that feels the greatest need for expansion and exerts the greatest pressure on Plaka.

These conditions, which developed through a process of evolution starting in the mid-1950s and attained their climax in the mid-1970s, ended up by creating new strong financial interests on the one hand and, on the other, by provoking an ever-increasing consciousness of the growing extent of the destruction of Plaka. This feeling manifested itself in a rising wave of public reaction. The inhabitants, various learned institutions, the daily press and periodicals have all expressed frequent and strong protests over a number of years concerning the fate of Plaka and have called for measures on behalf of the government to put an end to the problem and save Plaka.

Periods which were marked by inertia on the part of the State gave rise to a fresh wave of protests on the part of Plaka residents and public opinion generally. There were even protests from abroad about growing tourist commercialization of the district, its progressive disfiguration and vulgarization and the more frequent occurrence of anti-social incidents within its boundaries.

THE STUDY OF THE 'OLD CITY OF ATHENS'

The first serious discussions concerning the problem of Plaka took place in the Athens Municipality in 1964. It was a period when another danger was threatening Plaka. This was a proposal that the entire area should be expropriated and demolished to make way for the completion of excavations aimed at bringing to light the ruins of ancient Athens; the entire site was to be turned into an archaeological park. This, of course, was not a new threat but it reappeared at that time, supported by noteworthy personalities who regarded it as a duty owed by modern to ancient Greece. It seems almost certain that this was averted thanks only to the lack of funds for such an immense undertaking and also because of the sharp reaction on the part of many members of professions and the inhabitants of Plaka themselves.

Some years later, towards the end of 1972, the Ministry of Public Works, at that time responsible for area planning in Athens, decided to entrust a group of professionals with the task of compiling a study of this overall problem which became known as the 'study of the Old City of Athens'. This main objective caused the study group to set down certain basic principles which can be summarized as follows:

- As a fundamental requirement, it was agreed that there should be protection and preservation of the whole of Plaka, as it was regarded as a uniform and indivisible entity.
- It was also laid down that Plaka should be maintained as a living city quarter, all thought of preserving it as a 'museum piece' or a 'monument' deprived of the presence of modern life was ruled out.
- It was established that the meaning of area protection should be made to include, without any doubt whatever, protection of its functional structure while recognizing the need to introduce the conveniences of modern living.
- It was also established that protection and conservation of the district would have to take place within the framework of existing Greek legislation.

STUDY OF THE MEANS OF IMPLEMENTATION AND STRATEGY OF INTERVENTION

The study group proposed a specific strategy which would have two aims:

1. To ensure the broadest possible consensus for the measures and to minimize possible reaction to them.
2. To provide opportunities for the adoption of general measures of immediate effect while also making possible intervention by stages which, through a long-term programme, could lead to the desired final result.

Problems and solutions

The first problem was that of the exact boundaries of today's Plaka. A second very important step was the legal coverage of the existing pattern of the streets of Plaka which would protect the district from any future alterations and would preserve its urban form as it has been handed down to us. As to the nature and extent of intervention thought necessary, the first to be studied and implemented was the pedestrianization of a large number of Plaka streets in order to restrict motor traffic only to that essential in servicing the district's needs. The success of this measure was critical. Today, most of Plaka's streets have been pedestrianized. This means that its narrow and irregular streets have regained their original functional purpose, their use by motor vehicles has been drastically cut, and so have noise and pollution. The district's urban pattern, which, indeed, forms a 'monument to be conserved' can once again function properly to its full capacity and can give the inhabitants and the pedestrians a genuine picture of the space and scale of Plaka. Special regulations lay down the hours during which shops and residences can receive supplies, and the exceptions for emergencies and car parking at appointed locations by special permits for the area's inhabitants.

It was thought necessary to complement the fundamental functional change brought about to Plaka streets by pedestrianization with a series of works which, on the one hand, would emphasize this change while, on the other, would restore the streets' earlier appearance.

Measures taken

A great number of works have been planned and have been executed by stages. They include construction, replacement or improvement of the underground service networks as well as resurfacing streets and pavements. In this connection, it has to be stated that in many parts of Plaka the services are very old or even non-existent. Therefore, there has been renovation of water supply, drainage, electricity, town gas and telephones.

Finally, arrangements have been made for the laying of an underground TV central antenna cable in order to abolish the forest of TV antennae protruding from rooftops and terraces. As for the surfaces of streets, pavements and small squares, use is being made of natural stone slabs such as were always used for this purpose in Plaka – samples of this older form of paving have survived to this day in certain parts of Plaka. All street lighting standards are also being replaced with exact replicas of the old lamps that used to exist there. The final aim is the removal of all overhead electric lighting wiring. Naturally, the ultimate object is to restore the character and quality of Plaka by using elements historically connected with it and not to have new ones intruding.

The measures described are, of course, of a decisive nature in the drive to restore to the area its historic character and to prevent any further disfiguration but they are insufficient. The study group therefore went ahead with the drafting of a series of legislative measures aimed at further improvement and control of the image of the district and at defining the general framework within which it might evolve in future.

Obviously, any programme involving the conservation of Plaka but, at the same time, ensuring its balanced functional evolution and its re-establishment in the life of Athens as a whole – from which the mass operation of tourist entertainment had almost cut it off – had to be a complicated and ever-adjustable programme. Studies of the implementation of various works often have to be revised in practice, when, for example, digging for the construction of underground services brings to light important archaeological finds, such as occurred with work being carried out in St Katherine's Square. Such finds have to be investigated. The same occurred in the nearby Square of Lysicrates. It is equally obvious that there will be a time lapse before the definite results of these measures can become apparent.

However, already many changes have been brought about. Plaka streets are quieter, more beautiful and enjoyable for the pedestrians who can stroll their length free of the constant fear of motor cars. Allowing for the peculiar conditions encountered in the area, reconstruction of the underground services is going ahead at a satisfactory pace. Many private houses have already been repaired and others are now under repair. The trend towards a return to the quarter's old character is now quite strongly evident, although the loudspeakers blasting from numerous places of entertainment still create a noise problem which provokes complaints.

Active participation by the inhabitants in this conservation project is an important result. Their various associations keep a close eye on the progress of the work, and they offer advice and criticism which is constructive and helpful.

NOTES

1.   The main source of this case study is D. A. Zivas (1983) *The Saving of Plaka*. Athens: Monumentum (ICOMOS).
2.   J. Travlos (1960) *Townplanning Evolution of Athens*. Athens: J. Travlos, 1f, p. 71.
3.   For additional data, refer to D. A. Zivas (1980) 'The future of the old sector of the city of Athens', in D. Appleyard (ed.) *Conservation of European Cities*. Boston: MIT Press, pp. 154–63.

SUGGESTED READING

Altman, I. and Zube, E. H. (eds) (1989) 'Public places and spaces', in *Human Behaviour and Environment (Advances in Theory and Research*, vol. 10). New York: and London: Plenum Press, p. 316.
Breitling, P. (1975) *Historische Städte, Städte für Morge*. Deutsches Nationalkomitee für das Europäische Denkmalschutzjahr, Deutsche UNESCO-Kommission.
Conservation of the Architectural Heritage in the Context of Urban and Regional Planning (1975) Congress on the European Architectural Heritage, Amsterdam, 21–5, October 1975. Biornstad Margareta: Council of Europe.
Fazio, M. (1995) 'La tutela dei Centri Storici', *Italia Nostra*, Bollettino 324.
Feilden, B. M. and Jokilehto, J. (1993) 'Guide de Gestion des Sites du Patrimoine Culturel Mondial'. Rome: ICCROM.
Fitch, J. M. (1982) *Historic Preservation: Curatorial Management of the Built World*. McGraw-Hill Book Company. (Third edn 1995, University Press of Virginia, Charlottesville and London.)
Gazzola, P. (1975) *The Past in the Future*. Faculty of Architecture, University of Rome, Rome: ICCROM.
Larkham, P. J. (1996) *Conservation and the City*. London and New York: Routledge.
Papageorgiou, A. (1971) *Integration Urbaine*. Paris: Vincent, Fréal et Cie.
Papageorgiou, A. (1994) *Hauptstadt Athen*. Berlin: Deutscher Kunstverlag.
UNESCO (1972) *Preserving and Restoring Monuments and Historic Buildings*. Paris: UNESCO.

CHAPTER 3

The Case of Kaunas

Kaija Lindroth

Aim

This case study is about tourism in Kaunas, Lithuania. It aims to present the situation which faced the tourism industry of the country after the transition from a Soviet Republic to an independent nation. Students are invited to consider the challenges of planning and developing tourism in this new situation.

Keywords

transition economy; tourism planning and development; privatization; reorganization; search for new markets

Summary

After 50 years of Soviet rule Lithuania is independent again, together with the two other Baltic countries Estonia and Latvia. During the Soviet period the tourism industry was strictly in the hands of the state, and heavily centralized. Today the tourism industry is seen as one of the economic alternatives to generate foreign currency, to create jobs and thus add to the general well-being of the citizens.

However, there are many problems to be solved. On the one hand there are a lot of entrepreneurs eager to take speedy action to develop tourism services to meet the expectations of Western customers. On the other, the state is slow to adapt, struggling with a plethora of structural problems and inadequate resources to implement all the necessary reforms that would make the task of entrepreneurs easier. Local decision-makers seldom have the expertise to plan and develop tourism in an efficient and innovative way. Also co-operation between the different actors in the field is something still to be desired.

During the Soviet era Lithuanian resorts received a continuous flow of Russian tourists without any promotional effort. With the collapse of the Soviet system this came to an end and the country was faced with the serious problem of finding new customers to replace the Russian clients who had disappeared. After newly won independence curious Western tourists did turn up in quite large numbers but after the first years of interest the visitor numbers have started to go down. The organizations involved in developing tourism in Lithuania are aware of the expectations of Western tourists as well as of the existing problems but have been rather slow in taking adequate action.

This case study describes the situation in Lithuania using the city of Kaunas as an example to illustrate the problems of developing tourism industry in a new situation brought about by a sudden change in external circumstances.

Learning outcomes

The case study gives Western European tourism students an introduction to a completely different economic environment as well as helping them understand the problems of the former Soviet states now aiming at membership of the European Union.

The students should be able to identify the structural problems, to develop a critical perspective to tourism planning in this environment, to evaluate the measures taken, and to analyse the situation in order to suggest improvements.

Discussion topics

- What is the relevance of investing in tourism as opposed to other types of industry in an economic situation like this? Should tourism be part of the structural development of transition economies?
- Can Lithuania learn anything from the way tourism has been organized in other countries?
- Who should be responsible for tourism development in Kaunas?
- What type of tourists can Kaunas attract?
- What measures should be taken when making long-term tourism plans for Kaunas? Analyse the situation and make an action plan.

Theoretical background

This case study is written from the perspective of a transition economy recovering from the collapse of the centralized Soviet system. It takes up the economic problems of transition economies and questions the relevance of investing money in the tourism industry in an area with ill-adapted facilities and lack of planning authorities, struggling to find new markets to replace the former numerous Russian tourists.

INTRODUCTION

The aim of this case study is to present an image of the tourism industry in Kaunas, Lithuania, today. First a short account of the industry in the country during the Soviet period will be presented to help the reader understand the current state of affairs. The case study then moves on to deal with the present situation and the problems companies all over Lithuania were faced with after independence. The city of Kaunas will then be used as an example to illustrate the situation of the Baltic resorts struggling with the problems brought about by a drastic change in external circumstances.

The Republic of Lithuania, indigenously known as Lietuva, is the largest (65,300 sq km) and the most populated (3.8 million) of the three Baltic countries of Estonia, Latvia and Lithuania. Some 80 per cent of its residents are Lithuanian and the largest national minority is Russians with 9 per cent of the population. Estimates of the number of Lithuanians living abroad vary between 2 and 3 million.

After about 50 years behind the Soviet iron curtain Lithuania is independent again. The regaining in 1991 of its lost independence was the country's first step back to the free world. Since regaining their independence in 1991 the economies of the Baltic States have radically changed. Transition has taken place from an economy based on state ownership to one where private sector ownership is actively encouraged. GDP growth in Lithuania in 1997 was approximately 5 per cent and the EU Commission forecast growth of 5.4 per cent for 1998. Despite the growth in exports, trade deficit is 19 per cent of GDP, which is among the highest of all the transition economies. Inflation has been reduced from 40 per cent in 1995 to 8.4 per cent in December 1997. The official unemployment rate is around 10 per cent (closer to 15 per cent according to the International Labour Office). However, the share of labour in agriculture is very high, one-fifth. Since agriculture is unlikely to employ so many people in the future, job creation in other sectors should be encouraged.

TOURISM INDUSTRY IN LITHUANIA

During the Soviet period 1940–90, domestic tourism dominated. It was centrally ruled according to the Soviet ideology which preferred to develop tourism within the Soviet Union, keeping international tourism very restricted. Few Lithuanians were able to travel abroad and even in those few cases the destination was often within the Soviet empire. Lithuania was traditionally one of the key holiday resorts for the citizens of the former Soviet Union and Eastern Europe. The largest centres of tourism in Lithuania at the time were the capital Vilnius, Kaunas, Klaipeda, and the resorts of Palanga, Birstonas and Druskininkai.

The monopolistic state organization Intourist assisted foreign tourists in the USSR and Soviet tourists going abroad. Intourist controlled the industry in Lithuania as well. However, there were some other tourist organizations involved in travel and tourism in Lithuania during the Soviet period: the Lithuanian Tourism Union was established in 1929 in Kaunas with the aim of developing inbound foreign tourism and the Lithuanian Travelling Union was established in 1937 to take care of domestic tourism in the country.

Only when Lithuania became independent did opportunities to develop international tourism as well as finding new dimensions in domestic tourism emerge. Tourism in Lithuania does not yet have the same importance as in the West even if the country has seen a relatively large growth in the number of tourists mainly from Western European countries and the United States. This compensates in part for a vast reduction in the numbers of tourists visiting Lithuania from the former Soviet Union.

After independence the Intourist organization was unable to satisfy the increasing

Table 3.1: Lithuania border crossing statistics 1997 – number of arrivals.

| Country | Mode of transport | | | | | Compared with 1996 |
	Road	Air	Sea	Rail	Total	
Latvia	699,846	2,331	2,894	36,186	943,259	13.1%
Estonia	286,488	3,275	756	9,588	300,107	1.4%
CIS	1,081,948	13,299	19,701	774,202	1,889,150	9.0%
Poland	232,303	3,652	6,322	21,458	263,735	−21.6%
Central Europe	33,271	2,253	492	2,492	38,508	6.7%
Germany	36,781	18,966	16,497	8,825	79,069	−12.4%
USA	7,165	10,019	353	2,225	19,752	29.1%
Other countries	58,222	85,103	16,673	8,019	168,017	7.0%
Total	2,636,026	138,898	63,680	862,995	3,701,607	5.8%
	71.2%	3.8%	1.7%	23.3%	100.0%	

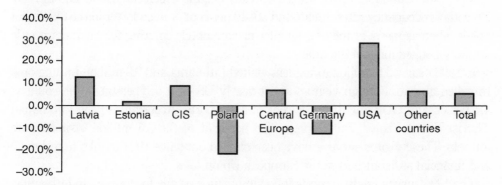

Figure 3.1: Number of arrivals in Lithuania (1997 compared with 1996).

Table 3.2: Lithuania border crossing statistics 1997 – number of departures.

| | Mode of transport | | | | | Compared with 1996 |
	Road	Air	Sea	Rail	Total	
Residents of Lithuania	2,503,197	107,240	67,864	302,838	2,381,139	4.1%
	84.0%	3.6%	2.3%	10.2%	100.0%	

demand and restructuring was inevitable. The State Tourism Service was established in 1992. It is the only state institution directly responsible for the development of tourism in Lithuania and is nowadays called the Lithuanian Tourist Board. The National Programme of Tourism Development was confirmed in April 1994. The programme provides recommendations for the improvement of the country's tourism infrastructure.

Statistics about tourists crossing the Lithuanian frontier have been collected since the middle of 1992. Until 1996, visitors coming by rail were not registered. Since 1996 information has been presented on a monthly basis, according to means of transport and citizenship. Registration is carried out according to citizenship, not according to country of residence, which makes it impossible to distinguish transit travellers from same-day visitors and tourists. Registration is not always very precise so statistics can at times be rather confusing.

The first years of the opening up of the country attracted a lot of foreign visitors making 1989–90 the peak years of Lithuanian tourism. Visitors filled the existing accommodation, shooting occupancy levels up to 80–90 per cent in bigger towns and even 60–70 per cent elsewhere. After the first years of great curiosity the total number of inbound foreigners started a steady decline which came to an end in 1996. Nowadays occupancy rates are around 30–40 per cent or even lower in the old Soviet hotels whereas many of the new smaller private hotels catering for business people are fully booked most of the time.

In 1996 nearly 3.5 million foreigners visited Lithuania and 2.9 million Lithuanians travelled abroad. Foreign visitors spent nearly US$ 350 per person in the country, 4.4 per cent of GDP and 10.5 per cent of all exports. According to the Lithuanian Tourist Board Visitor Exit Survey, 23.8 per cent of the 3.5 million visitors were tourists. These visitor surveys have been carried out since 1994 thanks to technical and financial assistance from the European Union.

The 1996 survey resulted in the following visitor profile for tourists to Lithuania:

- 43 per cent travelled on business, 32 per cent visited relatives, 22 per cent were on holiday and 3 per cent had some other purpose;
- 18 per cent of the respondents were born in Lithuania and 64 per cent had relatives or friends there;
- 73 per cent visited the country for the second time, 55 per cent had been there three or more times;
- information on Lithuania was received mainly through friends and relatives (59 per cent).

The following information on travel behaviour resulted from the study:

- a vast majority arranged their own trip, only 7.5 per cent came on package tours;

- 48 per cent came alone, 30 per cent with family members and the rest in non-family groups;
- 21 per cent visited also other countries than Lithuania: 25 per cent visited Estonia, 10 per cent Russia, Poland and the Scandinavian countries;
- average duration of visits was 10.1 nights for all and 6.4 nights for those who stayed in established accommodation.

The same tourist survey carried out in 1996 by the Lithuanian Tourist Board shows the following feedback from foreign tourists. There were a lot of complaints about infrastructure: roads, signs, toilets, cold hotels, and bad waste collection. Many also pointed out bureaucracy, bad customs work and the general difficulty of obtaining information. People were said to be serious, not very service-minded, and lacking in language skills. Several visitors were also bothered about the obvious poverty in the country. However, many tourists could see a lot of progress in service, more people capable of speaking English and a wealth of new private businesses. The beautiful landscape and the magnificent architecture were among the most frequent reasons for praise.

KAUNAS

Both in population (415,000) and significance, Kaunas is Lithuania's second city. It is a city of very old and established cultural traditions and a place where generations of Lithuanian artists, composers and writers have lived and left their imprint. The city is sometimes called the encyclopaedia of Lithuania's culture and literature.

The architectural significance of Kaunas' old town is second only to that of Vilnius. The city is marked by Gothic and Baroque churches and castles as well as the headquarters of Hanseatic merchants. However, Kaunas is also known as a business and industrial centre. The Soviet times gave the city a large number of industrial facilities. It also had a reputation of having a great number of underground capitalists with the biggest percentage of private cars and the largest private houses in the USSR. Kaunas has well-developed textile, clothing, wood and food processing, electronics and machine building industries. The years of transition to market economy have seen a constant increase in private shops, trade, crafts and service enterprises. International co-operation is extensive with most contacts with Sweden, Denmark, Norway, Germany and the United States.

The city has two universities and five higher education institutions to guarantee a significant research and development potential. Nowadays tourism can also be studied at Kaunas Technical University. Kaunas is one of the least Russian cities in the country and usually seen as the most Lithuanian town in Lithuania.

TOURISM IN KAUNAS

Much of what Kaunas has to offer tourists is concentrated in the pedestrianized street Laisves Aleja and the old town. There are many museums, art galleries, and monuments. There are also three professional theatres: drama, musical and puppet. The Kaunas Philharmonic Society arranges classical concerts and festivals. The range of restaurants is wide; everything from small bars to first class restaurants. Tourists who want to try Lithuanian cuisine have many places to choose from and most of the restaurants can be found in the old town. Hotels in Kaunas are mostly situated in the centre and the size and the quality vary a lot; there are the large Soviet-style hotels, and new, expensive private hotels aimed at businessmen. Shopping is concentrated around Laisves Aleja but most of the shops are not very inviting. The prices are good for Western tourists but the range of goods is rather limited.

In 1994, 7,652 foreign tourists were registered in Kaunas: a very low figure for this once very popular holiday resort. The average length of stay was only 1.16 days so the problem is not only to attract more tourists but also to make them stay longer and spend more money.

Table 3.3 shows the number of guests accommodated/the number of guest nights provided in Kaunas in 1995–96 as registered by Kaunas City Department of Economic Development and Investments. According to this information the numbers of Russians and CIS citizens are still decreasing whereas Western Europe is now seen as the most promising market. The City Council is responsible for planning and developing tourism in Kaunas. In practice the work is carried out at the Department of Economic Development and Investments. The department deals with many issues and there is not a specific tourism section or anyone solely in charge of tourism. There is no tourist information office. Visitors wondering what to do in Kaunas can find information at travel agencies or hotels.

Kaunas is quite accessible. It has an international airport with services to Helsinki, Budapest, Prague, Oslo and Hamburg. The railway network is well developed and a trip from Vilnius to Kaunas takes 1.5 hours. Kaunas is also situated on the main railway route from Tallinn to Warsaw. Regular buses go through small towns and villages so tourists are advised to use express buses. It takes 1.5 hours to get to Vilnius by express bus and 6 hours to reach the port of Klaipeda. City transport includes buses and trolley buses. Lithuanian roads are the best in the former Soviet Union. There are three highways, two of which reach Kaunas.

Kaunas has high hopes for road E 67, better known as the Via Baltica. This is a route connecting Helsinki and Warsaw through the three Baltic republics of Estonia, Latvia and Lithuania, a total of 950 kilometres. The road is constantly being improved. Partly with international support, around US$ 230 million are being invested in bridges, bypasses, widening, resurfacing, etc. over the period 1996–2000.

Table 3.3: Number of guests/number of guest nights in Kaunas in 1995 and 1996.

	1995	1996
Lithuania	16,106/22,157	10,685/14,984
North Europe[1]	4,420/8,812	4,971/9,551
United Kingdom	649/1,388	813/1,611
West Europe[2]	4,589/9,579	4,859/9,666
Germany	3,157/6,190	3,214/6,033
South Europe[3]	791/1,653	1,083/2,655
East Europe[4]	1,808/4,117	2,384/6,146
Poland	1,063/2,687	1,499/4,192
Latvia	1,089/1,896	1,225/1,835
Estonia	1,154/1,755	1,306/1,900
CIS	9,937/14,919	9,472/14,118
Russia	7,511/11,548	6,825/9,632
Belarus	605/754	907/1,179
North America[5]	1,431/3,373	1,102/2,442
USA	1,304/2,983	908/2,009
Canada	126/389	190/428
Latin America[6]	148/283	59/129
Australia and Oceania	73/165	197/513
Asia	525/1,058	548/1,512
Africa	16/32	46/146

Notes:
[1] Denmark, Iceland, Norway, Finland, Sweden, United Kingdom.
[2] Austria, Belgium, France, Germany, Luxembourg, Holland, Switzerland.
[3] Greece, Spain, Italy, Portugal, Croatia, Slovenia, Cyprus, Turkey.
[4] Poland, Czech Republic, Slovak Republic, Albania, Hungary, Bulgaria, Romania.
[5] Greenland, USA, Canada.
[5] Argentina, Brazil, Cuba, Mexico, Venezuela, Nicaragua and other.

Traffic is still fairly scarce on the Via Baltica even if roadside services are fairly good now as travellers can fill up at international service stations. These service stations also have well-equipped shops where paying by credit cards is possible. Unfortunately, however, there is not yet a sufficient number of good roadside restaurants. There is a wide variety of lodging available but most places have one thing in common: paying by credit card is seldom possible.

PROBLEM AREAS

In 1995 tourism students from Porvoo Commercial College spent two weeks in Kaunas interviewing dozens of tourism entrepreneurs representing the whole range of the industry: cafés, restaurants, hotels, activities, sights, travel agencies and tour operators. Interviews with tourism entrepreneurs revealed that the conditions for private entrepreneurship in Kaunas leave a lot to be desired: establishing a business is a bureaucratic maze and often involves bribery; company legislation lags behind;

high interest rates force businesses to seek alternative forms of financing to bank loans. Running a business in Lithuania involves several problems:

- lack of service-minded, trained personnel with good command of foreign languages;
- heavy taxation;
- restaurants have problems finding good and reasonably priced raw materials;
- not enough resources for marketing;
- few companies can afford electronic reservation systems;
- few Lithuanians can afford to spend money on restaurant and hotel services.

The entrepreneurs were also of the opinion that the general infrastructure of the country is poor and investment in tourism is insufficient at all levels: national, regional and municipal, as tourism industry is not yet seen as a valuable part of economy. According to them, the country is not well known abroad and is thus unable to attract large numbers of tourists. Most entrepreneurs also pointed out that they have not yet learnt to co-operate with each other to achieve better results, and that there is also one active actor they need to take into consideration in their operations: the Mafia.

CONCLUSION

Foreign investment is needed to improve tourism infrastructure in Lithuania. Privatization of large infrastructure companies has switched into a higher gear during 1997 and the first months of 1998. The country tripled its foreign investment to US$ 1 billion last year and the positive trend seems set to continue. Americans are the leading investors at the moment and over the coming years they are expected to increase their share. This is partly due to the fact that the newly elected President of Lithuania only recently returned to Lithuania after five decades in the United States. This should signal to the investors that Lithuania has shifted clearly to the West. The president served as a highly respected environmental regulator in the USA, and he is said to be eager to increase public awareness of environmental issues. This sounds promising for the country's tourism industry, which still has not taken advantage of the country's attractive and relatively unspoilt countryside. Government decisions reflect directly on entrepreneurs. At the moment private businesses are still facing a lot of problems in Kaunas, as well as in the whole country, e.g. in the areas of legislation, taxation, infrastructure, training and customs formalities.

SUGGESTED READING

Aldcroft, D. H. and Morewood, S. (1995) *Economic Change in Eastern Europe since 1918*. Cornwall: Edgar Elgar Publishing Ltd.

Anciunaite, D. and Lukauskaite, L. (1994) 'Tourism services in Kaunas', Final Bachelors thesis, Kaunas College of Technology.

The Baltic States No. 34 May/June 1998. Tallinn: City Paper OÜ.

City of Kaunas (1997) *Statistics 1996*. Department of Economic Development and Investments.

Hall, D. R. (ed). (1991) *Tourism and Economic Deveopment in Eastern Europe and the Soviet Union*. London: Belhaven.

Hall, D. R. (1992) 'The challenge of international tourism in Eastern Europe', in *Tourism Management*, **13**(1), 41–4.

Krastotvarka Tourism Agencies in Kaunas, Klaipeda and Vilnius. *Acquaintance with Lithuania: Places of Interest. Tourist Services 1995*.

Lindroth, K. (1996) 'Liettua matkailumaana'. Unpublished seminar paper, given at Finnish Network University, 6 May.

Lithuanian Investment Agency (1996) *Data of Foreign Investors*. Vilnius.

Lithuanian State Tourist Board (1997) *International Tourism Trends in 1995*. Vilnius.

Lithuanian State Tourist Board *Possibilities of Tourism Development in Lithuania*. Vilnius.

Lithuanian State Tourist Board *South-West Lithuania Area Guide*. Vilnius.

Lithuanian State Tourist Board *Welcome to Lithuania*. Vilnius.

Medlik, S. (1990) 'Focus on Eastern Europe', in *Tourism Management*, **11**(2), 95–8.

Ministry of Foreign Affairs of the Republic of Lithuania (1994) *Lithuania: Partner in a World Economy*. Vilnius.

Ministry of Transport of the Republic of Lithuania (1997) *Transportas 1990–1995*. Vilnius.

Nordicum: Scandinavian Business Review (1998), **3–4**, Helsinki: Publico Ltd.

Porvoo Commercial College (1995) *Tourism in Kaunas: A Study Based on Interviews with Entrepreneurs*. Unpublished course work.

Tiusanen, T. and Talvitie, K. (1998) 'The Baltic States in the 1990s. Western companies in Estonia, Latvia and Lithuania', *Studies in Industrial Engineering and Management* **4**, Lappeenranta University of Technology.

Via Baltica Touristica – User's Manual (1998). Helsinki.

Website: Http://www.tourism.lt

4

Calvià, Mallorca

Michael Morgan

Aim
Calvià is a typical area of mass market beach resorts which grew rapidly in the 1960s and 1970s but are now showing signs of decline. This case study outlines the problems faced by a mature resort and the strategies adopted by the local planners to try to overcome them.

Keywords
beach tourism; tourism area life-cycle; resort development; tourism planning; tourism marketing; destination marketing; distribution channels in tourism; sustainable development; Agenda 21

Summary
Calvià is a district of the Spanish Balearic island of Mallorca which includes a number of beach resorts including Palma Nova and Magaluf. There is a resident population of 23,000 but at peak times there are 100,000 visitors with a total of around 1.3 million visitors a year. There are 178 hotels with 46,000 beds, plus another 60,000 beds in self-catering apartments. Some 15,000 people are employed directly in tourism with 99 per cent of the adult population earning at least part of their income from it.

Many of the problems faced by Calvià are typical of those facing Spanish and other established Mediterranean beach resort areas. Uncontrolled development in the 1960s and 1970s had produced resorts where high-rise hotels crowded together right up to the beach. The hotels were overdependent on high volume, low-yield package tours from the British and German markets but the major tour operators dictated the prices. The accommodation stock was now in need of refurbishment but the low profit margins meant that funds to do so were not available. As a result, the resorts now had a down-market image attracting 'lager louts' whose behaviour deterred the family market. These factors combined with wider market factors had led to declining numbers and the resorts now had surplus capacity.

To counter the problems of a mature tourism destination, the local authorities adopted a number of measures. Planning controls were introduced to control the spread of urbanization. In 1988 Calvià published plans for a Magaluf Renewal Project which included a public esplanade along the beach and other improvements to the public environment and infrastructure. This was the first of a series of projects in all the resorts, costing £78 million in Calvià and £180 million for Mallorca as a whole. Legislation was introduced banning external noise from bars and discotheques after midnight. The municipality was given powers to close sub-standard holiday accommodation and to give grants for the refurbishment or demolition of obsolete buildings. To boost winter visitor numbers, Calvià launched a programme of activities and events under the title of 'Mallorca Calvià Club'. In 1996 Calvià launched a new strategy to ensure a sustainable future for tourism under the banner of Local Agenda 21. The immediate action taken was to modify the Calvià Master Plan, suspending the current zoning of land for development in order to halt urbanization programmes.

Calvià's efforts to tackle the problems of a mature tourist resort have received considerable publicity and this has helped to improve the image of Mallorca as a destination. Visitor numbers to Mallorca have recovered, partly as a result of wider market trends but without the refurbishment the resorts would not have been able to provide the quality holiday experience which tourists at the end of the twentieth century expect.

Learning outcomes

After examining and discussing this case study, students should be able to do the following:

- identify the key factors underlying the problems faced by a tourism destination at the mature stage of its life-cycle;
- identify the key players and stakeholders in the tourism industry and understand how their roles, objectives and relationships affect resort development and marketing;
- suggest potential strategies for resort regeneration;
- evaluate the success of the strategies adopted by Calvià.

Discussion topics

- What lessons could newer resorts learn from the problems encountered by the Calvià region?
- To what extent are the public sector responsible for the problems of the resort? To what extent are the private sector responsible?
- What solutions would you propose to the problems? Who should be involved in the implementation of your plan? Discuss the roles and responsibilities of the various 'players'.
- Is the concept of sustainable tourism development (a) desirable; (b) achievable in a region such as Calvià?

BACKGROUND

The Ayuntamiento (district or municipality) of Calvià is situated in the south-west of the island of Mallorca. It takes its name from the village of Calvià, 14 km west of the island's capital, Palma, and 7 km inland from the coast. Though the centre of administration for the district, it has the appearance of a sleepy Spanish village grouped around a church of medieval origins. The district covers 145 km^2 and comprises the resorts of Illetes, Portals Nous, Palma Nova, Magaluf, Santa Ponsa and Paguera, plus a number of smaller settlements.

Calvià has 54 km of coastline with 23 beaches along which, since the 1960s, the resorts have grown where originally there were only marshes, sand-dunes and coves. Once an agricultural area with 3,000 inhabitants, today there is a resident population of 23,000 but a peak times there are 100,000 visitors a year. There are 178 hotels with 46,000 beds, plus another 60,000 beds in self-catering apartments. Some 15,000 people are employed directly in tourism but the economy of the district is entirely dependent on tourism, with 99 per cent of the adult population earning at least part of their income from it. Magaluf/Palma Nova is the biggest resort on the island after the capital, Palma de Mallorca, and the south coast of Mallorca claims to have more hotel beds than the whole of Greece. Four out of the eight golf courses in Mallorca are located in Calvià, along with five marinas with 1,700 moorings. Attractions include the island's only casino, the Marineland dolphin show, a Wild West village, waterparks and innumerable bars, restaurants and clubs. The island's biggest nightclub, BCM, is located in Magaluf. Outside the resorts there are many opportunities for walking on the coast and inland in pleasant hilly country with pine woods and olive groves.

Mallorca is part of the Autonomous Region of the Balearic Islands, Spain. Tourism promotion is shared between the Spanish National Tourist Office in Madrid which promotes the country as a whole, the Balearic Islands Tourism Council, the Fomento del Turismo del Mallorca (a consortium of the public and private sectors on the island) and the 53 Balearic municipalities of which Calvià is one. Planning and funding tourism are the responsibility of the Balearic Islands government acting through the municipalities. Tourism generates 140,000 million pesetas for the local economy which has given Calvià both the highest tax income and the highest expenditure budget for any municipality outside the capital.

PROBLEMS AND ISSUES

Many of the problems faced by Calvià are typical of those facing Spanish and other established Mediterranean beach resort areas.

Uncontrolled development

The growth of beach tourism in the 1960s and early 1970s was encouraged by the central government and under the Franco dictatorship local communities had little say in planning decisions. In any case, tourism was seen as an opportunity to be seized, and local businessmen competed to erect hotels as close to the beaches as possible to meet the demand from the British and German tour operators. The Calvià

Master Plan of 1971 actively encouraged bigger and higher developments. As a result of this, particularly in Magaluf and Santa Ponsa, walls of tower-block hotels loom over the beaches which are lined with hotel grounds and café frontages. The developments continued to spread around the coast with the hitherto unspoilt cove of Cala Vinyes west of Magaluf becoming crowded with apartment blocks as late as 1989.

Ageing accommodation stock

The largest hotel in Mallorca is the Guadeloupe Sol in Magaluf with 503 rooms and employing 160 staff. It was built in 1973 by the Palma-based Grupo Sol, the largest hotel company in Spain. Most of its business comes from tour operators: 50 per cent of them British, also German, Italian, Scandinavian and Spanish. For these mixed nationalities it provides a self-service buffet restaurant and a multilingual programme of activities by day and entertainment by night. It is very similar to other large 3-star hotels in Magaluf run by Sol, Med Playa and other companies. By the late 1980s their decor appeared dated and in need of refurbishment.

Over-dependence

These hotels depend on high volume/low yield business from the major tour operators. In exchange for regular block bookings throughout the year, the tour operators negotiated rates as low as £7 or £8 per person per night which formed the basis for very affordable package holidays for the British mass-market. The market leader in British tour operations, Thomson Holidays, described this as virtuous circle (Figure 4.1), but for hotels in desperate need of revenue for reinvestment the circle

Figure 4.1: Thomson Holidays' Virtuous Circle of tour operating.

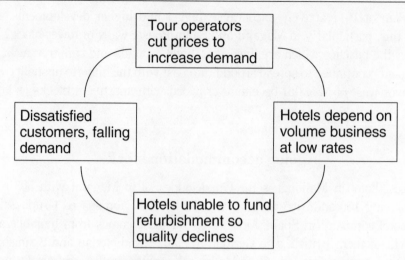

Figure 4.2: The Spanish hotels' vicious circle.

was in fact a vicious one (Figure 4.2). When in 1984 they attempted to raise prices, the result was an immediate fall-off in visitors. The price wars between British tour operators such as Thomson, Intasun and Airtours in the late 1980s fuelled the growth in the market but furthered the operators' determination to hold hotel rates down. In Mallorca as a whole the British and German visitors made up 70 per cent of the market, but in Magaluf 90 per cent of the visitors were British. The Germans preferred smaller resorts such as Paguera.

Down-market image

The low price of package holidays encouraged many young people to enjoy the beaches, the low bar prices and all-night opening hours of the resorts. Magaluf in particular developed an image as the haunt of the 'lager louts' – noisy drunken young men whose behaviour threatened to drive the family market from the resorts. These and other problems such as noise and dust from building work, over-booking, substandard accommodation, flight delays and pollution began to give the Mediterranean beach holiday a poor image in the British press.

Declining numbers

From 1989 onwards the number of visitors to Mallorca went into decline (see Table 4.1 and Figure 4.3), with an 8 per cent fall in the British market in 1989 and a 6 per cent fall in all foreign visitors, Calvià was particularly badly hit with an estimated 20 per cent fall in British visitors in 1990. Commentators attributed this to many factors, including disillusion with the quality of the product (Astles, 1989), growing

Table 4.1: Incoming passengers to Palma de Mallorca Airport by nationality (in thousands).

Nationality	1985	1986	1987	1988	1989	1990	1991	1992	1993	1994
German	1,067.5	1,126.1	1,316.8	1,376.7	1,351.3	1,542.3	1,697.2	1,715.8	1,886.7	2,264.9
Austrian	36.0	34.6	37.5	39.8	60.5	48.3	62.7	60.5	63.8	76.1
Belgian	67.6	68.0	77.7	79.3	79.5	82.2	81.7	83.4	102.2	105.4
Danish	97.1	113.6	133.4	121.6	96.5	87.2	64.9	62.0	57.5	65.7
Finnish	15.8	52.8	61.1	64.4	61.6	50.5	42.4	20.0	12.3	13.3
French	249.6	244.3	249.3	282.0	269.8	292.9	322.0	251.4	267.8	281.2
Dutch	121.4	115.2	133.2	147.2	121.8	97.8	103.7	95.6	89.0	120.9
Irish	23.8	28.6	45.5	52.5	47.4	31.1	34.0	36.6	50.5	67.1
Italian	121.7	99.7	98.6	106.5	90.5	85.7	96.1	113.5	125.2	115.1
Lux	18.5	20.8	25.0	26.0	25.2	25.5	30.6	29.2	27.7	40.4
Norwegian	110.9	123.8	149.5	110.5	69.1	78.7	69.0	65.4	61.2	58.5
British	1,177.0	1,629.3	1,822.3	1,753.4	1,599.2	1,212.6	1,130.4	1,223.5	1,408.5	1,679.2
Swedish	70.9	90.0	141.9	167.1	162.4	150.2	162.9	148.2	110.9	122.2
Swiss	133.6	137.5	152.6	150.3	150.5	160.1	172.7	180.6	172.0	181.3
Others	16.8	19.2	34.8	27.5	29.9	36.0	32.0	41.3	71.6	103.4
Total	3,328.2	3,903.5	4,479.2	4,504.8	4,215.2	3,981.1	4,102.3	4,127.0	4,506.9	5,294.7

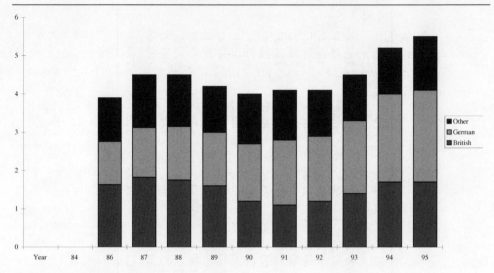

Figure 4.3: Arrivals at Palma Mallorca Airport.

competition from the Eastern Mediterranean, a switch to long-haul beach holidays, particularly to the USA, and to independent self-drive holidays with France threatening to overtake Spain as the UK's favourite holiday destination (Figure 4.4). Underlying these trends were economic factors such as the British recession forcing customers to become more value-conscious, demographic factors with a new generation of experienced travellers seeking new destinations and activities, and growing environmental awareness (Morgan, 1994). The growing prosperity of Spain

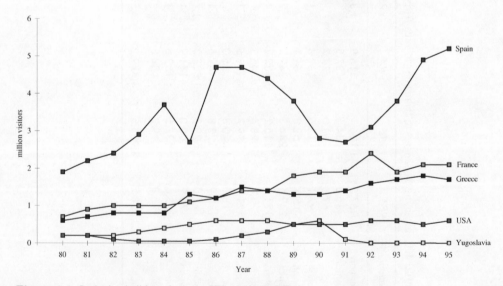

Figure 4.4: Inclusive holidays from the UK, 1980–95 (BTA).

as a member of the EU meant that it was no longer a low wage economy for the tourism industry, nor a destination for the tourists. The Managing Director of Thomson Holidays summed up the crisis when he wondered, in print, whether the package holiday as we know it was going out of fashion (Newbold, 1989, quoted in *Travel News*, 31 March).

Seasonality

The fall in visitor numbers was particularly marked in the winter months. Mallorca's climate is mild in winter but not as warm as other 'wintersun' destinations such as the Canaries. From 1989 to 1992 foreign visitor numbers fell, and fewer hotels, bars and shops stayed opened. The shortfall was made up to some extent through social tourism – Spanish senior citizens on winter holidays subsidized by the state to reduce unemployment in the hotel industry. However, such customers spent much less on food and drink than the foreign visitors.

Surplus capacity

In the boom years from 1986 onwards, around 70,000 extra hotel beds had been provided to meet the demand. By 1990, with the fall in numbers and the switch to self-catering apartments and villas, it was estimated that in Mallorca as a whole there were between 50,000–70,000 surplus hotel beds in the 1–3 star categories. Some of these hotels dated back to the 1960s.

THE PROBLEM IN BRIEF

Calvià as a tourism product would appear to have reached the mature stage of the product life-cycle (Butler, 1980) and begun to decline. In such situations, managers are faced with a choice of strategies – market penetration, market development, product development or diversification (Ansoff, 1957) – aimed at reviving the current product or replacing it with new ones. Those in the municipality responsible for resort planning and management, however, face constraints not shared by managers of other products and services. They do not have direct control of many of the tangible elements of the product – or of the human elements – the people who deliver the services to tourists in hotels, bars, etc. They can devise a promotional image for the resort but it is delivered to the end-users, the tourists, through a marketing channel dominated by the foreign tour operators and over which the resort has little control. Finally, it does not directly benefit from the sale of the product, so that the justification for investment is complex and subject to political controversy and restraints on public spending.

ACTIONS TAKEN

Planning controls

From the mid-1980s, the Balearic Islands belatedly began to introduce legislation to control the spread of urbanization. From 1985 new hotels could be no more than three storeys high and had to be built on a plot of 30 m^2 per bed. The Cladera Act of 1987 increased this to 60 m^2 and this was intended to prevent any more high-rise clusters but also to price out speculative building. Development was banned from areas of special natural beauty. However, the new controls were difficult to enforce and did not apply to licences issued prior to the legislation. In 1991 the law of Protected Areas preserved 45 per cent of the land surface of the Balearic Islands from construction.

'Dressing up' the resorts

In 1988 Calvià published plans for a Maguluf Renewal Project aimed, according to the brochure, at making it 'once again an esteemed and sought-after holiday resort'. The work which took place over the next four winters included a public esplanade along the beach, replacing privately owned hotel and café frontages; pedestrianization; traffic calming measures and off-street car parks; tree planting and the creation of new parks; better lighting, paving, seats, litter bins and other street furniture; and a 'Spanish-style' shopping precinct.

This was the first of a series of projects in all the resorts costing £78 million in Calvià and £180 million for Mallorca as a whole. The intention was to create an environment that would not only attract the tourists but also encourage investment in improvements by hotel companies and others in the private sector. Similar schemes in other Spanish resorts meant that Calvià was unlikely to gain a long-term competitive advantage, but would benefit from an improved image for Spain as a destination. At the same time Palma airport terminal was enlarged, a ring road round Palma improved access to Calvià, and improvements were made to the water supply.

Controlling the lager louts

Legislation was introduced banning external noise from bars and discotheques after midnight. Police patrols were increased.

Hotel modernization

Under a law of 1989, the municipality was given powers to close substandard holiday accommodation and to give grants for the refurbishment or demolition of obsolete buildings. The aim was to remove from the market low-priced, low-quality beds and to create new public spaces along the seafront. The demolition of the Hotel Atlantic in Magaluf in 1996 resulted in world-wide publicity for the renewal programme. In all, some twelve hotels have so far been demolished and 25 refurbished, some grant-aided and some as commercial ventures. (The Guadeloupe Sol, mentioned above, was refurbished in 1992.)

Winter activities

To boost winter visitor numbers, Calvià launched a programme of activities and events under the title of 'Mallorca Calvià Club'. For no additional supplement visitors could take part in guided walks, cookery and photography classes, keep-fit sessions and enjoy afternoons and evenings of dancing, music and entertainment.

Sustainable tourism

In 1996 Calvià launched a new strategy for the future of tourism under the banner of Local Agenda 21 – the guidelines laid down at the 1992 Rio Earth Summit. Avoiding the extremes of uncontrolled expansion and total restriction, it aims to ensure the future of the tourism on which the region depends by preserving and improving the features that originally attracted the visitors. It pledges to involve the local community in working out a plan for sustainable development through consultation and consensus. The objectives include 'to break free from the seasonal nature of local tourism, to generate wealth and welfare for its residents, to conserve the environment and to defend Calvià's heritage' (*Calvià*, 1996). The immediate action taken was to modify the Calvià Master Plan, suspending the current zoning of land for development in order to halt urbanization programmes that could be at odds with the ultimate goals of the project.

EVALUATION

Calvià's efforts to tackle the problems of a mature tourist resort have received considerable publicity and this has helped to improve the image of Mallorca as a destination.

As Table 4.1 shows, visitor numbers to Mallorca have recovered. By 1994 British visitors were back to 1986 levels while the growth in domestic Spanish visitors and in the German market following reunification had resulted in an overall figure 33 per cent higher than in 1986. To what extent the refurbishment programmes are responsible is debatable. As Figure 4.4 shows, Spain as a whole has benefited from the upturn in the Western European economies and from the reaction to the wars in the Balkans. The familiarity of the established resorts has perhaps become an asset again. Nevertheless, without the refurbishment, the resorts would not have been able to provide the quality holiday experience which tourists at the beginning of the twenty-first century expect.

REFERENCES

Ansoff, I. (1957) 'Strategies for diversification', *Harvard Business Review*, September–October, 114.
Astles, R. (1989) 'Overseas package holidays – where next?', *Leisure Intelligence* **2**, 4.
Butler, R. (1980) 'The concept of a tourism area cycle of evolution', *Canadian Geographer* **24**, 5–12.
Calvià (1988) Magaluf's dressing up publicity brochure by Ajuntament de Calvià, Mallorca.
Calvià (1996) 'Calvià Agenda Local 21', *Entorn*, June.

SUGGESTED READING

The product life-cycle in tourism

Haywood, K. (1986) 'Can the tourism area life cycle be made operational?' *Tourism Management* **7**, September, 154–61.
Kotler, P. (1988) *Marketing Management: Analysis, Planning, Implementation and Control*. 8th edn. Englewood Cliffs, NJ: Prentice-Hall, p. 369.

Destination marketing

Bergsma, J. and Goodall, B. (1990) 'Destinations as marketed in tour operators' brochures', in G. Ashworth and B. Goodall (eds) *Marketing Tourism Places*. London: Routledge, p. 173.
Middleton, V. (1994) *Marketing in Travel and Tourism*. 2nd edn. London: Butterworth Heinemann, Chapter 20, pp. 227–43.

Distribution channels in the tourism industry

Morgan, M. (1996) *Marketing for Leisure and Tourism*. Hemel Hempstead: Prentice-Hall, Chapter 10, pp. 126–30 and Chapter 13, pp. 187–96.

Resort regeneration

Fayos Sola, E. (1992) 'A strategic outlook for regional tourism – the White Paper on Valencian Tourism'. *Tourism Management* **13** March, 45–9.
Morgan, M. (1991) 'Dressing up to survive: marketing Majorca anew', *Tourism Management* **12**, March, 15–20.
Morgan, M. (1994) 'Homogeneous products: the future of the established resorts', in W. Theobald (ed.) *Global Tourism: The Next Decade*. London: Butterworth Heinemann, pp. 378–95.

Sustainable tourism

Middleton, V. and Hawkins, R. (1998) *Sustainable Tourism: A Marketing Perspective*. London: Butterworth Heinemann, Chapters 7–10, pp. 82–130.
Stabler, M. (ed.) (1997) *Tourism and Sustainability: Principles and Practice*. Wallingford: CAB International, Chapter 1, pp. 1–19.

CHAPTER 5

Faro: A Tourist Town?

A hypothesis under study

Ana Ferreira, Alexandra Rodrigues and Claudia Almeida

Aim

This case study aims to analyse the present tourism situation in Faro and to define future measures for its development and to identify potential tourist attractions.

Keywords

sustainability; urban regeneration; cultural entertainment; marketing and promotion; local tourism policy; accessbility

Summary

A sustainable urban policy allows the development of towns and also improves their socio-economic growth. Although the way to attain the goal of sustainable urban policy can vary, there are, according to the Development Scheme of the Community Space (DSCS),[1] five fundamental aspects which play a relevant role, including the control of urban expansion, the mixing of employment activities and social groups within urban spaces, prudent management of the urban ecosystem and the development of efficient means of access, which at the same time are not prejudicial to the environment or to cultural heritage.

According to the same document, urban tourism has a 28.3 per cent share of the European tourist market and shows a tendency to grow at a rate of 4.7 per cent – a rate which is higher than that of sun and beach resorts or mountain resorts, whose expected growth rates are 2.3 per cent and around 3 per cent, respectively.[2]

Clearly it is important to consider the best ways of making the sustainable development of towns compatible with tourist activity, whilst minimizing potential negative impacts such as those which have already been felt in Venice, Florence and Bruges where the carrying capacity has been surpassed in spite of the efforts of local authorities to avoid this.[3] Thus 'plurisectorial and integrated strategies'[4] need to be devised, to assess 'carrying capacity', not only physical and environmental, but also with social and psychological perspectives.

The peripheral large towns and cities of southern Europe (where the Algarve is situated), have developed a network of air links with many European urban centres due to the demands of mass tourism – principally the search for sun and beach – a market which, although already consolidated, now has other demands as this market segment is generally comprised of experienced, sophisticated consumers.

The primary reasons for visiting a town or city are, according to Law:[5] meetings, exhibitions, urban attractions, culture, sports and events. At a secondary level, accessibility, transport, accommodation and information services are also taken into account. This kind of tourism has the advantage, in relation to the beach product, of not being subject to a clear seasonality. Tourism plays a very important role in urban planning policy as regards economic regeneration and reconversion, image and promotion, and the revaluation of both space and heritage.

Learning outcomes

After examining this case study, students should be able to do the following:

- identify the problems of combining urban tourism with sustainable development;
- identify the importance of the Strategic Plan of Faro.

Discussion topics

- The Strategic Plan of Faro allows for many configurations to meet organizers' needs since it was based on extensive consultation with active and dynamic agents of the local activities and other experts. Determine the importance of this element.
- 'The Strategic Plan of Faro places a strong emphasis on cultural and sports events'. Discuss.
- 'In the case of Faro, there is no tourism marketing strategy, market research or customer feedback'. Discuss the importance of these marketing tools.
- 'Faro has been greatly affected by poor accessibility'. Discuss.
- Is urban tourism an alternative or a complement to the offer of 'sun and sea' products? Justify your answer.
- Identify achievements, hopes and limitations to the development of a cultural tourism product in Faro.

CHARACTERIZATION

Geographical location

Faro is the capital of the Algarve and one of the southernmost towns in Portugal. It lies almost at the geographical centre of the Algarvian coastline, separated from the Atlantic Ocean by a series of salt-water lagoons and sandbank islands, which are part of the Ria Formosa Natural Park (see Figure 5.1).

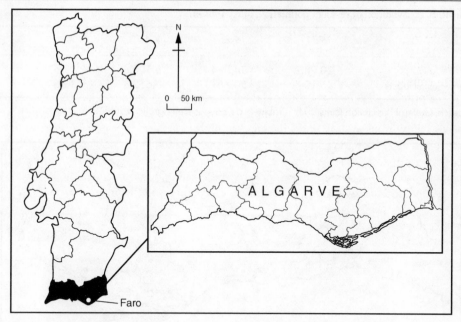

Figure 5.1: Geographical location of Faro.

Climate

The climatic features of the *Conselho* (municipality) of Faro are obviously a determining element of its biophysical aspects and play a decisive role in economic activities such as agriculture and tourism. The climate is not homogeneous throughout the whole district – the influence of the sea that can be felt along the coastal belt lessens the further inland one goes, where the weather becomes progressively drier and warmer. This contrast is strong enough to encourage the development of tourism that is not greatly affected by marked seasonal changes. The town of Faro itself has a mild, moderate climate, with low rainfall throughout the year.[6]

Demography and economy

The last population census (1991) put the number of inhabitants in the town of Faro at 34,094 (see Table 5.1). If we include the population of the immediate surrounding area (municipality), this figure rises to just over 50,000, meaning that Faro falls within the population scale of medium-sized European towns, which vary between 50,000 and 500,000 inhabitants. Combining the population figures of Faro and the neighbouring towns of Olhão (8 km to the east) and Loulé (12 km to the north-west) and their respective municipalities (see Figure 5.2), the total reaches 133,800 – or 39.3 per cent of the total population of the Algarve. There is also a very significant

Table 5.1: Evolution of resident population, Faro, 1981–91.

	1981	1991	V.A.	%
Faro – town	28,986	34,094	5,108	7.6
Faro – municipality	45,109	50,761	5,652	12.5

Source: General Population Census XIII, Gabinete de Estudos Demográficos, INE.[7]

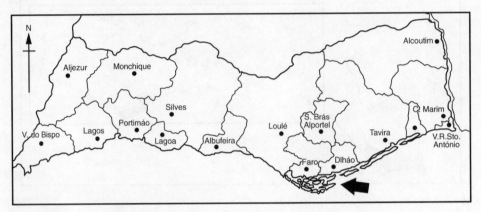

Figure 5.2: Municipalities of the Algarve.

Table 5.2: Resident and floating population in Faro.

		Floating population		
Municipality	Resident population	Low season	Mid season	High season
Faro	50,761	1,087	34,400	36,507

Source: Regional Plan of the Bureau of Tourism of the Algarve (1995).

'floating' population in Faro, connected to tourism and leisure, as can be seen from Table 5.2.

Most employment, both in the town itself and indeed throughout the municipality, is offered by the service industries – in fact 72.4 per cent of the total employed population (see Table 5.3).

ACCESSIBILITY

Accessibility, both within the town itself and the directly surrounding area (internal accessibility) and to and from other national and foreign centres (external accessibility) is fundamental for the future of Faro.

Table 5.3: Statistical indicators (municipality of Faro).

Area/square km (1993)	197
No. of parishes (1993)	5
Medium area (square kms)	40.2
Number of small villages	39
Resident population (Census 91)	50,761
Men	24,403
Women	26,358
Population density (inhabitants per square km – 1994)	261.2
Age groups in 1994 (%)	
0–14	17.2
15–24	15.8
25–64	52.6
65+	14.3
Ageing indicator, 1994 (%)	83.1
Illiteracy rate, 1991 (%)	9
Doctors per 1,000 inhabitants (1994)	5.3
Total of employed population (1991)	22,330
Primary sector (%)	10.1
Secondary sector (%)	17.5
Tertiary sector (%)	72.4
Activity rate, 1991 (%)	46.2
Unemployment rate, 1991 (%)	4.7
Enterprises	
No. of enterprises (1994)	6,778
No. of people employed	12,485
Tourism (1994)	
No. of establishments	30
Capacity (No. of beds)	1,499
Overnight stays	148,080
Guests	93,944
Electricity per 1,000 inhabitants (1995)	489.7
Electricity, kwh per capita (1994)	884

Source: Co-ordination Commission of the Algarve Region[8] (CCRA).

Railway connections

Railway transport in Portugal is generally slow and needs to be upgraded. Investment in the modernization of railways and other infrastructures of CP (Portuguese Railways) has been insignificant. However, projected plans for the future include the electrification of the line between Faro and Lisbon, with a view to reducing the journey time (currently 4.5 hours); the general improvement of the east–west Algarvian railway line (Vila Real de Santo Antonio to Lagos); and the modernization of Faro railway station and the lines within the town area. CP is also studying the development of a railway link to Faro international airport in two phases, including an underground station at the airport.

Road network

Public transport in the town continues to be inefficient and insufficient, although some additional bus routes have recently been introduced and the bus fleet has been renewed. Road access to the town has been improving over the last three years. A new road link to the airport has been built to replace the former main airport junction whose traffic lights previously caused long traffic jams in both directions, especially in the summer.

The main road into Faro from Olhão, which was another point of intense, slow traffic, has also been improved by means of a new ring road leading directly to the sea port, thus diverting heavy goods vehicles from the town centre. The main road between Faro and Loulé is still rather slow, due to a number of sets of traffic lights that cause long queues during the rush hour. Within the town, roads are still congested and access from one point of the town to another can be difficult. However, progress has been made.

> The implementation of the National Road Plan and the construction of the Via Longitudinal do Algarve (VLA)[9] and the bridge across the Guadiana River,[10] have contributed to the significant improvement of both the external accessibility of the region (the Algarve) and accessibility within the region itself.... Indeed, the construction of the VLA and the Seville–Huelva motorway has meant that inter-regional access has been greatly enhanced and the opening of national borders has brought new relations and inter-dependencies in the south of the Iberian Peninsula.[11]

Sea connections

Access by sea is the worst of all. The commercial port of Faro is not operating to its full capacity; this is due in part to the fact that the port is situated within the Ria Formosa Natural Park which imposes limitations on the use of the port in order to protect the environment, but none the less the lack of good road and rail access, limited cargo handling machinery and a disputed market do not aid the situation. The use of the port is also conditioned by the natural characteristics of the harbour entrance, which is difficult to navigate due to narrow channels of access and a number of sandbanks.

Air connections

The total movement of passengers embarking and disembarking at Faro international airport in 1996 was 3,533,994.[12/13] In 1996, if compared to the same period of time the year before, there was a decrease of 2.2 per cent – or 80,472 passengers. The present air terminal was built for 3 million passengers a year. However, work has been started to extend the terminal in order to increase capacity from the present 1,600 passengers per hour to 4,700 at the busiest times. Check-in desks will increase from 23 to 70, security control gates will increase from 3 to 6 and departure gates will increase from 10 to 21. New car parks will also be built.

Air transport to and from Faro is mainly based on charter flights that channel organized tourist fluxes into the region. Scheduled flights, which are the key to effective inter-regional accessibility, are relatively few and scheduled routes are limited.

Although the very existence of an international airport offers exceptional potential for links with large urban tourist-generating centres, the connections which must be guaranteed by other means of transport are still insufficient, and therefore prejudicial for Faro. In summary, transport services show weaknesses, which are unlikely to be overcome in the short or even medium term, in particular, the railway, which has extremely deficient infrastructures that require a complete overhaul (see Table 5.4).

Table 5.4: External connections to and from Faro.

Means of Transport	Comments
Railway	Faro–Lisbon (4.5 hrs). Daily connections from Lisbon to Madrid, to Vigo, Paris
	Algarve line: Lagos–Faro–Vila Real de St. Antonio
Road	Faro–Lisbon: 290 km[14]
	Infante D. Henrique motorway[15] Faro–Ayamonte (Spanish border town): 60 km
	National Route 125 connects all Algarvian towns
Sea	Routes to seven countries
Air	Faro international airport – 5 km from town centre
	Daily flights to many European cities; domestic flights to Lisbon
	(connections to major international cities)

Other information

Faro also offers the following:

- 25 accommodation units (total 810 rooms);
- youth hostel (56 beds);
- 50 restaurants;
- 43 'tourist taxis';[16]
- guided tours: trips to *Ria de Faro*, *Farol* and *Culatra* islands;
- 2 Tourist Information Offices – town centre and at the airport.

URBAN EVOLUTION

Faro's origins date back to prehistoric times. During the Roman occupation it was known as Ossónoba and was one of the most important urban settlements in the Algarve. At that time, the town was already divided into two main nuclei; the first, known as the *Vila-a-Dentro* (walled town) was where the forum was situated, along with the temple and other administrative and commercial buildings. The second area was centred on the *Ribeira* (waterfront) and was inhabited by the most important and wealthiest townsfolk. A third area – the *Baixa* – which nowadays is the commercial centre, was developed later. It is these three areas which combine to make up the town centre, the focal point for the development of urban tourism.

The layout of the city did not change much throughout the Visigoth and Arab occupations, or even after the Christian Reconquest in the thirteenth century (when the Algarve became definitively part of the kingdom of Portugal). It was only in the sixteenth century that the town began to undergo any significant development. Expansion and development continued through the seventeenth and eighteenth centuries – it was during this period that most of the noteworthy buildings were built. Moreover, many existing buildings were restored and enlarged at this time, some even needing to be completely rebuilt, due to a series of catastrophes suffered by the town, such as the sacking and arson by British troops under the Count of Essex in 1576, and the earthquakes of 1722 and 1755. Unfortunately, such disasters also meant that a great deal of the town's heritage was irretrievably lost. However, the most significant changes to the town occurred in the nineteenth century, when the railway reached the Algarve and industrial development began.

TOURIST EVOLUTION

The *Comissão Regional de Turismo do Algarve* (Algarve Regional Tourist Board) was created in 1970 and has been largely responsible for regional tourism policy since then. However, according to the *Plano Estratégico de Faro* (Strategic Plan for Faro – Faro Municipal Council 1996), during the 1970s and 1980s Faro 'didn't assert its role, in view of the new tourist motivations and the need to add complementary products to [the region's] products of excellency – sun, sea and golf – as a focal point for and management centre of regional tourism'.

The Plan also points out that population growth has led to an increase in housing demand which in turn has led to a sharp increase in the density of high-rise buildings, even within the town centre. Indeed only the historic nucleus of the old walled town has been spared, due to its intricate structure – an Arab legacy – which has made it impossible to construct tall buildings.

The Plan goes on to suggest various strategies and plans of action to affirm Faro's role as capital of the Algarve. As regards tourism, the most important points concern the re-thinking of town planning and development policies, a greater effort towards conservation, and the need for an increase in cultural resources and entertainment. Clearly an offer of urban tourism based in Faro would diversify and complement the regional offer, which is currently highly dependent on the sun and sea product. Faro has an interesting historical and environmental heritage, which can and should be used to create a more positive image of the town.

Faro is included in the 'tourist towns' of the Atlantic Arc[17] and is twinned with the cities of Tangiers (Morocco), Newark (USA) and Huelva (Spain). The Atlantic Arc urban tourism network is made up of ten cities, all past or present regional capitals with strong cultural identities (Cork, Cardiff, Exeter, Rennes, Poitiers, Bordeaux, Bilbao, Cordoba, Lisbon and Faro). The network aims to permit the exchange of ideas and experiences relating to urban tourism and to act as a stimulus for cohesion throughout the network, ensuring the promotion of other Atlantic destinations through local Tourist Information Offices.

Urban tourism in the present

Some of the available data concerning tourist flows in Faro is collected via the *Posto de Turismo* (Tourist Information Office) located near the main entrance to the old walled town, which records the number of visitors who come in seeking information.[18] Between 1992 and 1996, the number of tourists visiting the Tourist Information Office in Faro accounted for 11.2 per cent (3,737,058 visitors during this period, giving a yearly average of 747,412 visitors) of the total number of visitors to all seventeen Tourist Information Offices throughout the Algarve. However, the municipality of Faro only received 1.9 per cent of the total bed-nights spent in the Algarve in 1995 (DGT[19] and INE 1996). From these figures, it is clear that the town receives mainly day visitors.

A survey carried out by the *Escola Superior de Gestão, Hotelaria e Turismo* (School of Business Studies, Hotel Management and Tourism, University of the Algarve) between July and September 1995 in the departure lounge of Faro international airport to determine the profile of the tourist in the Algarve, revealed that only 2.3 per cent of passengers had stayed overnight in Faro. The accommodation available in the district of Faro (see Table 5.5) is obviously limited, which partly explains why its share of overnight visitors is so small. According to a survey carried out in Tourist Information Offices in the Algarve region,[21] only 21.1 per cent of visitors to the Faro Tourist Information Office stayed overnight in the district – one of the lowest rates in the Algarve. The figures for overnight stays can be related to the following: local capacity to attract visitors for more than one day; location/accessibility (centrality vs. periphery); and

Table 5.5: Accommodation, restaurants, bars and discos (municipality of Faro).

Types	Number
Hotels	5
Pensions, hostels, guesthouses	15
Youth hostels	1
Other accommodation types	4
Accommodation capacity (No. of beds)	1,494
Restaurants	50
Bars/discos	30

Source: Ambifaro.[20]

the type of trip (organized vs. independent).[22] Faro's share in the total offer of accommodation in the Algarve has decreased over the last two decades – 6.6 per cent in 1975, 3.6 per cent in 1980, 3.7 per cent in 1985 and 2.1 per cent in 1990 (INE 1976, 1981, 1986, 1991).[23]

Cultural resources and urban heritage

The classification of the Ria Formosa – an area of 18,400 hectares – as a nature reserve has meant that it can be managed in such a way as to preserve its unique characteristics, while encouraging environmentally friendly tourist and leisure activities. For example, the Visitor Centre at Marim, whose main objective is to increase environmental awareness, can cater for small groups of tourists who can engage in such activities as bird watching or following a nature trail. The *Plano de Estrutura Verde* (Green Plan) for Faro, drawn up by the Municipal Council in 1997, created the Waterfront Park Project, at the edge of the Ria Formosa, which is geared towards sports, recreation and leisure. This urban park, when finished, besides catering to the interests of the resident population, is a potential tourist attraction. Another green belt area of Faro, the *Mata do Liceu,* is also being rehabilitated and now has a fitness circuit and cycle track.

The existing historical heritage is being gradually restored and promoted, mainly thanks to the work done by the *Gabinete Tecnico Local* (Local Technical Office), who drew up the *Plano de Pormenor de Salvaguarda e Valorização dos Núcleos Históricos* (Plan for the Protection and Valorization of the Historical Nuclei). The walled town has been the object of serious attention, and the local authorities recently announced that its total restoration would begin shortly.

Within the historical centre of the town, two more museums will be created, besides the existing Archaeological Museum that is located in a sixteenth-century former convent. One of the new museums will be an open-air complex, based on archaeological findings revealed in ongoing excavation works in the town. The other will be installed in a former brewery, and will be dedicated to the works of Algarvian artists.

Also in the old part of the town, the local Council has already rehabilitated two former military buildings which are now art galleries, *Trem* and *Arco*. These two cultural spaces have enriched the architectural heritage of the *Vila-a-Dentro*, which includes the Cathedral, started in the thirteenth century, the sixteenth-century Bishop's Palace, and the eighteenth-century Seminary, although it must be said that the whole area is noteworthy for its balance and harmony.

Yet another example of rehabilitation is the acquisition of the former São Francisco Monastery, which dates from the seventeenth century, by the National Institute for Training in Tourism who have transformed the space into the site for the Algarve Hospitality and Tourism School.

The *Baixa* (commercial area) is currently the object of a development project to revitalize traditional commerce, within the framework of the *Programa de Apoio à Modernização do Comércio* (Programme of Support for the Modernization of Trade), a project which aims to transform the area into an open-air shopping centre. The entities responsible for the project are *Ambifaro* (a local development agency) and ACRAL – *Associação dos Commerciantes da Região do Algarve* (Association of Commercial Retailers of the Algarve). The project involves the improvement, diversification and modernization of shopping and other commercial facilities and will doubtless enrich the tourist attractions of the town.

The Lethes Opera Theatre, which dates from the nineteenth century, has been totally restored and now has the facilities to offer a cultural entertainment programme of high quality. Urban tourism, besides benefiting from this recent effort to restore and rehabilitate the town's heritage, can also act as an incentive to its continuation by playing a role in urban sustainability.

Centres of interest/tourist attraction poles

The Strategic Plan for Faro points out four main competitive advantages of the town: a good climate by European standards; its southern location and identification with the region of the Algarve; the fact that it is the capital of Portugal's best-known and most important tourist region; and the good access provided by an international airport. Urban tourism is mainly cultural, so cultural and leisure resources are of great importance. Table 5.6 shows the principal cultural and leisure facilities and amenities in the district of Faro. Entertainment and recreation amenities serve as a means of promoting the town in question. The main tourist attractions of the town, according to the Municipal Inventory, can be seen in Table 5.7. Due to the

Table 5.6: Culture and leisure facilities (municipality of Faro).

Types	Number
Libraries	3
Museums	5
Cinema screens	2
Art galleries	3
Theatres	1
Music schools	1
Sport pavilions	2
Archives	2
Cultural centres/houses	2
Youth support centre	1
Musical groups	6
Theatre groups	2
Folkloric groups	1
Philharmonic band	1
Other cultural associations	9
Local radio stations	4
Local press	6

Source: Ambifaro[24] and Municipal Inventory – Algarve Region (1995).

Table 5.7: Tourist attractions (municipality of Faro).

Types	Number
Casino and other gambling rooms	1
Natural parks	2
Beaches	4
Marina and recreation parks	2
Exhibition centre	1
Entertainment centres	3
Night entertainment venues	9
Handicrafts	Yes
Nautical sports	Yes
Monuments and historical buildings	Yes
Hunting and fishing	Yes
Religious events	yes

Source: Municipal Inventory, Algarve Region (1995).

geographical location of the town, it has the advantage of being able to offer a marina, a recreational port, beaches, nautical sports and the Ria Formosa Natural Reserve. Nightlife in Faro is lively and plentiful, largely due to the student population (around 8,000).

As regards sports, it should be mentioned that Faro lacks certain facilities that are found in other towns, such as an indoor swimming pool, an athletics stadium or a golf course. However, the town does offer a fair variety of sporting amenities (see Table 5.8), the most noteworthy being the tennis centres and the sports clubs and associations. Town parks are associated with leisure activities, and such green spaces within the town are important for its image, from the point of view of both residents and visitors. The most noteworthy parks in Faro are *Manuel Bivar, João de Deus* and the *Mata de Liceu*.

Urban centres are focal points for congresses, conferences, business meetings and incentive trips. Faro has various venues for receiving this market segment, including four hotels which are well equipped for business tourism: Hotel Eva, Hotel Faro, Hotel Ibis and Hotel Monaco, as well as several auditoriums located at both campuses of the University of the Algarve, the Institute of Youth, the regional headquarters of the National Association of Young Entrepreneurs and the Algarve Hospitality and Tourism School. Of these venues, the Hotel Eva (a 4-star hotel in the town centre) and the Auditorium at the Gambelas Campus, University of the Algarve (4 km from the town) are those with the largest seating capacities (about 300 people).

However, although Faro is able to cater for most business events, from small-scale (e.g. business executive meetings) to large-scale (congresses and conventions), it must be said that there are several weaknesses in the town's offer, such as the absence of a multi-lingual simultaneous translation service and a Convention

Table 5.8: Sports (municipality of Faro).

Types	Number
Open–air swimming pool	1
Sports pavilions	5
Sport grounds (large)	3
Sport grounds (small)	5
Tennis courts	9
Riding school/centre	2
Fitness circuit	1
Shooting ground	1
Associations/clubs	9

Source: Municipal Inventory, Algarve Region (1995).

Bureau, the low bed capacity of the town's hotels and indeed the inadequate standard of accommodation to cater for this market segment (there is only one 4-star hotel), and the general quality of the facilities available, which could be improved, particularly in terms of acoustics and audio-visual equipment. It is difficult to draw any real conclusions about the potential of Faro as a business tourism centre, as no statistics or studies are available on this subject.

AGENTS INVOLVED IN THE ELABORATION OF THE STRATEGIC PLAN OF FARO

The Strategic Plan for Faro was drawn up between December 1994 and June 1995. The body responsible for the co-ordination of this project was the Local Development Agency *Ambifaro*, and the partners/agents involved in the process are listed below:

- *Associação dos Comerciantes do Algarve* (ACRAL)/Association of Commercial Retailers of the Algarve
- *Associação Nacional dos Jovens Empresários* (ANJE)/National Association of Young Entrepreneurs
- *Câmara Municipal de Faro* (CMF)/Faro District Council
- *Cine Club*
- *Caminhos de Ferro Portugueses* (CP)/Portuguese Railways
- *Comissão de Coordenação da Região do Algarve* (CCRA)/Algarve Regional Co-ordination Commission
- *Confederação dos Empresários do Algarve* (CEAL)/Confederation of Algarve Business Owners
- *EVA Transportes*/National Bus and Coach Company
- *Gabinete de Cidade*/Town Consultants
- *Globalgarve*
- *Instituto do Emprego e Formação Profissional* (IEFP)/Institute of Employment and Professional Training
- *Junta Autónoma de Estradas* (JAE)/Portuguese Roads
- *Núcleo dos Empresários da Região do Algarve* (NERA)/Nucleus of Business Owners of the Algarve
- *Universidade do Algarve* (UAL)/University of the Algarve

Faro is also involved in several working groups supported by the World Federation of United Cities that are aiming to identify ways of using the concepts of sustainability in urban centres.

NOTES

1   DSCS is the first provisory official version from the meeting of Ministers responsible for the Territory Management of the Member States of the European Union, Noodwijk, 9 and 10 June 1997, p. 59.
2   DSCS, p. 38.
3   Jan van der Borg (1994) 'Tourism and urban development: the impact of tourism on urban development: towards a theory of urban tourism and its implications to the case of Venice', thesis, Amsterdam.
4   Ibid.
5   C. Law (1993), *Urban Tourism: Attracting Visitors to Large Cities*, London: Mansell.
6   *Director Plan of Faro* (1995), Municipal Council, Faro.
7   Portuguese National Statistic Institute.
8   http://www.ccr-alg.pt/
9   Motorway running east–west across the Algarve.
10   The Guadiana River borders the south of Spain (50 km from Faro).
11   *Strategic Plan of Faro* (1996), Faro Municipal Council.
12   *ANA (Airport and Air Navigation)* (1995) Faro airport.
13   This figure includes about 50,000 tourists per year who use Faro airport but spend their holidays in Spain, according to AHETA, Association of Hotels and Tourist Enterprises of the Algarve.
14   The main route from Faro to Lisbon is currently a mixture of single carriageways, dual carriageways and stretches of motorway. Eventually the motorway will be extended to cover the entire route, thus shortening the journey time considerably.
15   Motorway built at the time of the commemoration of the 5th Centenary of the Portuguese Discoveries, running from Albufeira to the Spanish border (Ayamonte).
16   The drivers of 'tourist taxis' are qualified tourist guides. A tourist taxi can be booked via a central reservations office, or via hotel receptions, etc.
17   The Atlantic Arc network of tourist towns dates from December 1993 and includes ten French, British, Irish, Spanish and Portuguese towns. The Atlantic Arc Commission was created in October 1989, following the Congress of European Peripheral Maritime Regions, and is constituted by 32 regions which cover 2,500 km of Atlantic coast, from Andalusia to Scotland.
18   *Movimento dos Postos de Turismo* (visitor numbers in Tourist Information Offices) 1992–96 RTA (Algarve Regional Tourism Board), Planning and Studies Department.
19   *Direcção Geral de Turismo*, Portuguese Tourism Board.
20   Data collected by Ambifaro (Local Development Agency) published in its brochure.
21   Suzana Miguel (1996) 'Data base of a survey designed to identify the services sought by visitors to Tourist Information Offices in the Algarve', Project for Postgraduate Diploma in Marketing, ESGHT, Universidade do Algarve.
22   Paulo Águas (1997) 'Tourism and urban entertainment', conference paper, ESGHT, Universidade do Algarve.
23   Ibid.
24   Data collected by Ambifaro (Local Development Agency) published in its brochure.

REFERENCES

Ashworth, G. J. and Larkham, P. J. (1994) 'Tourism, culture and identity in the New Europe' in J. G. Ashworth and P. J. Larkham (eds) *Building a New Heritage*. London: Routledge.
Ashworth, G. J. and Turnbridge, J. E. (1990) *The Tourist Historic City*. Chichester: John Wiley.
Buswell, J. (1993) *Case Studies in Leisure Management Practice*. London: Longman.
Law, C. (1993) 'Attracting visitors to large cities', in *Urban Tourism*. London: Mansell.

Law, C. (1996) *Tourism in the Major Cities*. London: International Thompson Business Press.

Laws, E. (1995) 'Issues in analysing and managing tourist destinations', in *Tourist Destination Management*. London: Routledge, pp. 7–39.

Uzzell, D. (1989) *Heritage Interpretation: The Natural and Built Environment*, vol. 1. London: Belhaven Press.

Uzzell, D. (1992) *Heritage Interpretation: The Visitor Experience*, vol. 2. London: Belhaven Press.

van der Borg, J. (1991) 'Tourism and urban development: the impact of tourism and its implications. The case of Venice', Italy. Thesis, Amsterdam.

van der Borg, L., van der Borg, J. and van der Meer, J. (1995) 'Performance and strategies in eight European cities', *Urban Tourism*. Brookfield: Avebury.

CHAPTER 6

Vilamoura

How to reconcile the present and future of a resort

Celia Veiga and Manuela Guerreiro

Aim

To establish forms of resort management, maintaining harmony between the present Vilamoura and the Vilamoura envisaged in the XXI Project.

NEDO/Tourism Society defines a resort as an established town which has a significant range of tourist facilities (Laws, 1995). Resort or destination marketing requires not only the identification and definition of the existing tourist products but the devising of strategies for the introduction of new products in relation to the existing product line (Ashworth and Voogd, 1990).

Bad planning, carelessly devised or unfulfilled strategies can compromise the strategic positioning of the entire resort, thus affecting its image. Furthermore, an incorrect match between the existing and the new product may lead to problems, namely internal competition or cannibalization.

For the creation or maintenance of an appropriate image, adequate promotion should be used. Branding is a powerful promotional tool and it aims, through the use of visual symbols and written means to convey a distributive and pleasing identity (Lumsdon, 1992).

Keywords

tourism resort management; strategic positioning; image

Summary

Vilamoura, located in the southernmost province of Portugal, the Algarve, is one of the largest developments of its kind in Europe. The first master plan for the urbanization of Vilamoura was approved in 1966 and then revised in 1980, when it was decided to increase significantly the population density of the urban area. This plan was revised again in 1993 with new proposals: to improve town planning and land use by redistributing building areas and by reducing population density and the number of floors for new buildings. This is the 2nd phase of Vilamoura, known as Vilamoura XXI Programme.

The underlying concept of this programme is the development of tourist, residential, sports and leisure facilities in a coherent and balanced way, at the same time, respecting the natural environment. The major question here is how to reconcile the present Vilamoura with the Vilamoura XXI Programme in order to create a unique resort, with a unique position and promotion strategy.

Learning outcomes
- to understand the concept of destination/resort marketing;
- to examine the development of strategies aimed at guaranteeing a unique image for a seaside resort;
- to examine the relationship and the importance between product development and promotion.

Discussion topics
- Will Lusotur be able to guarantee the same strategic positioning that it now has, for Vilamoura XXI, thus creating a unique resort?
- Is there a danger of 'cannibalization'? If so, how can this be avoided?
- Taking into account its strategic positioning and the brand name, which promotion techniques should Lusotur adopt to ensure a global promotion strategy?
- Can you apply the product life-cycle model to Vilamoura resort? What is the required information?
- What segmentation bases and approaches are used by Lusotur for the definition of Vilamoura relevant segments?
- According to the Ansoff matrix for defining strategic direction, in which *stage* would you classify the Vilamoura resort product?

THE ALGARVE

The Algarve is the southernmost province of Portugal. It is the main tourist destination of the country, for both domestic and international tourism. Its climate is basically Mediterranean, with some subtropical features. Long dry summers (about 3,000 hours of sun per annum) alternate with wet winters (averaging 600 mm rainfall a year).

The 1960s was the turning point for tourism development in the Algarve. The first hotels and other tourist infrastructures, such as the international airport of Faro (1965), were built during this period. The main tourist products of the Algarve are the sun and sea, and more recently, golf. In recent years the Algarve has diversified its portfolio and is offering other products such as rural, sport and cultural tourism.

It is estimated that the Algarve is responsible for about 60 per cent of the national gross income generated by tourism. Moreover, the region absorbs around 50 to 60 per cent of the national tourist investment.

The Algarve accounts for about 40 per cent of all Portuguese bed spaces available in the hotel sector. Even more significant is the Algarve's share of bednights which was 45 per cent of the national total in 1996.

The tourists who visit the Algarve are mainly from other countries: international tourism accounts for 73 per cent (10,390,444) of the total bednights compared to the 17 per cent (2,187,265) taken by the domestic market (1996). The traditional international markets of the Algarve are the British (39 per cent of the bednights in classified accommodation in 1996), the Germans (31 per cent of bednights) and the Dutch (10 per cent of bednights). These figures represent for the British and the Dutch tourists, 72 per cent of these nationalities' bednights in Portugal. Meanwhile the German bednights in the Algarve represent 62 per cent of the total German bednights in Portugal.

In 1996, Faro international airport recorded an annual movement of 3,553,994 passengers.

VILAMOURA

Location and accessibility

Vilamoura, located in the municipal district of Loulé, in central Algarve, benefits from a privileged location with good connections. By road, it takes three hours to Lisbon, the capital of Portugal. The new motorway linking Lisbon to the Algarve is expected to be completed by the end of the decade thus reducing the journey time. The Spanish border is only a 40 minute ride by car. The provincial capital of the Algarve, Faro, is 20 minutes away from Vilamoura. Faro international airport is about a 3-hour flight from the main European capitals and it is served by a large number of airlines, offering both regular and charter flights. Light aircraft and helicopters can use the local Vilamoura airstrip.

Background

The first master plan of urbanization of the Algarve, 'the preliminary master plan of Vilamoura', was approved by the government in 1966. It covered a 1,700 hectare area named *Quinta de Quarteira*. This initial plan was for an overall built-up area of 2,578,394 m^2 for approximately 60,000 inhabitants.

The preliminary plan of Vilamoura included the careful planning of supporting facilities, entertainment, services and basic infrastructure. From the beginning Vilamoura developed around three main focus points: the marina, golf and the beaches. The plan started with 1,631 ha, of which 1,053 ha were allocated for tourist developments. The remaining area was left undeveloped and reserved for pine wood and agricultural and cattle-raising activities.

In 1980 a revision plan was devised. The basic concept was maintained, but the revised plan envisaged a significant increase in the population density of the urban area leading to a general increase in the height of the buildings at the resort.

After changes were made to Lusotur's (Vilamoura's developer) shareholding structure, in 1988 a team of renowned international architects made recommendations to modify the 1980 Master Plan. At that time, a total of 1,560 145 m^2 had already been built on, which corresponded to an approximate capacity of 35,000 residential or tourist beds.

In 1993, a revised plan embodied considerations regarding improved town planning and land use, mainly in connection with redistributing building areas, reducing population density factors and the number of floors for new buildings (a return of the 1966 Plan). In 1995, the importance of the development of this second phase of Vilamoura was acknowledged and accepted by the Portuguese government.

In 1996, the André Jordan group acquired controlling interest in LUSOTUR S.A. The re-launching of Vilamoura resort was decided.

Vilamoura today

Vilamoura is one of the largest developments of its kind in Europe, with over 35,000 available beds, more than 6,000 permanent residents and around 350,000 visitors (tourists and temporary residents) per year.

The three main development features for the resort, golf, the marina and the beaches, are served by a wide range of accommodation, leisure facilities and complementary services in order to support the tourist development of the zone.

Vilamoura accommodation supply includes seven hotels (5 or 4 stars) (see Table 6.1), three aparthotels (self-catering complexes), tourist villages, villas and private apartments.

The area is served by about 100 restaurants and bars, twelve entertainment complexes, with particular reference to the Casino and discos, as well as six bank

Table 6.1: Hotel accommodation supply in Vilamoura.

Number of stars	Hotel	Number of rooms
*****	Vilamoura Marinotel	385
****	Vila Galé Vilamoura	243
****	Hotel Ampalius	330
****	D. Pedro Golf	261
****	D. Pedro Marina	155
****	D. Pedro Portobelo	55
	Motel do Golfe	52
*****	Atlantis Vilamoura	310
	Estalagem da Cegonha	10
	Total	1,801

Source: Lusotur, SA.

branches. Furthermore, Vilamoura has an international school, a horse-riding centre, an international shooting range, and various sports and cultural facilities, of which the Roman ruins of *Cerro da Vila* are of particular note.

Vilamoura has an extensive shopping centre where multinational companies are represented and it also provides excellent conditions for the organization of events (congresses, meetings and business conferences). Meetings can be organized for over 1,200 people within the existing facilities, which have a total seating capacity of approximately 5,000. The short distance between the hotels allows great ease and flexibility in organizing such events. A regular transport system (minitrain-trailer vehicle) is available for visitors and residents for trips to and from the various Vilamoura tourist village complexes, the beach, the town centre and the marina.

The marina

The initial construction phase of the marina took place in 1971. By 1974, 615 mooring berths had been completed. The second phase started in 1981, increasing the capacity to 1,000 berths and this also allowed vessels of up to 43 m (140 ft.) in length to be docked.

The marina includes services and support facilities such as a fuelling station, catering and provisions services, electricity and drinking water supplies, daily collection of rubbish and waste oil, laundry, shower blocks, permanent security and a boatyard. The annual movement at the Marina was around 2,700 vessels entries in 1997, with the period of July and August representing more than 50 per cent of the total (Table 6.2).

Table 6.2: Annual movement at the marina by months, 1997.

Month	Vessels	%
January	30	1
February	28	1
March	116	4
April	115	4
May	144	5
June	230	9
July	587	22
August	956	36
September	239	9
October	130	5
November	62	2
December	24	1
Total	2,661	100

Source: Lusotur, SA.

Table 6.3: Marina movement by nationality.

Nationality	1996 Entries	%	1997 Entries	%
Portuguese	1,525	57.7	1,577	59.3
British	388	14.7	374	14.1
German	162	6.1	146	5.5
Spanish	155	5.9	137	5.2
French	128	4.9	133	5.0
Dutch	99	3.6	129	4.9
Total	2,457	92.9	2,496	93.8

Source: Lusotur, SA.

In terms of nationalities, the Portuguese are the main users of the marina with around 60 per cent of the total entries followed by the British with 14 per cent (Table 6.3).

The marina comprises a Yacht Club and the International Marina Club, which is responsible for the organization of nautical events. The Vilamoura marina area is an important leisure and entertainment centre where national and international events (music and fashion shows, vintage car rallies, parades, new vehicle launches, etc.) take place. A Boat Show comprising the exhibition of vessels and accessories takes place annually.

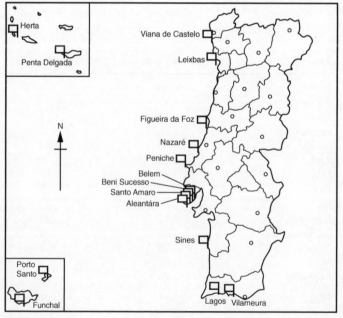

Figure 6.1: Marinas of Portugal.

Several companies operating at the Vilamoura marina rent out craft or organize deep-sea fishing along the Algarve coast. Very recently, the marina of Vilamoura has been facing competition from the marina of Lagos, although this marina has a smaller capacity: 462 berths and allowing only vessels up to 20 m (65 ft) (see Tables 6.4 and 6.5).

Table 6.4: Prices at marina of Vilamoura.

	High Season				Low Season				
Class	Day	Week	Month	3 months	Day	Week	Month	3 months	6 months
I	2.150	14.500	58.000	165.000	650	4.300	18.000	50.000	82.000
II	2.600	17.500	71.000	204.000	850	5.600	23.000	65.000	107.000
IIa	2.800	18.000	74.000	211.000	1.050	7.000	28.000	80.000	132.000
III	3.000	20.000	80.000	229.000	1.200	8.000	32.000	92.000	151.000
IIIa	3.200	22.000	88.000	248.000	1.350	9.000	36.000	102.000	170.000
IV	3.900	26.000	106.000	306.000	1.550	10.300	42.000	119.000	195.000
IVa	4.250	28.000	115.000	330.000	1.750	11.700	47.000	134.000	221.000
V	5.200	35.000	143.000	407.000	2.300	15.300	62.000	176.000	290.000
Va	5.900	39.000	162.000	462.000	2.600	17.300	70.000	199.000	328.000
VI	8.200	54.000	225.000	638.000	3.500	23.300	95.000	268.000	441.000
VIa	9.100	61.000	250.000	715.000	3.800	25.300	102.000	291.000	479.000
VII	11.700	78.000	320.000	924.000	4.500	30.000	122.000	344.000	567.000
VIII	14.900	99.000	405.000	1.166.000	5.700	38.000	154.000	436.000	718.000
IX	16.600	110.000	450.000	1.296.000	6.700	44.600	181.000	513.000	844.000

Source: Lusotur, S.A.

Table 6.5: Prices at marina of Lagos.

	High Season – 01 April–30 September				Low Season – 01 October–31 March				
Class	Day	Week	Month	3 months	Day	Week	Month	3 months	6 months
I	2.600	17.400	70.400	203.500	850	5.500	22.000	63.400	105.040
I-A	2.700	18.000	73.400	211.200	1.000	7.000	28.000	80.000	131.040
II	2.950	19.700	79.900	228.800	1.200	8.000	32.000	91.500	150.800
II-A	3.200	21.200	86.000	247.500	1.350	9.000	36.000	104.000	170.560
III	3.700	24.500	99.700	289.200	1.560	10.300	41.200	119.600	196.560
III-A	4.000	26.700	108.700	312.000	1.770	11.750	47.000	135.200	222.560
IV	4.900	32.800	132.800	384.800	2.300	15.200	60.800	175.000	288.080
IV-A	5.600	37.200	151.100	436.800	2.600	17.300	69.200	198.500	327.600
V	7.700	51.400	208.400	603.200	3.400	22.800	91.200	263.000	432.640
V-A	8.600	57.300	232.400	676.000	3.700	24.800	99.200	286.000	472.160

Source: http.//www.marlagos.pt

Golf

The Algarve has nineteen golf courses, around 50 per cent of the total golf courses in Portugal (see Figure 6.2). Vilamoura is ranked as one of the prime European golf destinations. It has three courses. *The Old Course of Vilamoura*, opened in 1969 and designed by golf architect Frank Pennink, was recently renovated, which included the rebuilding of all tees, fairways and greens, the installation of new drainage and sophisticated sprinkler systems, reaffirming it as one of Europe's best golf courses. It is a par-73 layout with an overall length of 6,250 metres, set among umbrella pinewoods on undulating terrain. A new clubhouse was constructed and inaugurated when the course was re-opened for play.

The Pinhal Golf Course (formerly Vilamoura II) is a par-72 course of 6,300 metres in length, and is lined by pine trees. It will be renovated in the near future. *Laguna Golf Course* (formerly Vilamoura III) has 27 holes with tricky playing characteristics, which makes it well respected by both local and foreign players.

A further 27 holes are planned for Vilamoura, built along the lines of existing layouts, and consequently making a total of five complete 18-hole courses in the resort.

Before long, work will start on the building of a golf academy, close to The Old Course. This will include a clubhouse, driving range, putting and chipping greens, sand bunkers and three practice holes. Vilamoura has also an Adventure Golf (mini golf) centre to provide entertainment and leisure for beginners, experienced golfers and families in general.

Golfing visitors to Vilamoura can travel between the main hotels, tourist complexes and the courses by the regular Golf Shuttle bus service. The traditional

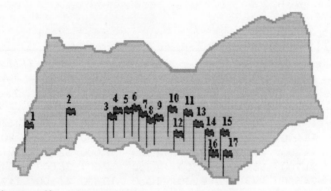

Figure 6.2: Algarve golf courses.

1	Parque Floresta	7	Vale do Milho
2	Palmares	8	Salgados
3	Penina	9	Pine Cliffs
4	Alto Golf	10	The Old Course
5	Vale Pinta	11	Pinhal Golf Course
6	Quinta do Gramacho	12	Laguna Golf Course

13	Vila Sol
14	Ocean Course and Royal Golf Course
15	Pinheiros Altos
16	Quinta do Lago and Ria Formosa
17	San Lorenzo

Table 6.6: Golf players by nationality January to April 1998.

Nationality	Number golf players	%
British	29,976	50.4
German	8,446	14.2
Swedish	6,446	10.8
Portuguese	2,573	4.3
French	2,414	4.1
Others	9,630	16.2
Total	59,485	100.0

Source: Lusotur, SA.

golf markets of Vilamoura are the British and the Germans, together representing over 60 per cent of the total (see Table 6.6). The prices of Vilamoura golf courses are competitive compared to other courses in the Algarve.

Beaches

Vilamoura has two sandy beaches, the Marina and the Falesia, which total about 3km, and have both been granted the European Blue Flag. They are accessible beaches where the regular practice of water sports (windsurfing, water skiing, para-sailing, fishing) is possible throughout the year due to a mild climate. Vilamoura beaches are served by several restaurants and bars offering traditional gastronomy.

VILAMOURA XXI

Urbanization plan of Vilamoura – Vilamoura XXI Programme

Lusotur, SA is planning the Vilamoura second development phase, known as the Vilamoura XXI Programme. The underlying concept of this programme is the development of tourist, residential, sports and leisure facilities in a coherent and balanced way, at the same time respecting the natural environment.

The development of the project will be based on two priority guidelines. On the one hand, the revival of Vilamoura's currently built-up area as a means of enhancing the value of the already established investments, on the other, a general intervention in terms of architecture, engineering and landscaping where the local environmental features are to be entirely respected. This is perceived as a guarantee of a better standard of living for all, residents, visitors or tourists.

Strategic objectives

In order to establish Vilamoura as a properly structured tourist centre, Vilamoura XXI has incorporated the following strategic objectives: to keep the quality of

Vilamoura and to preserve the environment. Building with nature is the main concept for the Vilamoura development. All the development will be carefully planned in order to place Vilamoura according to the defined concept.

Vilamoura's privileged segment targets are Portuguese, British and German individuals and families with a high social and economic status.

Revitalization of the urban area

The revitalization of the present urban area will be based on diversified operations, namely the improvement of connections, reorganization of the cleaning and refuse collection services, improved security, golf course renovation, new landscaped areas, entertainment centres and beach facilities.

The urban revitalization will be the result of new architectural methods, the correction of present anomalies and development of new and integrated landscaping concepts. Several support areas will be developed, such as areas providing children's entertainment, leisure and social areas, repairs to dilapidated buildings, information for both tourists and residents and new beach facilities.

The Vilamoura urbanization plan

The general urbanization plan of Vilamoura aims for a built-up area of 860 ha in a total of 1,700 ha. New tourist, residential, social, sport and leisure facilities will be built. Particular emphasis will be put upon the development of transition areas linking the previously built-up zones with the 'new' Vilamoura.

The project will involve the creation of different zones, considering the local topography, vegetation and landscape frameworks, but also keeping their functional characteristics – vocation, attraction poles and type of market. It consists of the development of thematic villages which are well differentiated and located in terms of landscape. According to the defined concept 'building with nature', the proposals for the building area and the total forecast population will not exceed 11 per cent of the total area.

The following areas were established and considered as the basis for the development and structuring of the second phase of the Vilamoura project:

- *Aldeia Hípica* (equestrian village) 24 ha – to provide facilities for the horse riding centre with building permission covering an area of 45,000 m^2.
- *Pinhal Velho*, a 99-ha luxury condominium area with 45,000 m^2 of approved building area.
- *Aldeias da Ribeira*, an area planned for a sports complex. The total area allocated is 28 ha with 15,000 m^2 of building area authorized.

- *Colinas do Golfe,* a series of quality tourist villages with a total area of 119 ha and building permission covering an area of 130,000 m^2.
- *Encosta das Oliveiras,* planned as a permanent residential area totalling 57 ha with building permission for 150,000 m^2.
- *Praia da Falésia,* a 34-ha area to connect with and facilitate access to the beach.
- *Fonte do Ulme,* a zone reserved for an exclusive luxury residential condominium complex. Total area of 15 ha with building permission for 15,000 m^2.
- *Cerro da Vinha,* an area set aside for hotels, and other tourist and residential accommodation. The new golf courses, horse riding areas, a theme park and a sports centre suitable for international meetings will be built here. With a total area of 313 ha and 160,000 m^2 of building area authorized, this zone will include protected green areas within an ecological framework.
- *Cidade Lacustre* (Lakeside city) an urban residential centre around a series of lakes and canals spread over an area of 140 ha with building permission for 340,000 m^2. It will comprise a variety of occupational activities linked directly with the inner marina, lakes and canals.
- *Canais do Golfe,* a residential zone located between the present built-up area of Vilamoura and Cidade Lacustre, covering an area of 26.2 ha and approved building area totalling 63,000 m^2.

Green globe

In 1996, Lusotur SA became associated with Green Globe, a worldwide programme established by the World Travel and Tourism Council. The Green Globe define guidelines for sustainable development with full respect for the environmental balance and the protection of nature. Lusotur, whose main objective is to establish and implement a sustainable development programme has already received the Green Globe progress award for the work done.

REFERENCES AND SUGGESTED READING

Ashworth, G. J. and Voogd, H. (1990) *Selling the City.* London: John Wiley and Sons.

Cooper, C. *et al.* (1993) *Tourism, Principles and Practice.* London: Pitman Publishing.

Laws, E. (1995) *Tourist Destination Management: Issues, Analysis and Policies.* London: Routledge.

Lickoust, L. (1994) *Developing Tourism Destinations: Policies and Perspectives.* Harlow: Longman.

Lumsdon, L. (1992) *Marketing for Tourism: Case Study Assignments.* London: Macmillan Press.

Lusotur (1997) *Vilamoura,* April, **3**.

Lusotur (1998a) *Vilamoura XXI Program – Building with Nature,* from the 6th Annual US/Latin America Resort and Tourism Development Conference.

Lusotur (1998b) *Vilamoura Magazine,* Winter/Spring 98, **2**.

Seaton, A. V. and Bennet, M. M. (1996) *Marketing Tourism: Products, Concepts, Issues, Cases.* Oxford: Alden Press, Chapter 14.

HELLO Tourism

Evangelos P. Karavangelis

Edited by Thomas Mavrodontis

Objectif

Les principaux objectifs d'étude du présent article sont:

- aborder la problématique de la gestion améliorée d'un flux touristique, afin d'obtenir une meilleure protection de l'environnement et de la culture d'une localité touristique d'accueil. En d'autres termes, obtenir un meilleur équilibre entre la localité concernée et le flux des touristes accueillis.
- aborder la question de la mise en pratique de la gestion susmentionnée à deux sites touristiques de la Grèce présentant une offre touristique similaire, mais des taux de croissance divergents: l'île de Milos (Cyclades) et Dion, lieu historique aux pieds du Mont Olympe (Région de Pieria – Macédoine grecque).

Mots Clés

étalement touristique; optimisation de la demande; nouvelles technologies d'information; bornes inter-actives; 'éducation' (visiteur et autochtone)

Résumé

Le projet pilote HELLO Tourism (Heritage Environment Leisure Learning and Organization of Tourism Management) est un système novateur de gestion environnementale et culturelle d'une destination touristique. Le projet a été réalisé durant la période entre les mois de décembre 1995 et juillet 1997 dans le cadre du Plan d'Action Communautaire en faveur du tourisme pour l'année 1995. Les entités responsables de la matérialisation du projet sont l'association à but non-lucratif MEWCAT qui a son siège à l'île de Milos et l'association non-lucrative 'Alexandros' qui a son siège à la ville de Katerini (Grèce). Les mairies de Milos et de Dion ainsi que la commune de Adamas (Milos) ont également participé à la réalisation du projet.

La promotion de son produit final a été effectuée par le tour opérateur allemand Last Minute Tours qui a son siège à Munich et le tour opérateur chypriote Kinisis Travel and Tours qui a son siège à Nicosie.

L'achèvement du projet a conduit à la production de deux CD-ROM, qui sont utilisés par les touristes à des Centres d'Information (Info-kiosks) installés aux entrées principales des deux régions étudiées (île de Milos et site de Dion/Pieria). Ces CD-ROM ont été diffusés par les tour opérateurs ci-dessus mentionnés.

Le projet a été basé sur l'œuvre théorique de Pierre Défert (1967), considérée comme classique, reflétant le concept de 'l'offre touristique' d'une localité et le moyen d'obtenir un équilibre optimum par rapport à la demande touristique, soit Tf(t) = 100.

La méthodologie du projet a été réalisée selon les sept types d'actions suivants:

- études de faisabilité;
- recherche et recueil du matériel pour la production des CD-ROM;
- ébauche du contenu des CD-ROM;
- procédure technique de la production des CD-ROM en trois phases;
- mise en utilisation par le public des CD-ROM à des Centres d'Information (Info-kiosks) et évaluation de leur impact;
- mesures à prendre en termes d'un soutien supplémentaire;
- diffusion des résultats.

La structure du contenu des deux CD-ROM, qui constituent un 'produit touristique multimédia', comporte les sections suivantes:

Section 1: Histoire – Monuments – Objets d'Art
Section 2: Habitats Traditionnels – Attractions d'Esthétique Naturelle
Section 3: Plages – Zones littorales
Section 4: Mode de Vie – Activités – Manifestations Socioculturelles
Section 5: Loisirs des Visiteurs – Touristes
Section 6: Environnement Naturel
Section 7: Équipements – Offre de Services Touristiques – Renseignements

Le projet produit un impact éducatif en termes de management touristique et propose de manière 'intrinsèque' ou 'extrinsèque' les mécanismes régulateurs suivants:

1. Mécanisme pour un meilleur étalement des flux de visiteurs dans le temps.
2. Mécanisme pour la protection de l'environnement.
3. Mécanisme pour l'amélioration des effets didactiques et de communication à l'égard du public et des institutions impliquées.
4. Mécanisme, enfin, de renforcement des résultats positifs.

Pour en conclure, le projet a un caractère didactique et de par sa structure peut être appliqué à toute région touristique.

Résultats visés pour l'étudiant
Après l'étude du présent rapport et l'usage de son matériel d'appui (les deux CD-ROM) tout intéressé peut:

- comprendre comment l'offre touristique d'une localité peut être analysée et comment peut être estimé le seuil de son équilibre;
- apprendre à déployer le 'système de management touristique' HELLO Tourism afin d'assurer aux visiteurs l'amélioration de leurs expériences de vacances, d'organiser mieux les flux touristiques et d'améliorer la protection culturelle et environnementale;
- comprendre comment le système HELLO Tourism met en route, de manière

intrinsèque et extrinsèque, des mécanismes régulateurs concernant les flux de visiteurs au site examiné, la protection de son environnement, la fonction de diffusion des résultats grâce au matériel pédagogique-didactique et de communication, matériel qui peut s'appliquer à toute région méditerranéenne et européenne.

Points de discussion

- Formulez la structure de l'offre touristique d'une localité et le concept de son équilibre dynamique, selon la conception des CD-ROM HELLO Tourism.
- Imaginez que vous vous efforcez de mettre en pratique un plan d'action afin de gérer le flux de touristes d'une localité d'accueil: décrivez les sept types d'action de la méthodologie appliquée d'un plan d'action de ce genre, selon le projet HELLO Tourism.
- Vous avez à produire un CD-ROM, en deux langues, pour le management touristique d'une localité d'accueil: décrivez les sept sections qui correspondent à la structure de son contenu, selon la conception des CD-ROM HELLO Tourism; efforcez-vous de répertorier, basés sur la structure susmentionnée, les facteurs touristiques d'une localité d'accueil de votre choix, afin de produire votre CD-ROM bilingue.
- Ciblez le travail initial en terme de segmentation du marché. Argumentez.
- Élaborez un mécanisme régulateur afin de gérer le flux des visiteurs d'une localité d'accueil de votre choix. Objectifs recherchés: l'allongement de la période touristique – l'étalement dans l'espace de la demande touristique. Consultez le cas du projet HELLO Tourism.
- Élaborez un mécanisme régulateur pour la protection de l'environnement d'une localité d'accueil de votre choix. Suivez le cas du projet HELLO Tourism.
- Élaborez un mécanisme régulateur pour renforcer l'impact et la diffusion des résultats d'un plan d'action de management touristique pour une localité d'accueil de votre choix. Consultez le cas du projet HELLO Tourism.
- Formulez un questionnaire pour les visiteurs d'une localité de votre choix, afin d'évaluer leurs expériences touristiques en termes de:

  - facteurs géographiques;
  - facteurs historiques;
  - facteurs culturels;
  - facteurs écologiques;
  - facteurs proprement touristiques (p. ex. moyens de transport, d'hébergement etc.).

Fondement théorique

Le rapport concernant le projet HELLO Tourism est basé sur la notion de la 'structure de l'offre touristique' d'une localité et le concept relatif de la 'fonction touristique optimale'.

La thèse doctrinale de Pierre Défert 'La localisation touristique – Aspects théoriques et pratiques', ainsi que les travaux plus récents de R. Baretje, J.J. Schwarz, V. Middleton, S.F. Witt et L. Moutinho sont les sources théoriques de notions susmentionnées.

INTRODUCTION

Selon le Journal Officiel des Communautés Européennes N° C 106/7 et plus particulièrement selon le Plan d'Action Communautaire en faveur du Tourisme (95C 106/09) pour l'année 1995, toute action étant appelée à se réaliser dans le cadre de ce Plan devrait, d'une part, établir des relations de collaboration étroite entre les Pays Communautaires et ceux du Centre-Est d'Europe, du Maghreb, ainsi qu'avec Chypre et Malte; d'autre part, elle devrait promouvoir un lien d'équilibre entre le phénomène touristique émanant de cette action et son environnement.

Selon le même Plan d'Action Communautaire en faveur du tourisme et dans le champs d'intervention concernant le lien d'équilibre entre le courant touristique des visiteurs et la localité touristique d'accueil, un de ses objectifs primordiaux est d'améliorer la gestion du flux touristique. Cette gestion a comme objectif de garantir, moyennant la mise en pratique de projets pilotes, une meilleure protection des facteurs constitutifs de l'environnement et de la culture de la localité touristique d'accueil.

Dans le contexte susmentionné le projet HELLO Tourism a été réalisé entre les mois de décembre 1995 et juillet 1997. Dans une première partie de cet exposé nous verrons la structure théorique et méthodologique du projet en question, alors que dans la deuxième partie nous présenterons les points fondamentaux du management du site touristique d'accueil. Nous décrirons également le matériel pédagogique et de communication que ce projet propose.

STRUCTURE THÉORIQUE ET MÉTHODOLOGIQUE

Fondement théorique

La conception de la structure de l'offre touristique des deux localités touristiques d'accueil grecques, qui constituent l'objet d'approche du projet, est fondée sur le concept de l'offre touristique, telle qu'elle émane de l'œuvre classique de Pierre Défert (1967). D'une manière générale, cette structure correspond aux facteurs suivants:

- l'attraction du site;
- les coordonnées géographiques du site;
- les monuments et lieux historiques du site, ainsi que le patrimoine touristique culturel de sa population;
- les aspects du site non apparents au public (le cadre socio-économique de la vie quotidienne de la population);
- les aspects provenant de l'environnement naturel du site et leur mise en valeur;
- enfin, les modes d'hébergement, les équipements et les services publics et privés du site (séjour, restauration, loisirs, consommation de biens fondamentaux, tels circulation, éclairage, eau, etc.) satisfaisant la demande touristique.

La structure de l'offre touristique d'un site correspond aux notions de l'offre touristique originelle ('hydrome', 'phytome', 'lithome' et 'anthropome') et de l'offre touristique dérivée ('infrastructures de base', 'infrastructures touristiques', 'canaux de distribution touristique', 'facteurs conjoncturels').

Sur la base de cette offre touristique susmentionnée et pour ce qui est de chacune des deux localités touristiques d'accueil en question, nous essayons d'obtenir une fonction touristique optimale, à savoir un Tf(t) = 100, voir René Baretje et Pierre Défert (1972). Ce taux de fonction touristique correspond à un état d'équilibre dynamique entre l'offre et la demande touristique d'un site d'accueil. C'est précisément cet équilibre qui tend à diminuer les dysfonctionnements touristiques qu'engendrent une situation de déséquilibre quantitatif et qualitatif entre l'offre et la demande touristique du site précis.

MÉTHODOLOGIE APPLIQUÉE

Le projet HELLO Tourism, grâce à sa méthodologie, contribue à présenter un 'système de management touristique' offrant une information éducative sous forme d'un CD-ROM à l'usage du visiteur et du professionnel ainsi que sous forme de 'matériel d'appui supplémentaire'.

La méthodologie suivie consiste à une intervention identique dans les deux localités touristiques d'accueil choisies par le projet. Celle-ci vise à mieux gérer les courants touristiques s'y rendant et par conséquent mieux protéger l'environnement naturel et culturel de ces localités. Ce mode d'intervention correspond à sept types d'action qui constituent les sept modules du Plan d'Action du projet.

Ces modules sont, par ordre de priorité, les suivants:

Module 1: Étude de faisabilité.
Module 2: Recherche et recueil du matériel indispensable.
Module 3: Ébauche du contenu du CD-ROM.
Module 4: Procédure technique de la production du CD-ROM en trois phases.
Module 5: Mise en usage du CD-ROM dans des centres d'information (Info-kiosks) et d'accueil du public et évaluation de son impact.
Module 6: Mesures à prendre en termes d'un soutien supplémentaire.
Module 7: Diffusion des résultats positifs du projet.

La méthodologie précédente est complétée par un effort d'assurer une formation des groupes choisis dans la population concernée. Cette formation va dans le sens de l'amélioration de la protection de l'environnement naturel et culturel des sites touristiques d'accueil examinés.

Enfin, suit la diffusion des résultats, qui se fait à travers des canaux professionnels et vise les touristes potentiels des principaux pays émetteurs à destination de la Grèce et plus particulièrement à destination de l'île de Milos et du site de Dion/Pieria.

MANAGEMENT SOUTENU D'UN SITE TOURISTIQUE D'ACCUEIL: MATÉRIEL PÉDAGOGIQUE ET DE COMMUNICATION

Aspects généraux

Le choix des deux sites touristiques d'accueil, celui de l'île de Milos (région de Cyclades, Grèce) et celui de Dion (région de Pieria au sud-ouest de la Macédoine grecque), pour l'application de la méthodologie commentée plus haut n'a pas été fait au hasard. Ce choix a été imposé par le fait qu'ils présentent les mêmes conditions d'offre touristique, alors qu'en même temps leurs taux de croissance touristique divergent. Celle de l'île de Milos est en voie de développement, alors que celle du site de Dion/Pieria est considéré comme déjà acquise, mais caractérisée par une saisonalité aiguë, en juillet et août.

Ce contraste s'avère, en fait, un défi pour la 'capacité d'applicabilité' (possibilité de transfert et mise en application) du projet HELLO Tourism. C'est-à-dire la possibilité d'application de la même méthodologie à des produits/sites touristiques d'accueil similaires en ce qui concerne la structure de leur offre, mais différents en ce qui concerne leurs rythmes de croissance.

La similitude des structures de l'offre touristique de l'île de Milos et celle du site de Dion/Pieria est fondée sur les facteurs suivants:

Île de Milos	Site de Dion/Pieria
Site et monuments historiques	Site et monuments historiques
Musée archéologique	Musée archéologique
Ancien théâtre	Ancien théâtre
Temples, monastères, églises	Temples, monastères, églises
Climat méditerranéen insulaire	Climat méditerranéen continental
Montagne (Hàlakas)	Montagne (Olympe)
Villages montagneux (Pollonia, Plàka, Trypiti, Adàmandas, etc.)	Bourgs et villages montagneux (Litohoro, Vrondou, Milià, etc.)
Zones littorales	Zones littorales
Forteresse (de Ste Marine)	Forteresse (de Platamonas)
Gastronomie locale	Gastronomie locale
Coutumes locales	Coutumes locales

Les données présentées ci-dessus constituent la structure du contenu de la production touristique multimédia suivante:

Section 1:   Histoire – Monuments – Objets d'Art
Section 2:   Habitats Traditionnels – Attractions d'Esthétique Naturelle
Section 3:   Plages – Zones littorales
Section 4:   Mode de vie – Activités – Manifestations Socioculturelles
Section 5:   Loisirs des Visiteurs – Touristes
Section 6:   Environnement Naturel
Section 7:   Équipements – Offre de services Touristiques – Renseignements

Toutes ces informations sont adressées au grand public, aux segments choisis des populations concernées et aux professionnels intéressés en trois langues: grec, anglais et allemand (les touristes allemands et anglais constituent les plus gros consommateurs du produit touristique grec).

Les organismes responsables de la matérialisation du projet HELLO Tourism sont:

- L'Association Féminine MEWCAT (Milos European Women's Cooperation for Advancement in Tourism) qui siège à la commune de Plàka à Milos. Cette Association a conçu et présenté le projet devant les autorités compétentes de la Communauté Européenne.
- L'Association Alexandros Cooperation dont le siège se trouve à Katerini, capitale du Département de Pieria (au sud-ouest de la Macédoine grecque). Cette Association a réalisé tout le travail concernant le site de Dion/Pieria pour l'achèvement du projet.
- La Mairie de Milos et la Commune d'Adamantas à Milos.
- La Mairie de Dion/Pieria.
- Le tour opérateur allemand Last Minute Tours dont le siège se trouve à Munich. Il est chargé de la diffusion en Allemagne, Suisse et Autriche des résultats du projet et des deux CD-ROM produits, l'un pour l'île de Milos et l'autre pour le site de Dion/Pieria.
- Enfin, le tour opérateur chypriote Kinisis Travel and Tours dont le siège se trouve à Nicosie. Il est chargé du même type de diffusion en Chypre et dans les pays riverains.

Impact du projet et solutions proposées

Le projet HELLO Tourism contribue à mettre en place un système de management des sites touristiques d'accueil qui assure au visiteur une mise en valeur améliorée de son expérience de vacances. En même temps il contribue à mieux organiser les flux de visiteurs et à régler les questions concernant la protection des ressources culturelles et environnementales du site. En outre, le projet encourage la prise des vacances hors de la haute saison en offrant au visiteur une information relative aux activités pendant toute l'année.

L'achèvement du projet conduit donc à la production de deux CD-ROM, l'une pour l'île de Milos et l'autre pour le site de Dion/Pieria (Macédoine grecque). Les deux titres de production multimédia suivent une structure similaire (Shell), ayant comme but leur applicabilité à la plupart des destinations touristiques méditerranéennes. Leur contenu tend à favoriser la prise de conscience sur les grandes questions environnementales concernant les sites touristiques d'accueil et la participation active à la protection environnementale.

Le système d'Éducation–Information HELLO Tourism constitue un produit intégral et multidimensionnel. Ceci est un produit multimédia et interactif disponible au visiteur arrivant à sa destination touristique (p. ex. aux lieux de débarquement des bateaux, aux points d'information locale, etc.); il est diffusé également par un réseau d'Agences de Voyages en Allemagne, Autriche, Suisse et Chypre.

Les usagers de ce produit multimédia seront:

- principalement, les visiteurs des deux sites où le projet a été appliqué, à savoir l'île de Milos et le site de Dion/Pieria;
- ensuite, les professionnels et les autorités locales qui participent à l'industrie touristique, afin d'améliorer leurs services;
- enfin, la population locale.

Les partenaires impliqués dans la production de cet outil multimédia vont s'assurer qu'il convient aux principales destinations touristiques dans la région méditerranéenne. Le partenaire chypriote sera le premier à adapter le produit à ses besoins.

Enfin, les critères de choix des ressources touristiques, qui ont constitué le contenu des CD-ROM, sont les suivants:

- leur localisation: l'appartenance ou la non-appartenance à une région ayant des ressources touristiques qui constituent le champs d'application du projet;
- leur degré d'originalité écologique et culturelle: le niveau d'authenticité écologique et culturelle des ressources touristiques d'une localité qui a été retenue selon le critère précédent;
- leur caractère exclusif et différentiel: le niveau d'attraction des ressources touristiques d'une région où le projet s'applique par rapport à celui des autres localités. Cette supériorité comparée se traduit en termes de marketing touristique par la notion de USP – Unique Sales Propositions (en d'autres termes 'Propositions Exclusives de Vente');
- les possibilités de la localité choisie pour étaler l'encombrement du courant touristique avec plus d'efficacité qu'une autre destination;
- leur niveau de connaissance par le public: la mise en valeur et la promotion des localités les moins connues par le public.

PROPOSITIONS DE MANAGEMENT TOURISTIQUE SOUTENU – MATÉRIEL PÉDAGOGIQUE

Une des propositions du projet concerne la gestion des flux de visiteurs sur les deux sites d'accueil touristique retenus. Le projet propose un *mécanisme régulateur* qui fonctionne de deux manières:

1. *De manière intrinsèque* à travers le contenu de chaque CD-ROM qui, d'une part, encourage les arrivées touristiques durant toute l'année et par conséquent favorise l'allongement de la période touristique, et d'autre part décongestionne les arrivées touristiques sur les sites en leur proposant des lieux d'intérêt touristique à différentes 'chronodistances'.

2. *De manière extrinsèque* à travers des moyens supplémentaires d'intervention, tels qu'un *modem téléphonique* utilisé avant l'arrivée des groupes scolaires et touristiques sur les sites historiques fournissant l'information sur leur état d'encombrement touristique du moment; *un système de distribution des tickets/ time-ticketing* fonctionnant sur place aux points d'entrée des sites déterminant la priorité d'entrée des visiteurs; *un centre d'information* (Info-kiosk) pour l'utilisation du CD-ROM fonctionnant localement à l'entrée principale des sites; et enfin, des *prospectus* diffusés localement aux points d'arrivée des visiteurs les incitant à visiter le Parc de Distraction local ou à participer aux activités quotidiennes des habitants des sites (p. ex. aux soins des animaux domestiques, aux tavernes, etc.) durant l'encombrement touristique locale des sites à visiter.

Un autre mécanisme régulateur qui fonctionne de la même manière est celui qui est destiné à encourager la protection de l'environnement.

En effet, de manière intrinsèque à travers le contenu de chaque CD-ROM le projet commente de façon simple et argumentée les facteurs écologiques et environnementaux des deux sites et encourage tant la population locale et les professionnels locaux du tourisme que les visiteurs à participer activement aux actions de protection de l'environnement (p. ex. contre les incendies forestiers, contre la prolifération des ordures dans les zones urbaines et de campagne, etc.).

De manière extrinsèque le projet, par des moyens supplémentaires d'intervention, vise le même objectif de protection environnementale des deux sites retenus, par exemple: l'installation au niveau local de poubelles pour le ramassage des ordures, l'installation de poubelles de recyclage pour certains types d'ordures, la confection de sacs recyclables de petite et grande taille (portables) pour usage local afin de mettre en dépôt les ordures dans les poubelles existantes et, enfin, la diffusion locale d'affiches et de prospectus sur les mesures de protection environnementale, disponibles pour les visiteurs des sites retenus.

Enfin, un autre mécanisme régulateur qui intervient dans le projet est celui de caractère extrinsèque, visant à impliquer les organismes suivants:

- unions régionales de tout type d'hébergement touristique;
- unions régionales des agences de voyage et de tour opérateurs, ainsi que représentants nationaux et internationaux des agences de voyages qui commercialisent la Grèce;
- unions régionales de tout type de restauration touristique;
- unions de guides touristiques et de 'tour-leaders' concernés;
- collectivités locales et régionales;
- moyens d'information ('mass-média') locaux, nationaux et internationaux impliqués;
- enfin, organismes de formation de tout type au niveau local et régional.

Le matériel pédagogique–didactique et de communication du projet est par excellence le CD-ROM produit pour chaque site choisi. La structure, les récits écrits, les narrations, les moyens audiovisuels (photographies, vidéos, effets-sonores et visuels) et le 'design' de ces CD-ROM leur confèrent un caractère didactique, pédagogique et de communication de qualité supérieure.

En outre, il est question d'introduire prochainement dans le contenu de chaque CD-ROM, à des fins pédagogiques et de divertissement, un jeu de quiz comportant des questions qui couvrent toutes les données et informations fournies à l'usager ou à l'écolier, à l'étudiant et à quiconque voulant apprendre par cette méthode.

Un questionnaire applicable dans ce cas est celui qui comporte des questions ouvertes ou à choix multiples. Leurs facteurs d'évaluation peuvent être les facteurs géographiques/climatiques, historiques, culturels, écologiques et proprement touristiques de deux localités.

Pour en finir, le projet, afin de rentabiliser la procédure de ses mécanismes régulateurs et de l'impact de son matériel pédagogique a l'intention de mettre en marche un réseau de canaux de distribution de ses CD-ROM et de diffusion de ses résultats en Allemagne, Autriche, Suisse et en Chypre en collaboration avec les touroperateurs mentionnés au paragraphe 'Aspects Généraux'.

CONCLUSIONS: ÉVALUATION DES RÉSULTATS

La mise en usage des moyens multimédia constitue un instrument innovateur dans le domaine du management touristique. La Grèce se trouve en ce moment dans une phase d'initiation en ce qui concerne l'usage des nouvelles technologies dans le domaine du tourisme bien que principalement à des fins commerciales. En particulier, la mise en fonctionnement des 'Info-kiosks' – centres d'information et leur impact sur le comportement des touristes ne sont pas encore suffisamment évalués.

Le projet HELLO Tourism utilise cet important moyen d'éducation et d'information dans le but d'améliorer la qualité du tourisme alors qu'en même temps il contribue à la recherche et au développement de méthodes d'approche à l'usage des 'Info-kiosks' touristiques.

L'outil CD-ROM constitue une méthode agréable et motivante pour transmettre une 'Éducation–Information' au visiteur, à l'habitant et au professionnel pouvant facilement être adaptée aux autres régions méditerranéennes et aux autres destinations touristiques européennes. A présent, la transférabilité des résultats du projet HELLO Tourism dans une perspective de productions similaires en Chypre est prévue en collaboration avec des organismes des pays de l'Europe du Nord.

L'évaluation des résultats du projet HELLO Tourism se fait périodiquement – selon les saisons touristiques de chaque site à l'aide de questionnaires remplis par les visiteurs et les habitants aux points principaux d'usage de ses CD-ROM. Les résultats de ces analyses statistiques obtenues permettent, par une procédure de feed-back, d'améliorer l'application des mesures prévues.

À titre indicatif, nous présentons en langue anglaise certains thèmes du questionnaire déjà utilisé:

1. Social, demographic and economic characteristics of interviewees
2. Consumer behaviour and tourist requirements
3. Standards of tourist supply
   3.1 Accommodation
   3.2 Standard of facilities
   3.3 Standard of leisure facilities
   3.4 Sightseeing at the location
   3.5 Information on other locations of particular interest, e.g., local beauty spots
   3.6 Availability of information for access to the location, etc.

Il faut noter que jusqu'à présent (fin avril 1998) les plus importantes parties des procédure extrinsèques, des mécanismes régulateurs et d'analyse statistique du projet n'ont pas été achevés parce que la mise en usage des CD-ROM et Info-kiosk est en cours.

Ce projet touristique pilote a comme objectif principal d'obtenir une croissance touristique équilibrée de sites retenus respectant leur culture, leur environnement et la vie quotidienne de leurs habitants. Ce type de croissance touristique devrait être la base d'une croissance économique vitale pour les populations concernées.

DÉPÔT ET DISTRIBUTION DES CD-ROM

Toute institution intéressée, ainsi que toute entreprise et personne voulant à se procurer les CD-ROM HELLO Tourism – ce pour l'île de Milos et ce pour le site de Dion/Pieria (Macédoine grecque) – à la quantité désirée, doivent s'adresser à:

Milos: MEWCAT Association (Resp. Yvonne v. Beck Katsambi)
    Plaka, GR – 84800 MILOS,
    Tel/Fax (+ 30) 287 23220
    e-mail: mewcat@otenet.gr

Dion: ALEXANDROS Cooperation (Resp. Georges Balogiannis)
    Svoronos, GR – 60100 KATERINI,
    Tel/Fax (+ 30) 351 32788
    e-mail: alexand@spark.net.gr

REMERCIEMENTS

Je tiens tout particulièrement à remercier les personnes responsables de l'association Féminine MEWCAT de l'île de Milos, ainsi que Georges Balogiannis responsable de l'association Alexandros de Katerini (Macédoine grecque) qui m'ont permis d'utiliser le contenu du Projet HELLO Tourism pour la rédaction du présent rapport.

Je désire également remercier profondément mon collègue Professeur Dr Thomas Mavrodontis pour sa contribution concernant la publication de ce rapport ainsi que Professeurs Christine Pratley et Philomila Obessi pour leur contribution linguistique.

Ce rapport est dédié a mes parents Hélène et Périclés, à ma femme Maria, à mon fils Périclés, à Mme Euthalie, à mes mâitres, à mes amis et élèves!

BIBLIOGRAPHIE

Baretje, R. et Défert, P. (1972) *Aspects économiques du tourisme*. Paris: Berger et Levrault.

Défert, P. (1967) *La localisation touristique – Aspects théoriques et pratiques*. Berne: Collection AIEST.

Middleton, V. T. C. (1990) *Marketing in Travel and Tourism*. London: Heinemann Professional Publishing.

Schwarz, J.-J. (1984) *Pour une approche marketing de la promotion touristique*. Lausanne et Région du Leman: Office du tourisme du Canton de Vaud.

Witt, S. F. and Moutinho, L. (1989a) *Tourism Marketing and Management Handbook*. New York and London: Prentice-Hall International.

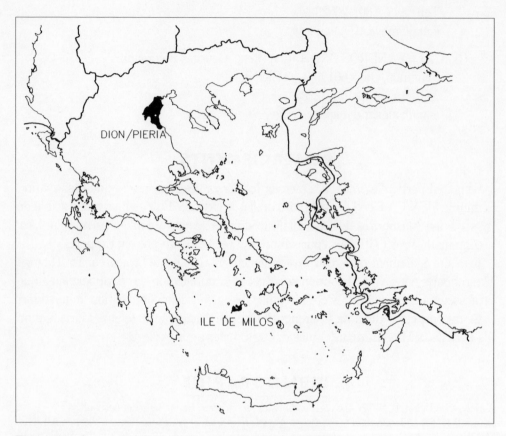

Figure 7.1: Carte de la Grèce, préfecture de Pieria et de l'île de Milos.
Map of Greece, showing Dion/Pieria and the island of Milos.

Figure 7.2: Carte de l'île de Milos.
Map of the island of Milos.

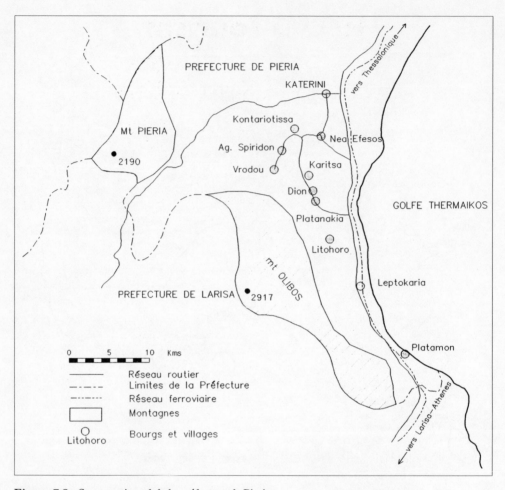

Figure 7.3: Carte partie sud de la préfecture de Pieria.
Map of the southern part of the region of Pieria.

HELLO Tourism

Evangelos P. Karavangelis

Edited by Thomas Mavrodontis

Aim

The main objectives of the study presented in this chapter are:

- to address the problem of tourist movement management in terms of improved environmental and cultural protection of tourist areas. In other words, how to provide a better balance between the needs of the site and the needs of visitors.
- to examine the implementation of the above mentioned management system at two tourist sites in Greece: the island of Milos (Cyclades) and Dion, an historic site at the foot of Mount Olympus (Pieria Region: Greek Macedonia); two places that are very similar in terms of the structure of their tourist offer but with very different tourism growth rates.

Keywords

management of visitor flows; demand optimization; new information technologies; inter-active information terminals; 'education' (visitors and local people)

Summary

The pilot project HELLO Tourism (Heritage Environment Leisure Learning and Organization of Tourism Management) is an innovative system for the environmental and cultural management of a tourist destination. The project was carried out from December 1995 to July 1997 as part of the 1995 Community Action Plan to promote tourism. The practical side of the project was carried out by the non-profit-making associations MEWCAT, which is based on the island of Milos, and 'Alexandros', which is based in Katerini (Greece). The councils of Milos and Dion and the village of Adamas (Milos) also helped with the realization of the project.

The final product was promoted by the German tour operator 'Last Minute Tours', based in Munich, and the Nicosia-based Cypriot tour operator 'Kinisis Travel and Tours'.

The project involved the production of two CD-ROMs, which are used by tourists in the Information Centres (Info-kiosks) to be found at the main points of entry to the two regions which were studied (the island of Milos and the Dion/Pieria site). These CD-ROMs were distributed by the two tour operators mentioned above.

The project was based on the classic theoretical work carried out by Pierre Défert (1967), which looked at the idea of the 'tourist offer' of a location and how to obtain the optimum equilibrium with respect to its tourist demand, i.e. Tf(t) = 100.

Project methodology involved the following seven actions:

- feasibility study;
- research and gathering of material for the CD-ROMs;
- design of the contents of the CD-ROMs;
- technical procedure, in three phases, for the production of the CD-ROMs;
- installation of the CD-ROMs in Information Centres (Info-kiosks) and their use by the public and evaluation of their impact;
- provision of supplementary support materials;
- distribution of results.

The two CD-ROMs, which make up a 'multimedia tourist product', were structured as follows:

Section 1: History – Monuments – Art Objects
Section 2: Traditional Habitats – Sites of Natural Beauty
Section 3: Beaches – Shorelines
Section 4: Lifestyle – Activities – Socio-cultural Events
Section 5: Visitor Activities – Tourists
Section 6: Natural Environment
Section 7: Facilities – Provision of Tourist Services – Information

The project has an educational impact in terms of tourist management and provides, in 'intrinsic' or 'extrinsic' ways, the following regulatory mechanisms:

1. A mechanism for providing a better spread of tourist movement over time.
2. A mechanism for protecting the environment.
3. A mechanism for improving the educational impact of a visit and communication between the public and the institutions involved.
4. A mechanism for reinforcing positive results.

In conclusion, the project is of an educational nature and, due to its structure, can be applied to any tourist area.

Learning outcomes

After studying this report and using the supporting material (the two CD-ROMs) the student will be able to do the following:

- understand how the tourist offer of a location can be analysed and how its equilibrium threshold can be calculated;
- learn how to use the 'tourism management system' HELLO Tourism, in order to ensure that tourists get the most from their holiday, to provide better management of tourist movement and to improve both cultural and environmental protection;

- understand how the HELLO Tourism system instigates, in both intrinsic and extrinsic ways, mechanisms which regulate the movement of visitors to the site concerned and mechanisms which protect the environment. It also facilitates the diffusion of results, due to its educational and communication systems; systems which can be applied to any Mediterranean or European region.

Discussion topics
- Formulate the structure of the tourist offer of a locality and the concept of its dynamic equilibrium, following the design structure of the HELLO Tourism CD-ROMs.
- Imagine that you are trying to implement an action plan in order to manage the movement of tourists at a locality: describe the seven types of action in the methodology. Produce an action plan of this type, following the HELLO Tourism model.
- You have to produce a CD-ROM, in two languages, for the tourist management of a locality: describe its seven-part structure of contents as laid down in the design structure of the HELLO Tourism CD-ROMs. For any one site, list the tourist characteristics that you would choose, based on the above mentioned structures, in order to produce your bilingual CD-ROM.
- Target the initial work in terms of market sector. Defend your choice.
- Draw up a regulatory mechanism in order to manage the movement of visitors through a locality of your choice. Objectives: extension of the tourist season – dispersion of tourists over the locality. Refer to the HELLO Tourism project.
- Draw up a regulatory mechanism to protect the environment of a locality of your choice. Refer to the HELLO Tourism project.
- Draw up a regulatory mechanism to reinforce the impact and improve the distribution of the results of a tourist management action plan for a locality of your choice. Refer to the HELLO Tourism project.
- Draw up a questionnaire for visitors to a locality of your choice, in order to evaluate their experiences as tourists in terms of:

  - geographical factors;
  - historical factors;
  - cultural factors;
  - ecological factors;
  - tourism factors (e.g. transport, accommodation, etc.).

Theoretical background
The report concerning HELLO Tourism is based on the concept of the 'structure of the tourist offer' of a location and the related concept of the 'optimum tourist function'.

Pierre Défert's doctoral thesis 'La localisation touristique – Aspects théoriques et pratiques' and more recent work by R. Baretje, J.J. Schwarz, V. Middleton and S.F. Witt and L. Moutinho are the theoretical sources of the above mentioned concepts.

INTRODUCTION

In accordance with the *Official Journal of the European Community* no. C106/7 and, more particularly, in accordance with Community Action Plan for Tourism (95C 106/09) for the year 1995, any project carried out under the auspices of this plan must, on the one hand, involve close collaboration between European Community countries and Central and Eastern Europe, North Africa, Cyprus and Malta and, on the other, ensure a balance between the tourism phenomena resulting from the action and the environment.

According to this same Community Action Plan for Tourism, and in the field of intervention concerning the equilibrium between the flow of visitors and the tourist locality, one of the primary objectives must be to improve the management of tourist movement. The objective of this management regime, based on the results of pilot schemes, is to provide a better level of protection for the constituent elements of the environment and culture of the tourist locality.

The HELLO Tourism project was carried out, within this context, between December 1995 and July 1997. In the first part of this chapter we will examine the theoretical and methodological framework of the project. In the second part we will present the fundamental points to be considered in a tourist locality management scheme. We will also describe the educational and communication material developed by this project.

THEORETICAL AND METHODOLOGICAL FRAMEWORK

Theoretical basis

The design of the structure of the tourist offer for the two Greek tourist localities involved in the project is based on the concept of tourist offer as described in the classic work by Pierre Défert (1967). In general, this structure takes into account the following factors:

- the attraction of the site;
- the geographical coordinates of the site;
- the site's monuments and places of historical interest, as well as the cultural heritage of its population;
- the aspects of the site not apparent to the public (the socio-economic framework of the daily life of the population);
- aspects arising from the natural environment of the site and its development;
- private and public services and facilities (catering, leisure activities, provision of essential services such as roads, lighting, water, etc.) and accommodation designed to meet the needs of tourists.

The structure of the site's tourist offer corresponds to the ideas of the original tourist offer ('hydrome', 'phytome', 'lithome' and 'anthropome') and to the derivative tourist offer ('basic infrastructure', 'tourist infrastructure', 'tourist distribution channels' and 'economic factors').

Based on the above mentioned tourist offer, we are trying to achieve an optimum tourist factor for each of the two sites in question, i.e. Tf(t) = 100; see René Baretje and Pierre Défert (1972). Such a tourist factor of 100 corresponds to a dynamic equilibrium between the tourist demand and the tourist offer of the site. It is this equilibrium which tends to minimize the operational problems which lead to quantitative and qualitative imbalances between the tourist demand and tourist offer of a particular site.

APPLIED METHODOLOGY

The methodology used in the HELLO Tourism project produces a 'tourism management system' which offers educational material in the form of a CD-ROM, to be used by visitors and professionals alike, and in the form of 'supplementary support materials'.

The same methodology was followed for both of the tourist localities chosen for the project. The aim was to improve the management of tourist flow and thereby protect the natural and cultural environments of the localities. This mode of intervention corresponds to the seven types of action which form the seven modules of the project's Action Plan.

These modules, in order of importance, are:

Module 1: Feasibility study.
Module 2: Research and gathering of essential material.
Module 3: Design of the contents of the CD-ROM.
Module 4: Three-phase technical procedure for the production of the CD-ROM.
Module 5: Installation of the CD-ROM in Information Centres (Info-kiosks) and tourist reception centres. Evaluation of its impact.
Module 6: Provision of supplementary support materials.
Module 7: Distribution of the positive results of the project.

This methodology is complemented by an effort to ensure the training of chosen groups within the populations concerned. This training is aimed at improving the protection of both the natural and cultural environment of the tourist sites examined.

Finally, the distribution of results through professional channels, aimed at potential tourists in the countries which provide the majority of tourists to Greece, and more particularly to the island of Milos and Dion/Pieria.

SUSTAINED MANAGEMENT OF A TOURIST SITE: EDUCATIONAL AND COMMUNICATION MATERIAL

General aspects

The two tourist sites chosen for the application of the methodology described above, the island of Milos (Cyclades region, Greece) and Dion (the Pieria region in the southwest of Greek Macedonia), were not chosen at random. The choice was dictated by the fact that both sites offer the same conditions of tourist offer even though their tourism growth rates are very different. The development of the island of Milos is ongoing, whereas Dion/Pieria is considered to be a mature site, albeit with a marked seasonal peak in July and August.

This contrast was considered to be a good test of the 'applicability' (possibility of transfer and implementation) of the HELLO Tourism project, i.e. the possibility of transferring the same methodology to products/tourist sites with similar tourist offer structures but different growth rates.

The resemblance between the tourist offers of the island of Milos and Dion/Pieria is based on the following factors:

Island of Milos	Dion/Pieria
Site and historical monuments	Site and historical monuments
Archaeological museum	Archaeological museum
Temples, monasteries, churches	Temples, monasteries, churches
Island Mediterranean climate	Continental Mediterranean climate
Mountains (Halakas)	Mountains (Olympus)
Mountain villages (Pollonia, Plaka, Trypiti, Adamandas, etc.)	Mountain villages and market towns (Litohoro, Vrondou, Milia, etc.)
Coastline	Coastline
Fortress (St Marie)	Fortress (Platamonas)
Local cuisine	Local cuisine
Local customs	Local customs

The above data provides the structure for the content of the tourist CD-ROM:

Section 1: History – Monuments – Art Objects
Section 2: Traditional Habitats – Sites of Natural Beauty
Section 3: Beaches – Shorelines
Section 4: Lifestyle – Activities – Socio-cultural Events
Section 5: Visitor Activities – Tourists

Section 6:   Natural Environment

Section 7:   Facilities – Provision of Tourist Services – Information

All this information is available in three languages: Greek, English and German, to chosen sections of the local population and to interested professionals. (German and English tourists are the most numerous foreign visitors to Greece.)

The organizations responsible for carrying out the HELLO Tourism project are:

- the women's organization MEWCAT (Milos European Women's Cooperation for Advancement in Tourism) which is based in the village of Plaka on Milos. This organization initiated the project and presented it to the relevant authorities in the European Union.
- The organization Alexandros Cooperation, based in Katerini, the capital of the Pieria Region (in the south-west of Greek Macedonia). This organization carried out all the work for the Dion/Pieria part of the project.
- Milos Council and the village of Adamantas on Milos.
- Dion/Pieria Council.
- The German tour operator Last Minute Tours, which is based in Munich. It is responsible for the distribution of the results of the project and the two CD-ROMs (one for the island of Milos, the other for Dion/Pieria) in Germany, Switzerland and Austria.
- The Cypriot tour operator Kinisis Travel and Tours, which is based in Nicosia. It is responsible for the same type of distribution in Cyprus and neighbouring countries.

Impact of the project and proposed solutions

The HELLO Tourism project is designed to set up a tourist site management system to ensure that tourists get more from their visit and have the best possible holiday experience. At the same time, it helps improve visitor flow and addresses the question of the protection of the cultural and environmental resources of the site. The project also encourages people to take their holidays outside the high season by offering visitors information about activities throughout the year.

The project led to the production of two CD-ROMs: one for the island of Milos, the other for Dion/Pieria (Greek Macedonia). The two multi-media productions use a similar structure (Shell) as the aim was to produce a format applicable to most Mediterranean tourist destinations. Their content is biased towards promoting an understanding of the environmental problems facing tourist sites and the active protection of the environment.

The HELLO Tourism Education–Information system is an integrated and multi-dimensional product. It is a multi-media, interactive system available to tourists on arrival at their chosen destination (e.g. tourist arrival points, local information points, etc.). It is also distributed by a network of travel agencies in Germany, Switzerland, Austria and Cyprus.

The users of this multi-media product will be:

- mostly, visitors to the two sites covered by the project, the island of Milos and Dion/Pieria;
- professionals and local authorities concerned with the tourism industry, in order to improve their services;
- the local population.

The partners involved in the production of this multi-media tool will confirm that it is applicable to most Mediterranean tourist destinations. The Cypriot partner will be the first to adapt it to its needs.

The criteria for choosing which tourist resources to include on the CD-ROM were as follows:

- location: whether or not they are part of a region with tourist resources covered by the project;
- degree of ecological or cultural originality: the level of ecological or cultural authenticity of the tourist resources of a locality is judged on their exclusive or unique nature and the level of attraction of tourist resources within an area covered by the project is evaluated relative to other localities. This comparative superiority is translated into tourism marketing terms by the idea of USP – Unique Sales Propositions;
- the possibilities of spreading tourist flux compared with other tourist areas;
- level of public awareness of the site: development and promotion of less well-known sites.

PROPOSITIONS FOR SUSTAINABLE TOURISM MANAGEMENT: EDUCATIONAL MATERIAL

One of the propositions of the project concerns the management of the flow of visitors to the two chosen sites. The project proposes a *regulatory mechanism* which works in two ways:

1. *In an intrinsic way* through the contents of the CD-ROM, which both encourages tourists to come throughout the year, thereby encouraging the extension of the tourist season, and spreads tourists over the whole site by suggesting different places of interest at different 'time distances'.
2. *In an extrinsic way* through supplementary materials such as:
   (a) *telephone modem links* to places of historical interest which can be used to advise groups on how busy a site is before they arrive;

(b) *a ticket distribution/time-ticketing system* at the entrances to sites in order to prioritize entry;

(c) *an information centre* (Info-kiosk) with CD-ROMs at the main entrances to sites;

(d) *leaflets and brochures*, distributed at visitor arrival points, encouraging them to visit the local Visitor Centre or to take part in the daily activities of the local inhabitants (e.g. helping out on farms or in taverns, etc.) when local tourist sites are overcrowded.

Another regulatory mechanism which works in the same way is aimed at protecting the environment.

In effect, in an intrinsic way, via the contents of each CD-ROM, the project provides a general outline of the ecological and environmental problems of the two sites and encourages locals and tourism professionals, as well as visitors, to actively participate in protecting the environment (e.g. prevention of forest fires, reducing litter in both urban and rural areas, etc.).

In an extrinsic way, the supplementary material included in the project is designed to work towards the same objective, for example, provision of rubbish bins, provision of recycling bins for certain types of rubbish, production of both large and small rubbish bags for local use so that litter can be easily transported to existing litter bins, distribution of posters and leaflets on environmental protection measures to visitors at local tourist sites.

Finally, another extrinsic regulatory mechanism included in the project is aimed at involving the following organizations:

- regional accommodation organizations for all types of accommodation;
- regional travel agent and tour operator organizations as well as national and international representatives of travel agencies which operate in Greece;
- regional organizations of restaurateurs and caterers;
- organizations of tourist guides and tour leaders for the areas concerned;
- local and regional councils;
- local, national and international press (mass media);
- all types of local and national training organizations.

The CD-ROM produced for each site provides the best possible educational and communication medium. Through its structure, with written material, narratives and audio-visual tools (photographs, videos, sound effects and visual effects), it is possible to produce an educational and communication tool of the highest quality.

In order to introduce more of an entertainment element, in future a quiz about the site will be included, containing questions on all aspects of the information provided by the CD-ROM. The type of questionnaire applicable in this case is one based on open or multiple-choice questions about such topics as: geography/climate, history, culture, ecology and tourism.

Finally, in order to reap the greatest benefits from the regulatory mechanisms and maximize the impact of the educational material, it is intended to develop a distribution network for the CD-ROM and the results of the project in Germany, Austria, Switzerland and Cyprus, in collaboration with the tour operators listed in the 'General Aspects' section.

CONCLUSIONS: EVALUATION OF THE RESULTS

The use of multi-media tools in tourism management is quite innovative. Greece is still a newcomer to the use of new technologies in the field of tourism, their use being mainly limited to the commercial side of the industry. In particular, the introduction of 'Info-kiosks' – information points – and their impact on the behaviour of tourists have not been sufficiently evaluated. The HELLO Tourism project uses this important educational and information tool not only in order to improve the quality of tourism but also as a contribution to research in this field and the development of ways in which tourist 'Info-kiosks' can best be used.

The CD-ROM provides an agreeable and motivational tool for educating and informing visitors, local people and professionals. It can be easily adapted for use in other Mediterranean or European tourist destinations. The transfer of the results of the HELLO Tourism project, in the form of similar projects in Cyprus, is currently being planned in conjunction with organizations in northern European countries.

Evaluation of the results of the HELLO Tourism project is carried out periodically – according to the tourist seasons of each site – by using questionnaires filled in by visitors and locals at the main points of use of the CD-ROMs. These results are statistically analysed and the information gained is fed back to the sites to enable continuous improvement of the measures in place.

An example of the themes covered by the questionnaires is given below:

1. Social, demographic and economic characteristics of interviewees
2. Consumer behaviour and tourist requirements
3. Standards of tourist supply
   3.1 Accommodation
   3.2 Standard of facilities
   3.3 Standard of leisure facilities
   3.4 Sightseeing at the location
   3.5 Information on other locations of particular interest, e.g., local beauty spots
   3.6 Availability of information for access to the location, etc.

It must be noted that at the time of writing (end of April 1998) the main parts of the extrinsic measures, the regulatory mechanisms and the statistical analysis of the project have not as yet been carried out because the installation of the CD-ROMs and 'Info-kiosks' is still ongoing.

The principal aim of this pilot project is to obtain a balanced growth in tourist numbers to the sites concerned while maintaining respect for local culture, environment and daily life. This type of tourist growth should be the basis of a vital economic growth for the local population.

AVAILABILITY AND DISTRIBUTION OF CD-ROMS

Any institution, company or individual interested in obtaining the HELLO Tourism CD-ROMs – for the island of Milos and/or Dion/Pieria (Greek Macedonia) – should contact the following addresses stating the quantity required:

> Milos: MEWCAT Association (Contact: Yvonne v. Beck Katsambi)
> Plaka, GR – 84800 MILOS
> Tel/Fax (+30) 287 23220
> e-mail: mewcat@otenet.gr

> Dion: ALEXANDROS Cooperation (contact: Georges Balogiannis)
> Svoronos, GR – 60100 KATERINI
> Tel/Fax (+30) 351 30193
> e-mail: alexand@spark.net.gr

ACKNOWLEDGEMENTS

I would especially like to thank the people in charge of the women's organization MEWCAT on the island of Milos, and Georges Balogiannis, manager of the organization Alexandros in Katerini (Greek Macedonia), who have allowed me to use the contents of the HELLO Tourism project in this chapter.

I would also like to thank my colleague Professor Dr Thomas Mavrodontis for his contribution to the publication of this chapter and Professors Christine Pratley and Philomila Obessi for their linguistic contributions.

REFERENCES

Braetje, R. and Défert, P. (1972) *Aspects économiques du tourisme*. Paris: Berger and Levrault.
Défert, P. (1967) *La localisation touristique: Aspects théoriques et pratiques*. Berne: Collection AIEST.
Middleton, V. T. C. (1990) *Marketing in Travel and Tourism*. London: Heinemann Professional Publishing.
Schwarz, J.-J. (1984) *Pour une approche marketing de la promotion touristique*. Lausanne et Région du Leman: Office du tourisme du Canton de Vaud.
Witt, S. F. and Moutinho, L. (1989a) *Tourism Marketing and Management Handbook*. New York and London: Prentice-Hall International.

CHAPTER 8

Renrike

A Scandinavian mountain resort

Solveig Böhn

Aim
The aim of this case study is to give students the chance to practise identifying and categorizing problems that can occur in a tourism business at a resort, and to find solutions to the problems.

Keywords
resort; tourism products; resources; actors; relationships; problems

Summary
The case study deals with conflicts that can occur in a resort when you have one company controlling the most important tourism resources. It is based on a discussion between small business owners, their relationships and about how to handle a proposal from the big company. The problems described in the case study could be in any resort in any area where the population is sparsely distributed and where you have one big actor and many small actors.

The case study will give the students the opportunity to practise identifying key resources for a resort: core products, relationships/links between actors, different problems that can occur, and discussing different possible solutions to the problems.

The case study can be used as a role-play or in the form of a seminar. It is blind case study, which means there are no solutions to the problems.

Learning outcomes
After examining this case study students should be able to do the following:

- identify and solve problems;
- identify factors in the environment that affect a tourism activity;
- identify a resort's resources: physical resources, guests, financial facilities and market/reservation systems;
- identify and categorize different kinds of links/relationships between actors in a resort;
- identify the tourism product, core and support products;
- state what it means to have control over tourism resources.

Theoretical background

As early as in the middle of the nineteenth century 'fresh air fiends', as they were called, found the Scandinavian mountains. Many writers and painters who had described and painted this particular landscape and its wilderness inspired them. Wealthy Englishmen also came for the hunting and fishing.

Coming to the area for winter sports started at the beginning of the twentieth century. Wealthy and experienced travellers came mainly from Stockholm and other major cities in Sweden. The accommodation facilities were few and small but a few big hotels were constructed and became very popular. They still are, although they do not look the same and have different services and guests.

Development came during the 1960s and 1970s, when special recreation areas were appointed in Sweden. These interested investors and, at the same time, downhill skiing was becoming more popular. Now two out of three people go skiing, either cross-country or downhill.

The mountainous areas of Sweden are found in the province of Dalarna, in the south, and in the provinces of Härjedalen, Jämtland and Lappland, towards the north, a distance of about 1,200 kilometres. The areas are sparsely populated with fewer than six people per square kilometre. Most people who want to go there have to have a car. Only three resorts are accessible by train. There are airports all over Sweden but there is only good access by public transport to a few areas. From populated areas the closest mountain resort is about five hours' drive by car.

Today in these mountain areas tourism is of great economic importance. In the province of Jämtland 10 per cent of the population works in the tourism industry and a lot more are dependent on tourism.

In the 1990s tourism developed from a diverse industry with a lot of small private businesses, with substantial involvement by the public sector, to concentration on a few big resorts which control the main ski lift capacities. Also, the ski resorts now have one single owner controlling more and more of the facilities. This phenomenon is not unique for the tourism industry in Sweden. This process has been going on in other sectors of Swedish society.

The case study that follows is fictitious. Any similarities to existing organizations, individuals and situations are pure coincidence.

CASE STUDY

Alberta runs a small hotel, Järven (The Wolverine). It has 32 beds, in 15 double rooms and 2 single rooms. It also has a nice bar and a small restaurant with 50 seats. The cook, Bert, serves excellent food. You ask yourself, why does he work at a hotel in Renrike (Reindeer-land) in the Swedish mountain area? He could get a job at any restaurant in Stockholm or Gothenburg.

He says: 'Well, a couple of years ago I worked here at the mountain resort, Björnen (The Bear) as a kitchen boy. After that, I went to a restaurant school and got a job in Stockholm. Three years ago Alberta called me, and said she had bought a hotel and asked me to come and work for her. She worked at Björnen at the same time as I did. When I was working there I enjoyed nature and the quiet life up there in the

Scandinavian *fjällen* (mountains). Ten of my old work-mates at Björnen are back in the area again, not working at Björnen but running their own businesses in the surroundings. So why not, I thought. Now, one year later, I am not employed any longer, but leasing the restaurant at Järven.'

Alberta says: 'All we old friends have businesses like restaurants, ski-shops, hotels, boarding houses, holiday villages and an adventure park. We have quite a nice time together, and we also support each other. Our businesses are all very small compared to Björnen where there are around 5,000 beds in hotels/apartments and cabins. The Björnen company also owns restaurants and ski lifts, a shopping area, a sports arena, and indoor/outdoor swimming pools. However, we do not feel we are competing but more that we are a complement. Besides, they have more capacity in their ski lifts than they have beds.'

Swedish mountain areas are so sparsely populated that the day visitor market is limited. The products we offer are different from the one offered by Björnen. The accommodation has a more personal atmosphere and the restaurants are cosier. The shops have personnel with long experience and can give information about almost anything. You can get a story about the latest seen bear or where to find cloudberries in summer. At Björnen most employees come from the big cities in Sweden to work for a season. As a tour operator said, 'In the winter nothing works before the end of February.'

As well as Alberta and Bert in their group of close friends is also Curt, who has his adventure park but also guides tourists to different attractions and arranges events. One very active person in the town is David, who has just started up a restaurant/pub. There is also Erica who, together with her husband Fredrik, took over Hotel Älgen (The Elk Hotel), a hotel for younger people who want to go skiing but can't afford to stay at Björnen. Closer to the ski lifts George has built a holiday village, Varglyan, (the Wolf's Lair) with 105 self-catering cabins. No support services are offered.

All these businesses are within 15 minutes' drive from Björnen. In the next village, Svartsjö (Black Lake), which is about 50 minutes by car away from Björnen, you can find Helma with her boarding house, Lodjuret (The Lynx), and Ingvar, with his small but beautiful hotel, Svanen (The Swan). The group has good support from Jacob, who has been running his sports shop in Renrike for more than 40 years, and Curt, a young man from Stockholm, who has opened an agency for incoming tourists, selling summer package tours and, during the winter, distributing accommodation on a commission basis. Another actor in distributing accommodation is the tourist bureau, situated in the town of Renrike.

The whole area has had a steady increase in tourists. The Björnen booking department has had so many requests that they have been able to recommend other hotels and cabins in the neighbourhood. At the same time they have been expanding their lift capacity and have now become more dependent on visitors coming up to the ski lifts from the surrounding area than before.

In many ski resorts in Sweden the profit, which makes it possible to expand, comes just from the ski lifts. This means that capital for investments is dependent on how well the ski lift departments are running. The Björnen company, as well as other big companies running ski lifts in Sweden, has prepared itself for winters with a low snowfall by investing in artificial snow machines, and for early darkness by investing in lighting plants. But when other factors in the environment occur that could reduce the number of visitors, are they prepared?

In 1995, for the first time after members of the group of friends had started their businesses, they could see a decline in the visitor numbers. The beds closest to the ski lifts were occupied as usual in peak season but the further away from the ski lift the lodging camps were situated the bigger difficulties they had, but not all of them. There were many reasons for the decline, which we are not able to discuss in detail in this case study.

Businesses dependent on the tourists came from within an area of about one hour's drive by car from the town of Renrike. The local tourist manager called for a crisis meeting. More than 50 people came, but some companies didn't feel it was a decline: 'There have always been ups and downs.' The Björnen company had noticed a drop in income from their ski lifts. Both David and Alberta had had fewer guests. 'Maybe more people prefer to go cross-country skiing?' said Helma. 'I have had as many guests as in 1994 and George had more than last year.' The meeting ended without any agreement about what was to be done.

A few days later Curt called Alberta saying that the manager of the Björnen company had called and wanted to see those running accommodation businesses, and distributors, in the nearest area – about 15 minutes' drive from Renrike. 'He wanted to start to collaborate,' Alberta said. This was interesting. For the first time the Björnen company had proposed a meeting and said they wanted to collaborate. Now they must be in trouble!

The first issue to be discussed was to make the ski lifts at Björnen more accessible for the guests staying in the surroundings. The suggestion was to have a daily bus that could transport guests to the ski lifts. Maybe that would attract more young snowboarders to come the area, with cheap accommodation, a town, and good skiing? Erica found that idea interesting.

Ingvar was not at all interested. 'I have families as guests and want to go on with that. Besides, youngsters would destroy my new cabins, but I am interested in having transport to the restaurants in town in the evening as in Sweden there are tough restrictions on drinking alcohol and driving.

'Maybe we could attract more downhill skiers to come to our lodgings. If we had buses they could also go down to town in the evenings, so guests who maybe don't want to stay up at the resort in the evenings can visit our restaurants and have a nice meal without the need to drive a car.'

The result of the meeting was that a bus started to operate on the route from town up to the ski lift and back, but not one from Björnen to town and back during the evening.

Björnen is a progressive company and saw their need for a new booking system. Their booking office had not only their own beds in the system, but also beds in privately owned cabins around the ski lift establishment. 'Why not create the Renrike Mountain Area, made up of the businesses depending on tourism in an area of about 20 km from Björnen?' said the manager of the Björnen company. 'We have a booking system, you can buy a part of the system and be able to handle your own bookings and make reservations at Björnen accommodation, ski lifts, events and activities. You will get a commission of 10 per cent, but not in the peak season.'

'Why not in the peak season?' Curt said. 'As always you only give away the small pieces.' After giving this information out the manager for Björnen left and a wild discussion started.

The people at the meeting couldn't see why they couldn't agree as equals. David said: 'We who don't live on the mountain top always have to bow to Björnen. Now, we have our own businesses and we still depend on the Björnen company. We always have to ask ourselves – will we be cheated or not again? Why do they only offer the tourism businesses 20 km from Björnen association with the booking system? Is it expensive? They have already a system and it is paid for, why do we have to pay to belong? Is the Internet an alternative way to communicate with the customers and with the Björnen company?'

Fredrik stopped the questioning and said: 'Why don't they have big fights in Svartsjö? They discuss mutual problems and find solutions.'

'The differences,' George said, 'are that none of them has control of the main attraction, the landscape with its beautiful nature and that none of the business owners has enough money to buy out another.

'Back to our problems. We have to accept that during the winter the main attraction in the area is skiing, downhill and cross-country. The Björnen company controls about 95 per cent of the lift capacity. Those who are interested in following long trails by ski prefer to go to Svartsjö. We also have to accept that Björnen means downhill skiing and well prepared ski trails and has given an image to all of Renrike.'

'But when you have a booking system don't you control the market?' Alberta said. 'We in Renrike have telephones, faxes and some travel agencies working for us on a commission basis and a tourist office linked to Björnen. But how about opening hours in low season, on Sundays and in the evenings? When they are not open, how do the customers find us?'

Augusta wound up the meeting by saying, 'We have to think it all over very carefully. I am planning to join the Björnen booking system but first I will find out what our incoming bureau is intending to do. Maybe we should work closer with him instead. He is an agent for different tour operators and has close links with the ferry lines. He has also his own travel agency in Stockholm. We already have some links to travel agencies in Stockholm and maybe we can find some new travel agencies and bus tour operators. Maybe we can work towards getting more people during the summer, and I think it is possible to sell September too. The Scandinavian mountains are very colourful in the autumn and the sky can be very clear. That, I think, is the time when this area is most beautiful.

'Thank you all for coming to this meeting. See you again in two weeks when it is time to give an answer to the Björnen company about the reservation system.'

SUGGESTED READING

Ford, D. (ed.) (1997) *Understanding Business Markets*. 2nd edn. London: Dryden's Press.

Gunn, C. A. (1994) *Tourism Planning: Basics, Concepts, Cases*. 3rd edn. Washington, DC: Taylor & Francis.

Håkansson, H. and Snehota, I. (eds) (1997) *Developing Relationships in Business Network*. London: International Thompson Business Press.

Leiper, N. (1990) *The Tourism System: An Interdisciplinary Perspective*. Occasional Papers No. 2. Dept of Management Systems, Business Studies Faculty, Palmerston: Massey University.

Mill, R. C. and Morrison, A. (1992) *The Tourism System: An Introductory Text*. Englewood Cliffs, NJ: Prentice-Hall.

Smith, S. (1994) 'The tourism product', *Annals of Tourism Research*, **21** (3), 582–95.

CHAPTER 9

Metsovo, Greece

High on top of Pindos

Fotis Kilipiris

Edited by Thomas Mavrodontis

Aim

The aims of the chapter are as follows:

- to identify the basic tourist elements of the Metsovo area that contribute to the synthesis of the local tourism product;
- to show historically the role of the private sector in the development of the area;
- to demonstrate how mountainous cultures and products contribute to the synthesis of the local tourism product; and
- to identify existing problems directly related to the future tourism development of the area and the role of the public sector.

Keywords

ecotourism; benefactors; sustainable tourism development; charitable foundations; national park; local information system; cultural tourism; tourism merchandise

Summary

A favourable geographical position in a mountain passage connecting Western to Central Greece spurred Metsovo's economy to a high degree of economic integration. Particularly favourable conditions have proved to be the key to development

For many centuries, due to its geography, the Ottoman administration had granted Metsovo a favourable tax regime and a high degree of administrative autonomy, which turned it into an attractive location. The combination of a harsh local climate and a favourable geographical position turned its inhabitants to commerce, bringing them into close economic contact with the Ottoman, Central and Eastern European markets and enriching local culture. Outgoing orientation led to the emergence of the major economic phenomenon: the benefactors, who are Metsovitans who emigrated and started sending capital home. This systematic injection of resources into the local economy further enriched local infrastructure and boosted local income. Moreover, these transfers of resources sustained a level of income and social and cultural cohesion once favourable conditions were repealed early in the nineteenth century.

The end of the civil war was a turning point for rural life in Greece. The emergence of what could be termed 'institutional benefactors' saved Metsovo from the exodus that emptied and impoverished other regions. The actions of non-profit-making, non-government organizations, and recently of local government, have permitted post-war Metsovo to maintain sustainable income levels through the pursuit of traditional activities.

Today, in Metsovo a sustainable tourism development model can partially ensure the town's future survival in the twenty-first century.

Learning outcomes
The learning outcomes from this case study will include:

- proposals for maintaining a sustainable tourism development for the area; and
- proposals for improving local tourism infrastructure such as the development of a local information system through the application of multi-media systems.

Discussion topics
- Explain the role of the so-called institutional benefactors in the development of an area.
- In what ways can the association of a rural area with universities and other institutions be beneficial for the area?
- What are the implications of a Local Information System for the visitor?
- Identify the key elements that play an important role in the development of remote rural areas.

LOCATION: GEOGRAPHICAL CHARACTERISTICS

Metsovo is characterized as one of the most traditional settlements of mountainous Greece. The town is unique for its architectural and natural environment and lies 350 km north-west of Athens in the region of Epirus, the most mountainous area of mainland Greece. The greater Metsovo area is part of Pindos, the greatest mountain complex of Greece. The town is surrounded by the mountain peaks of Katara (altitude 1,801 m), Zygos (altitude 1,650 m), and Lakmon or Peristeri (altitude 2,295 m). The town itself lies on an altitude of 1,156 m. Some of the most important rivers of Greece have their sources in the broader Metsovo area: Aoos which flows towards the Adriatic Sea, Aheloos and Arachtos flowing towards the Ionian Sea, and Pinios and Aliakmon rivers flowing towards the North Aegean Sea. The town has the second highest degree of rainfall in Greece, next to that of Corfu. Heavy snowfall in winter is a common natural phenomenon in the area. Finally, the town lies on the main road that connects Epirus with Thessaly and Macedonia, two other major regions of Greece. The broader Metsovo county covers an area of 267.5 km^2 and in the last population census (1990), registered 5,829 permanent inhabitants. In the major Metsovo area 56.9 per cent of the land is under pasture, 37.3 per cent is forested and only 5.8 per cent is cultivated land.

HISTORY

Metsovo was founded on the ruins of ancient Parorea, land of the Epirotic tribes of Tymphaei and Atintanes. Strabo, a geographer of the first century AD (67 BC–23 AD) repeating the historical sources of Ecateos, the Greek geographer of the sixth century BC, mentions eleven tribes living in the Epirus area: Haones, Thesproti, Kassopei, Amphilohii by the sea, and Mollosi, Athamanes, Aethikes, Tympaei, Paravei, Orestes and Atintanes on the top of the Pindos mountains.

Tympaei and Atintanes, the ancestors of today's Metsovitans, traditionally used to follow a pastoral way of semi-nomadic life, moving their sheep and goat flocks from the plains to the mountain and vice versa: six months in the summer on the top of Pindos and six months in winter to the Thesprotian and Thessalian plains.

In 168 BC the entire Hellenic peninsula, including Epirus, was conquered by the Romans. For more than 500 years the Roman language was spoken in the area, and this linguistically affected the native Greek populations, especially those of mountainous Greece. As a result, some of these populations today speak together with the Greek, a latinophone dialect, the so-called Vlach language, as it is known in Metsovo.

Historically Metsovo for the first time is mentioned in 1380. In 1430, after the occupation of the area by the Ottomans, the Emperor Mourat the Second gives to Metsovo and the surrounding area important privileges. Metsovitans for more than three centuries enjoyed a high degree of political, ecclesiastical and judicial autonomy, paying in return only an annual tax to the Ottomans. The result was that from the beginning of the seventeenth century Metsovo became a major economic centre establishing commercial ties with major economic centres of that period: Venice, Livorno, Vienna, Odessa, Constantinople, Bucharest, Alexandria, etc. That led to the economic and cultural development of the town, thanks also to the wealth accumulated by numerous Metsovitan benefactors living abroad. Numerous buildings and monuments of that period contribute to the uniqueness of Metsovo's profile today.

THE ROLE OF THE PRIVATE SECTOR

There are a variety of reasons that historically played a very important role in the development of Metsovo. One was mentioned earlier, the autonomy and freedom that Metsovo enjoyed during the years of Ottoman occupation. Another important factor was the role the private sector played and still plays in the development of modern Metsovo. The Metsovitan benefactors through their donations created the infrastructure that contributed largely to the town's prosperity and development.

Today the private sector in Metsovo still plays a very important role basically through the three foundations that Metsovitan benefactors established. It is worthwhile mentioning them to show how their activities contribute to Metsovo's development, including that of tourism.

Baron Tositsa's Foundation

The Foundation was founded in 1959 by the last descendant of the Tositsa's family, Baron Mihail Tositsa who by that time lived in France. The Foundation operates the following establishments in the town:

- ski pistes: in Metsovo one of the three ski pistes is owned and operated by the Foundation as is a restaurant in the same area.
- dairy products factory: the dairy products factory plays a very important role in Metsovo's economic life. It offers employment to the locals and also produces some of the most famous cheeses in Greece. The products are not only consumed locally by the tourists but are also distributed all over Greece and abroad.
- wood factory: the Foundation's wood factory process locally produced wood. This wood is mainly used by the local family-operated establishments to produce wood-carved products for the tourists as well as barrels used for wine and cheese packing.

Averoff's Foundation

This Foundation was established in 1979 by Evangellos Averoff, a prominent Metsovitan and an important politician of contemporary Greece. The Foundation operates the following establishments:

- the Katogi Winery: the Foundation operates wine fields in Metsovo that produce the famous local 'katogi' wine. The wine is locally consumed and together with local cheeses contributes to the famous Metsovitan cuisine.
- Metsovo Art Gallery: the art gallery is one of the most important private collections in Greece and attracts visitors from all over Greece.

Egnatia–Epirus Foundation

The Foundation was established in Metsovo in 1991. It operates offices both in Athens and Ioannina, the capital of Epirus. Its mission is to protect and promote the local Epirotian cultural heritage, including that of Metsovo. Its activities include economic, social and cultural activities compatible with the traditional and natural environment of the area. The Foundation operates the following establishments:

- Diaselo Convention Centre: this first started operating in April 1991. It is totally constructed out of traditional materials like stone and wood and offers a variety of facilities including convention rooms, traditional restaurants and other amenities; and
- other establishments: the Foundation operates in Ioannina the 'Office for Energy Technologies'. The office undertakes initiatives related to the above activities that mainly work for the benefit of the broader Epirus area.

THE ROLE OF THE PUBLIC SECTOR

When talking about the public sector in Metsovo we mainly refer to the Municipality (local authority), the Prefecture (regional authority) and other organizations that are directly associated with the town, such as Mestovitan National Polytechnic University of Athens.

The Municipality

Municipal authorities in Metsovo in recent years have played an important role in the development of the town. The Municipality operates various offices that manage development activities for the area. One of the most important offices run by the Municipality is the Metsovitan Development Office. This is an office that mainly exploits development opportunities for the town basically through EU funding programmes. During the last five years the following projects have been implemented:

- town roads restoration: the entire city road cluster was restored to its original structure and appearance. Some 30 km of asphalt-made town roads were transformed into stone-paved traditional streets;
- building restorations: old buildings including the town hall, various public service buildings (schools, kindergardens, etc.) were restored to their traditional appearance using only stone and wood as basic materials for construction;
- fountain restorations: Metsovo had a very interesting water-supply system through fountains situated in various parts of the town. All these fountains were restored in a way to be easily accessed both by locals and tourists; and
- sports complex: two of the three ski pistes in Metsovo are operated by the local development office. Also in 1996 an indoor sports facility started to operate, offering a broad range of sports activities. At the end of the year (1998) four tennis courts will start to operate nearby.

Ioannina Prefecture

Ioannina Prefecture represents the national authority in the area. The prefecture operates various offices responsible for developing projects related to road construction and preservation, environment protection, promotion of the area, including that of tourism. Lately, under new legislation, prefectures will be granted additional authority that will allow them to undertake more initiatives locally.

The Metsovitan National Polytechnic University of Athens (MNPUA)

The MNPUA is one of the biggest educational institutions in Greece, a donation of great Metsovitan benefactors like N. Stournaris, G. Averoff, M. Tositsas and H. M. Tosistas. The town has for a long time worked closely with the University. Lately the University under the programme 'Paying back a part of the debt' undertook interdisciplinary initiatives for the Metsovo area, including integrated surveys of the natural, socio-economic and cultural assets of the town as well as interdisciplinary contributions to the development of integrated approaches for facing the problems related to the Metsovo province.

EMPLOYMENT AND TOURISM INFRASTRUCTURE

In the last decade, Metsovo has been developed as the most important tourism destination for the entire Ioannina Prefecture thanks to its natural environment, for example the Pindos national park of Valia Kalda, its traditional settlements and architecture as well as its winter sporting (ski) facilities.

Based on the latest available data in the entire Metsovo county the following arrivals and overnight stays for the period 1990–7 can be seen in Table 9.1. From the figures shown in the table we can see a stable increasing number in both arrivals and overnight stays although in 1992 there is a decrease in both figures due to a general economic recession in the country.

Table 9.1: Metsovo arrivals and overnight stays, 1990–7.

Year	Arrivals	Overnight stays
1990	17,697	34,151
1991	19,712	31,994
1992	17,472	30,389
1993	20,424	34,287
1994	21,688	35,350
1995	21,179	35,994
1996	21,039	35,111
1997	22,099	35,994

The town's tourism infrastructure includes thirteen small hotels with a total of 700 beds. Most of them are built in local traditional architectural style where stone and wood are in abundance. In addition, there are ten units of furnished apartments contributing 200 extra beds. In 1998 a local Hotel Association was founded.

SUSTAINABLE TOURISM DEVELOPMENT: SOME CONSIDERATIONS FOR METSOVO'S FUTURE DEVELOPMENT

It is well known that the post-war boom in tourism growth is reaching a saturation point where the marginal utility for every new offer is approaching zero or even registering a negative impact. It is also becoming evident that unspoiled natural and human environment attracts more and more tourists. For future development of a sustainable tourism model for the area, the following considerations for the locals and the environment must take place:

- Through careful land management and conservative infrastructural development, large nature reserves in addition to the existing ones (Valia Calda) will be created in order to preserve particularly valuable ecosystems in the area (Aspropotamos area).
- Socially responsible and environmentally conscious tourism development should encourage many forms of community participation and decision-making.
- In order to preserve Metsovo's traditional profile, infrastructural development policies must be based on restraint. Planners must be very careful when building new or extending the existing infrastructure, especially roads, parking lots, ski lifts, new public buildings, etc. The construction of the 'Egnatia Odos' (regarded as one of the most important regional EU projects) that will run through Greece, linking Western Europe with the Balkan and the Middle East, is expected to offer both opportunities but also threats to the area. A major opportunity will be the area's easier accessibility. But a negative impact is also expected to impinge on the aesthetic of the landscape as a consequence of the route chosen for the new connecting road to the town.
- As far as tourism development is concerned, the host population should decide on and participate in all matters relevant to the development of the town. It is local authority's responsibility to encourage community participation, especially in matters concerning nature preservation and local cultural activities.
- Alternative tourism activities in the area can bring economic benefits for local people. There is a growing number of family-operated hotels and tourist merchandise production, like wood-carved products and textiles. Since, worldwide, there is growing concern that little of the revenue of eco (alternative)

tourism activities reaches local people, it must be ensured that only locally produced merchandise will be sold to visitors.

LOCAL INFORMATION SYSTEM DEVELOPMENT

Apart from other initiatives a Local Information System (LIS) development using multimedia technology will improve Metsovo's tourism infrastructure. The proposed user-friendly system not only will offer visitors easier access to the various historical monuments and buildings but also will provide information on the various activities, products and tourism-related interests of the town.

The data that will be used can include:

- topographic mapping of the town;
- pictures of the monuments and the buildings;
- descriptive text;
- video and audio recorded information.

Specifically the operating menu will include information with the following choices:

- local topography;
- churches;
- historical houses;
- fountains;
- monuments;
- cultural places and activities.

Information kiosks where this LIS system will be installed must be created in strategic points. A considerable number of tourists are 'passing through' tourists who visit the town while travelling through the area. Installing this system will enable this type of tourist to browse the town's interesting points and possibly visit some of them. The entrances, as well as the central square of the town, may be the most strategic points to establish these information kiosks.

CONCLUSION

It is widely accepted that the geography of a mountain area plays a significant role in the economic, social and cultural development of its population. Specifically, a mountainous area leads to people's isolation and to a slow rate of change in their social background, which remains the same for centuries. However, one factor that makes a gradual transformation feasible is population immigration, the development of trade and handicrafts, elements that shake the mountainous area from its historical immobility. The rich past of the town in history, culture, architecture, professions and products works as a lever for future development and sustainable tourism activity.

ACKNOWLEDGEMENTS

Special thanks are due to: Dr Thomas Mavrodontis for his constructive suggestions and guidance; the Greek National Tourism Organization (Epirus Office); the Baron Tositsa Foundation; the Averoff Foundation; the Epirus–Egnatia Foundation and the Metsovo Municipal Authority.

SUGGESTED READING

Charisis, V. (1992) *Greek Traditional Architecture, Metsovo*. Athens: Melissa.

Deffner, A. (1992) *Cultural Activities in Greece: Tradition or Modernity?* Athens: National Centre of Social Research.

Egnatia–Epirus Information Centre (1993) *Ioannina*.

Greek National Tourism Organization (1998) *Report on Overnight Stays at Epirus Area*. Ioannina:

Hammond, N. (1967) *Epirus*. Oxford: Oxford University Press.

Healy, R. G. (1994) 'Tourist merchandise as a means of generating local benefits from ecotourism'. *Journal of Sustainable Tourism*, **2** (3), 137–49.

Muller, H. (1994) 'The thorny path to sustainable tourism development', *Journal of Sustainable Tourism*, **2** (3), 131–6.

Prefecture of Grevena (1990) *The Valia Calda, National Park of Pindos*. Grevena:

Rokkou, V. (1998) *The Culture of Mountain Environment*. Athens: The National Technical University of Athens.

Tritos, M. (1991) *History of Metsovo*. Metsovo: EMA.

Tsotsoplides, C. N. (1998) *Economic Integration and Development of Metsovo: A Future Scenario with a Past*. Athens: The National Technical University of Athens.

Vranousis, L. (1962) *The Ioannina Chronicle*. Athens: EMA.

CHAPTER 10

Nordseeheilbad Westerland, Germany

Hans–Dieter Ganter

Themenbereich der Fallstudie
Entwicklung einer Marketingstrategie für ein Seebad

Hauptziel
Kenntnisse zum Bädertourismus in Deutschland

Zusammenfassung
Sylt ist die viertgrößte Insel Deutschlands. Sie liegt in der Nordsee mit einer Grundfläche von 100 km^2 und hat 21,000 Einwohner, die in zwölf Kommunen leben. Es stehen ungefähr 50.000 Gästebetten zur Verfügung. 1997 verzeichnete die Insel mehr als 500.000 Besucher, die Anzahl der Übernachtungen betrug ca. 5 Millionen. Der Zugang zur Insel ist durch einen Eisenbahnbrücke vom Festland nach Westerland, der Hauptstadt der Insel, einfach. Außerdem gibt es Fährverbindungen sowie Flugverbindungen zu allen größeren deutschen Flughäfen. Für den Tourismus auf der insel sind medinzinische Kuren von höchster Bedeutung, und obgleich sie ganzjährig möglich sind, konzentrieren sie sich auf das Frühjahr, den Herbst und den Winter. Seit den sechziger Jahren zeichnet sich Sylt durch ein „High-Society-Image" aus, das aufrechterhalten werden konnte, obwohl mittlerweile viele Prominente ihre Ferien nicht mehr auf der Insel verbringen.

Westerland ist als Hauptstadt der Insel geographisch zentral gelegen. Die Einwohnerzahl beträgt 9.500. Die Stadt weist von 1855 bis heute eine lange Geschichte als Seebad auf. Die Stadt verfügt über zahlreiche Einrichtungen für alle möglichen Sportarten und einen sieben km langen Sandstrand, der in mehrere Bereiche unterteilt ist, darunter einige FKK-Gelände.

Seit 1964 existiert ein riesiges Hallenwellenbad, damit alle Einrichtungen eines Seebades unabhängig von der Witterung genutzt werden können. Außerdem gibt es das „Haus des kleinen Gastes", eine Einrichtung für Kinder, die Aktivitäten aller Art anbietet. Besucher Westerlands bezahlen eine Kurtaxe von DM 5,50 täglich, die für die Finanzierung der für ein Seebad dieser Art notwendigen Einrichtungen und Aktivitäten verwendet wird.

Westerland verfügt über 30 Hotels mit einem Angebot von insgesamt 3.707 Betten. Allerdings ist die Existenz von 15.377 Betten in Ferienwohnungen sowohl in quantitativer als auch in qualitativer Hinsicht bedeutsamer. 1997 betrug die Anzahl der Besucher nahezu 470.000, die der Übernachtungen 2,7 Millionen. Im Durchschnitt verbrachten die Besucher 9,8 Tage auf der Insel. Die Zahl der Besucher stieg von 1996 auf 1997 um 7%, wodurch der Rückgang im Jahr zuvor ausgeglichen werden konnte. Allerdings war trotz der geringfügig angestiegenen Zahl der Übernachtungsgäste ein leichter Rückgang in der Zahl der Übernachtungen zu verzeichnen. Hinsichtlich der Gäste- und Übernachtungszahlen zeigt sich ein deutlicher Schwerpunkt in den Monaten von Mai bis Oktober mit einer Konzentration im Juli und August. 77,5% der betten befinden sich in Ferienwohnungen, die auch einen Anteil von 61,5% der Gäste aufnehmen, wohingegen Hotels und ähnliche Einrichtungen lediglich einen Anteil von 14,7% der Betten, 27,2% der Gäste und 18% der Übernachtungen zu verzeichnen haben.

1997 kamen lediglich 2.779 Gäste aus dem Ausland, was nur einen Anteil von einem Prozent ausmacht. Die meisten deutschen Gäste kamen aus den benachbarten Bundesländern. 57% der Gäste sind älter als 40 Jahre. Die Alterskohorte zwischen 21 und 30 weist lediglich einen Anteil von 8% der Besucher aus, während der Anteil der über 70-Jährigen nahezu ebenso hoch ist.

Lernergebnisse

- Informationsvermittlung zu einem Seebad mit spezifischen Ressourcen und einer besonderen Geschichte
- Kenntnisse über die Gästestruktur und das Gästeverhalten
- Entwicklung von Kriterien für die Analyse empirischer Daten
- Schlußfolgerungen für eine Marketingstrategie

Diskussionspunkte

- Die Vermarktung des Seebades an andere Gruppen als die augenblicklichen Zielgruppen.
- Wie kam die spezifische Gästestruktur zustande?
- Probleme der Interpretation von Statistiken. Welche Daten fehlen? Auf welche Art lassen sich diese gewinnen?

EINLEITUNG: SYLT, DIE LAGE UND TOURISTISCHE MERKMALE

Sylt ist eine deutsche Nordseeinsel, die zur sogenannten Nordfriesischen Inselgruppe gehört und vor der Westküste Schleswig Holsteins liegt. Mit knapp 100 Quadratkilometern ist Sylt die größte deutsche Nordseeinsel und nach Rügen, Usedom und Fehmarn die viertgrößte deutsche Insel. Sylt hat eine Gesamtfläche von ca. 100 km^2 und ist 38 km lang, die größte Breite beträgt 12 km, an der schmalsten Stelle ist die Insel allerdings nur 600–800 m breit. Sie weist zwölf Ortschaften aus und hat ca. 21.000 Einwohner, die knapp 50.000 Gästebetten vermieten. Im Jahre 1997 besuchten die Insel insgesamt über 500.000 Gäste, die Zahl der Übernachtungen betrug ca. 5 Mio.

Trotz der Insellage ist Sylt vom Festland aus einfach zu erreichen: Seit 1927 gibt es zwischen Niebüll auf dem Festland und Westerland auf der Insel eine Bahnverbindung über den „Hindenburgdamm", die etwas mehr als eine halbe Stunde beanspruchtucht. So läßt sich Sylt sowohl direkt von vielen Städten der Bundesrepublik Deutschland aus mit der Bahn erreichen oder – mit dem privaten PKW – über den Autozug von Niebüll aus. Daneben gibt es natürlich noch zahlreiche Schiffs- und Flugverbindungen, Letztere von nahezu allen größeren Flughäfen in Deutschland – zumindest während des Sommers. 1997 betrug die Zahl der Flugbewegungen auf dem Flugplatz Westerländ nahezu 10.000 bei insgesamt ca. 80.000 Fluggästen.[1]

Die tages- und jahreszeitlich ausgeglichenen Lufttemperaturen und die im Bereich des Meeres dauernden Luftbewegungen sind für das gesundheitliche Wohlbefinden von besonderer Bedeutung. Kuren spielen für den Tourismus der Insel eine besondere Rolle. Sie sind zwar ganzjährig möglich, Frühjahr, Herbst und Winter eignen sich aber für die meisten Heilanzeigen besonders.

Für den Kurtourismus in Deutschland ist die Klassifizierung als Bade- oder Heilbadeort von besonderer Bedeutung. Damit Orte den Begriff „Seebäder" führen dürfen, müssen die folgenden Bedingungen erfüllt sein:

- Eine Lage an der Meeresküste oder in deren unmittelbaren Nähe (Entfernung der Orts- oder Ortsteilmitte nicht mehr als zwei km vom Strand);
- Eine Überprüfung des Lage- und Witterungsklimas und der lufthygienischen Verhältnisse;
- Das Vorhandensein artgemäßer Kureinrichtungen;
- Ein artgemäßer Kurortcharakter.[2]

Auf Sylt gibt es vier Orte, die als Seebad klassifiziert sind: List, Kampen, Rantum und Hörnum.

Darüber hinaus gibt es mit Westerland und Wenningstedt zwei Orte, die als Seeheilbäder qualifiziert sind. Als staatlich anerkanntes Seeheilbad werden dort folgende Heilanzeigen behandelt:

- Chronische Krankheiten der Atemwege;
- Herz- und Gefäßkrankheiten;
- Hautkrankheiten;
- Chronische Krankheiten des Bewegungsapparates;
- Frauenleiden;
- Krankheiten im Kindesalter;
- Allgemeine Schwächezustände.[3]

Sylt genießt seit der Mitte der sechziger Jahre den Ruf einer mondänen Insel. Damals wurde von Strandparties an Nacktbadestränden berichtet, die vor allem von Prominenten veranstaltet wurden. Dieser Ruf führte dazu, daß im Gefolge der

Prominenz immer mehr Inselbesucher auftauchten, die daran teilhaben wollten. Zum einen erklärt die Lage der Insel zwischen Watt auf der einen und wilder See auf der anderen Seite die Attraktivität. Die Schönheit dieser Lage ist seit Beginn dieses Jahrhunderts von zahlreichen Schriftstellern und anderen Künstlern, die sich hier regelmäßig aufhielten, immer wieder gerühmt worden. Zum anderen aber sind es die Ferienhäuser und damit auch der Aufenthalt von Prominenten aus allen gesellschaftlichen Bereichen, die für die Anziehungskraft Sylts sorgen. All dies hat dafür gesorgt, daß – vor allem in Westerland und Kampen – auch von dem Angebot an Waren und Dienstleitungen eine entsprechende Sogwirkung ausgeht. So haben insbesondere in den Hauptstraßen Westerlands nahezu alle Hersteller von Nobelmarken ihre Boutiquen, daneben gibt es dort viele Galerien. Das Preisniveau ist entsprechend hoch. Obwohl viele Prominente mittlerweile Sylt meiden, scheint das Image heute immer noch ungebrochen.[4]

WESTERLAND

Westerland ist mit ca. 9.500 Einwohnern der größte Ort und liegt geographisch ungefähr in der Mitte der Insel. Als Seebad hat es eine lange Tradition, bereits im Jahre 1855 wurde das Seebad eröffnet, zwei Jahre später eine Badeaktiengesellschaft gegründet. Sehr schnell galt es als eleganter Badeort. Schon um die Jahrhundertwende war der Zustrom von Badegästen groß, was zur Einrichtung eines Kurhauses führte und dazu, daß 1897 ein Telefonnetz eingerichtet wurde. Schließlich wurde 1902 ein Familienbad eingerichtet, zur damaligen Zeit deshalb außergewöhnlich, weil bis zu jener Zeit Männer und Frauen nur streng getrennt baden durften. Heute verfügt Westerland über einen Strand von sieben km Länge, der in mehrere Abschnitte unterteilt ist, darunter auch mehrere FKK-Strände. Darüber hinaus sind in Westerland zahlreiche Sporteinrichtungen vorhanden, so daß es die Möglichkeit gibt, nahezu alle Sportarten zu betreiben.

Damit der Kurbetrieb unabhängig von Witterung und Jahreszeit wird, wurde im Jahre 1964 ein Meerwasser-Wellenbad eingerichtet, das seither immer wieder modernisiert und vergrößert wurde. Heute verfügt die „Erlebniswelt Sylter Welle" über eine Wasserfläche von $450\,m^2$ bei einer Wassertemperatur von $28°$, wobei zweimal stündlich für jeweils zehn Minuten die Brandung simuliert wird. Darüber hinaus gibt es dort unzählige andere Möglichkeiten des Wassersports und der Gesundheitsanwendungen, u. a. Tauchkurse, Sauna, Wassergymnastik und Massage. Zusätzlich verfügt die „Sylter Welle" noch über einen Eltern-Kind-Bereich mit einem vielfältigen Angebot für Kinder. Insgesamt konnte die „Sylter Welle" im Jahre 1997 fast 200.000 Besucher verzeichnen, davon waren ca. ein Viertel Jugendliche.

Speziell für die Betreuung von Kindern wurde das „Haus des kleinen Gastes" eingerichtet, das ganzjährig geöffnet ist. Dort stehen Kindern Möglichkeiten zu entsprechenden Aktivitäten offen.

Westerland besitzt eine Spielbank, Kinos, Museen und Galerien. Von Mai bis Oktober finden täglich Konzerte an der Strandpromenade statt. Außerdem gibt es Konzerte und Galaabende.[5] Ca. 30 Lokale sind bis spät in die Nacht bzw. bis in den frühen Morgen geöffnet.

Als Seeheilbad ist Westerland mit einem Kurmittelhaus ausgestattet. Die Palette mit unterschiedlichen Kurmittelanwendungen ist umfangreich und reicht von Bädern und Packungen über Inhalationen, Liegekuren, Hydrotherapie und Atemgymnastik. Die Kuren werden in Kurkliniken oder auch als offene Kuren durchgeführt. Eine Besonderheit stellen Meerwasser-Trinkkuren dar, die in der Biomaris-Kurhalle an der Strandpromenade durchgeführt werden.

Besucher Westerlands sind zur sogenannten Kurabgabe verpflichtet. Die Entrichtung der Abgabe wird über die „Kurkarte" nachgewiesen. Die Kurabgabe beträgt zur Zeit pro Tag zwischen dem 1. Mai und dem 31. Oktober DM 5,50, in der übrigen Zeit die Hälfte dieses Betrages. Tagesgäste bekommen eine Tageskarte zum Preis von DM 6. Für Langzeitbesucher gibt es eine Jahreskurabgabe von DM 154. Die Erlöse der Kurabgabe dienen der Finanzierung von Einrichtungen und Aufgaben, die speziell den Gästen zugute kommen und nicht aus dem üblichen Haushalt einer Kleinstadt von der Größe Westerlands getragen werden können wie z. B.: Kurkonzerte, Instandhaltung und Pflege von Kureinrichtungen und Stränden, Kinderbetreuung, etc.

Für die Organisation und Durchführung von Kongressen, Tagungen und Seminaren ist im Städtischen Kurbetrieb eine Abteilung eingerichtet. Die Anzahl der im Jahre 1997 diesbezüglich durchgeführten Veranstaltungen betrug 27 bei ca. 4.200 Teilnehmern mit ca. 48.000 Übernachtungen.[6]

Westerland verfügt derzeit über etwa 30 Hotels aller Kategorien mit 3.707 Betten, zusätzlich über zahlreiche Ferienwohnungen und Appartments mit 15.377 Betten, Pensionen mit einer Bettenanzahl von 112. Aus Privatvermietungen stehen 4.720 Betten zur Verfügung. In Erholungsheimen beträgt die Bettenanzahl 332, in Sanatorien und Kliniken 682. Die Campingkapazität beträgt 1.000 Betten. Im Jahre 1997 konnten insgesamt nahezu 470.000 Tages- und Übernachtungsgäste sowie ca. 2,7 Mio. Übernachtungen verbucht werden. Die Gäste hielten sich 1997 durchschnittlich 9,8 Tage in Westerland auf.[7]

Im folgenden sollen einige der oben genannten Gästezahlen Westerlands näher betrachtet werden. Grundlage dieser Betrachtung ist die Tourismus-Statistik für Westerland und Sylt[8] sowie eine im Jahre 1996 in Westerland durchgeführte Gästebefragung.[9]

Die Gästezahlen Westerlands konnten von 1996 auf 1997 einen Zuwachs von 7,7 Prozent verzeichnen. Damit konnte der Rückgang um 6,1 Prozent von 1995 auf 1996 wieder aufgeholt werden. Auch die Zahl der Übernachtungsgäste nahm von 1996 auf

1997 leicht um 2,7 Prozent zu. Allerdings nahm die Zahl der Übernachtungen von 1996 auf 1997 um 2,8 Prozent ab.

Betrachtet man die Gäste- und Übernachtungszahlen in den einzelnen Monaten, so zeigt sich ein deutlicher Schwerpunkt in den Monaten Mai bis Oktober, wobei die Monate Juli und August sich noch einmal deutlich hervorheben.

Ein anderes Bild ergibt sich, wenn man sich die durchschnittliche Aufenthaltsdauer aller Übernachtungsgäste in den einzelnen Monaten ansieht. Hier bildet der Januar mit 20,0 Tagen durchschnittlicher Aufenthaltsdauer je Gast einen deutlichen Schwerpunkt, während die durchschnittliche Aufenthaltsdauer in den übrigen Monaten – mit Ausnahme des Dezembers – relativ ausgeglichen ist und zwischen 12,6 und 8,1 Tagen liegt. Eine Ursache dafür dürfte darin zu finden sein, daß im Januar medizinische Kuren gegenüber anderen Aufenthaltsarten überwiegen und somit eine längere Aufenthaltsdauer notwendig machen.

Hinsichtlich des Anteils der Gäste- und Übernachtungszahlen nach Beherbergungskategorien zeigt sich – der bereits erwähnten Struktur der Kategorien entsprechend – ein deutlicher Schwerpunkt bei den Ferienappartments und Privatvermietern mit einem Gesamtanteil an allen Betten von 77,5 Prozent und einem Anteil dieser Gäste an der Gesamtzahl aller Gäste von 61,6 Prozent. An der Gesamtzahl der Übernachtungen weisen diese beiden Kategorien einen Anteil von 68,6 Prozent auf. Für Hotels und Pensionen liegen die jeweiligen Anteile bei 14,7 Prozent der Betten, 27,2 Prozent der Gäste und 18,1 Prozent der Übernachtungen.

Diese Zahlen spiegeln deutlich die Struktur des Tourismus auf Sylt im allgemeinen und in Westerland im besonderen wider, die eine deutliche Betonung der Ferienwohnungen zeigt – auch von Zweitwohnungsbesitzern, die sich die Nutzung der Wohnung ausschließlich selbst vorbehalten. Diese Struktur wird auch deutlich, wenn man den Anteil der Übernachtungsgäste im Prozentsatz der Einwohner des jeweiligen Bundeslandes betrachtet, also die Marktdurchdringung. Die benachbarten Bundesländer Hamburg (1,21), Schleswig-Holstein (0,95) und Niedersachsen (0,66) nehmen mit Abstand die ersten Plätze ein. Dies macht deutlich, daß Sylt bzw. Westerland bevorzugt als Feriendomizil solcher Touristen gewählt wird, die sich nicht nur während zwei bis drei Wochen Sommerurlaub dort aufhalten, sondern ihre Ferienwohnung auch häufig für Wochenend- und andere Kurzaufenthalte nutzen wollen. Darüber hinaus zeigt sich in dieser Struktur auch die Position Sylts als Insel der „Reichen und Schönen", weil dadurch auch bestimmte Markteintrittsbarrieren sowohl für Anbieter als auch für Konsumenten errichtet werden.

Aus dem Ausland kamen 1997 lediglich 2.779 Gäste (32 weniger als im Jahr davor), die Übernachtungszahl ausländischer Gäste lag bei 21.340 (1996: 22.253), was einer durchschnittlichen Verweildauer von 7,7 Tagen entspricht (1996: 7,9 Tage). Der

Anteil ausländischer Gäste an der Gesamtzahl betrug nur 1 Prozent. Anders als „Prominentenferienorte" in anderen Ländern, wie z. B. St Tropez in Frankreich oder St Moritz in der Schweiz, kann Westerland außerhalb Deutschlands also nicht von seinem Image profitieren.

Die Herkunft der Übernachtungsgäste aufgeschlüsselt nach Bundesländern zeigt Nordrhein-Westfalen mit ca. 80.000 Gästen, ein Anteil von 28,9 Prozent auf dem ersten Rang. Niedersachsen hat einen Anteil von 18,4 Prozent und von dort kamen etwas mehr als 50.000 Gäste. Schleswig-Holstein und Hamburg stellten einen Anteil von 9,3 Prozent (25.856) bzw. 7,4 Prozent (20.642). Nennenswert ist noch der Anteil von 8,5 Prozent (23.766) der Gäste, die aus Hessen kommen.

Die Altersstruktur der Gäste zeigt ein deutliches Übergewicht der über 40-jährigen mit einem Anteil von nahezu 57 Prozent an der Gesamtzahl. Betrachtet man die einzelnen Alterskohorten, so fällt auf, daß die Kohorte zwischen 21 und 30 Jahren mit ca. 8 Prozent deutlich unterrepräsentiert ist. Zum Vergleich: Der Anteil der 71–80-Jährigen ist mit 7,17 Prozent fast gleich hoch. Auch an diesen Zahlen wird die Gästestruktur und das Image der Insel deutlich. Jüngere Gäste verfügen im allgemeinen nicht über ein verfügbares Einkommen, das ihnen den Ferienaufenthalt in Westerland problemlos ermöglichen würde.

Im Dezember des Jahres 1996 führten Mitarbeiter des Städtischen Kurbetriebs eine Befragung unter den Gästen durch. Befragt wurde eine Stichprobe von 302 Personen, die auf Sylt wohnen, die Insel besuchten oder dort Urlaub machten. Die Ergebnisse dieser Gästebefragung sind insofern mit einem Vorbehalt zu versehen, als sie im Dezember erfolgte, also dem Monat mit der geringsten Gästefrequenz. Unter dieser Voraussetzung ist es schwierig, den Daten einen repräsentativen Charakter zuzusprechen, eher handelt es sich dabei um eine Art Momentaufnahme. Sie ist zusätzlich dadurch geprägt, daß sie während der Zeit durchgeführt wurde, als auf Sylt der „Surf Cup" stattfand. Folgt man – mit dieser Einschränkung – der Gästebefragung, so nannten als Reisemotiv 68,9 Prozent der Befragten Erholung. 38,7 Prozent der Befragten gaben an, wegen des Strandes nach Westerland gekommen zu sein. Für 35,8 Prozent war Natur und für 34,1 Prozent Gesundheit der Beweggrund für die Reise. Weitere Motive waren Sport (17,2 Prozent), eine Kur (8,9 Prozent) und Kultur (4,6 Prozent). Bei dieser Frage waren Mehrfachnennungen möglich.

Befragt nach der Nutzung von Einrichtungen im Kurmittelhaus gaben ca. 50 Prozent der Gäste an, die Einrichtungen des Kurmittelhauses überhaupt nicht zu nutzen. Von der anderen Hälfte bekamen etwas mehr als ein Drittel medizinische Anwendungen. Der größte Teil der Gäste, die Einrichtungen des Kurmittelhauses nutzten, war mit dem Personal äußerst zufrieden.

Die Frage nach der Bewertung des Freizeitbades „Sylter Welle" ergab, daß ein Großteil der Befragten das Erlebnisbad noch nicht besucht hatten (65,5 Prozent). 19,2 Prozent der Befragten waren schon mehrmals dort gewesen, 13,2 Prozent einmal. Von der Altersstruktur her gehören zwar die 36–45-Jährigen zur stärksten Besuchergruppe, allerdings war es die Gruppe der bis zu 25-Jährigen, von der die meisten Wiederholungsbesucher gestellt wurden. Den Eintrittspreis für das Erlebnisbad beurteilten 57,1 Prozent derjenigen, die es bereits besucht hatten, als zu hoch, 41,9 Prozent hielten ihn für angemessen und für 1 Prozent war er zu niedrig. Eine genauere Betrachtung weist ferner aus, daß ca. 60 Prozent derjenigen, die das Bad schon mehrfach besucht hatten, den Eintrittspreis als zu hoch beurteilen.[10] Offensichtlich ist der hohe Eintrittspreis ein wichtiger Grund für Nichtbesucher.

SCHLUSSFOLGERUNGEN FÜR MARKETINGMASSNAHMEN

Die Rahmenbedingungen für das Reiseverhalten in Deutschland haben sich nach Ergebnissen der Reiseanalyse[11] gegenüber früheren Jahren verändert. Diese Veränderungen zeigen sich auch in den Zahlen zur Gästestruktur und dem Gästeverhalten in Westerland. Steigende Arbeitslosigkeit, steigende finanzielle Unsicherheiten, sinkende Haushaltsnettoeinkommen durch niedrige Tarifabschlüsse und höhere Abgabenbelastungen verbunden mit einem wachsenden Wettbewerbsdruck durch Billiganbieter von Auslandsreisen haben zu einem Rückgang der Urlaubsreiseintensität um 3,3 Mio. Reisen geführt, der insbesondere zu Lasten des Inlandsurlaubs ging. Insgesamt haben sich die Wettbewerbsbedingungen auf dem deutschen Reisemarkt Verschärft. Seiner Gästestruktur entsprechend war Westerland von dieser Entwicklung in besonderem Maße betroffen. Das Urlaubsverhalten der Deutschen in rezessiven Zeiten scheint der Reiseanalyse zufolge geprägt durch einen Verzicht auf Zweit- und Dritturlaub, eine Verkürzung der Aufenthaltsdauer sowie tendenziell rückläufiges Urlaubs-Ausgabeverhalten.

Hinsichtlich der Reiseziele im Inland konnten der Reiseanalyse folgend zwar Bayern und Schleswig-Holstein ihre führende Stellung in den vergangenen Jahren behaupten, jedoch mußte vor allem Schleswig-Holstein starke Marktanteilsverluste hinnehmen. Offensichtlich kann Mecklenburg-Vorpommern seine starke Stellung zu Lasten Schleswig-Holsteins ausbauen.

Zu den bevorzugten Informationsquellen der Deutschen über Zielgebiete von Urlaubsreisenden gehören nach der Reiseanalyse Empfehlungen durch Freunde und Verwandte, Erfahrungen durch Tagesausflüge, Presseberichte, Informationen durch Ärzte, durch Prospekte, durch TV und Rundfunk. Außerdem spielen Anzeigen sowie Reiseführer und Bücher bei der Informationsbeschaffung eine tragende Rolle.

Die Gästegruppen in Sylt lassen sich nach Angaben des Kurbetriebs Westerland in Natur- und Erholungsurlauber, Gesundheitsurlauber und Aktivurlauber unterteilen. Dies drückt sich auch in den bevorzugten Urlaubsaktivitäten der Westerländer Gäste aus, nämlich:

- Spazierengehen;
- ausschlafen, ausruhen;
- Einkaufsbummel;
- Ausflugsfahrten;
- Lesen;
- Wandern;
- Sonnenbaden;
- Radfahren.

Angesichts dieser Entwicklungen auf dem Tourismusmarkt ist es notwendig, für Westerland Marketingziele und Marketingstrategien zu erarbeiten, die den geschilderten Problemen gerecht werden.

ANMERKUNGEN

1. Kurbetrieb Westerland; Tourismus-Statistik 1997 – Westerland. und Insel Sylt, Westerland 1998, S. 20.
2. Statistisches Bundesamt (1996) Tourismus in Zahlen 1995, Wiesbaden, S. 262.
3. Deutscher Bäderverband e. V. (1979) *Deutscher Bäderkalender*, Bonn, S. 180.
4. Ausführlich dazu: Maak, Niklas (1998) 'Lebenslügen: Sylt', in *Süddeutsche Zeitung* vom 12. 8. 1998.
5. Kurbetrieb Westerland; Tourismus-Statistik 1997 – Westerland und Insel Sylt, Westerland 1998, 5. 18–21.
6. Kurbetrieb Westerland; Tourismus-Statistik 1997 – Westerland und Insel Sylt, Westerland 1998, 5. 18–21.
7. Kurbetrieb Westerland; Tourismus-Statistik 1997 – Westerland und Insel Sylt, Westerland 1998, 5. 18–21, S. 2, S. 9.
8. Kurbetrieb Westerland (1998) *Tourismus-Statistik 1997 – Westerland und Insel Sylt*. Westerland.
9. D'Aulnis de Bourouill, A., Mühlbronner, B. und Friedrich, U. (1996/97) *Marktstudie: Gästebefragung in Westerland/Sylt. FH Heilbronn: Hausarbeit zur Vorlesung Tourismusbetriebswirtschaftslehre*. WS 1996/97.
10. D'Aulnis de Bourouill, A., Mühlbronner, B. und Friedrich, U., *Marktstudie: Gästebefragung in Westerland/Sylt. FH Heilbronn: Hausarbeit zur Vorlesung Tourismusbetriebswirtschaftslehre*. WS 1996/97, S. 17.
11. *Reiseanalyse der Forschungsgemeinschaft Urlaub und Reisen e. V.* (1997) Hamburg.

LESELISTE

Bauer-Tertius, J. (1995) „Auswirkungen auf Prävention und Rehabilitation in Heilbädern und Kurorten" in *Heilbad und Kurort*, Zeitschrift für das gesamte Bäderwesen; Deutscher Bäderverband, Baden-Baden.

Berekoven, L. (1974) *Der Dienstleistungsbetrieb*. Wiesbaden: Betriebswirtschaftlicher Verlag Dr. Th. Gabler, Wiesbaden.

Bleile, G. (1991) „Zunehmender Wettbewerbsdruck erfordert neue Management-Konzepte und Marketing-Strategien", in *Heilbad und Kurort*, 2–3.

Bleile, G. (1994) „Heilbäder und Kurorte im Strukturwandel – Anpassungsprobleme der Kurhotellerie", in *Allgemeine Hotel- und Gaststättenzeitung*, 94. Jg., Nr. 16, 4, S. 18.

Böni, C. (1992) *Vom Kur- zum Gesundheitstourismus – Entwicklung und Chancen*, St. Gallen: Institut für Tourismus und Verkehrswirtschaft an der Hochschule St. Gallen.

Deutsches Seminar für Fremdenverkehr (Hrsg.) (1986) *Urlaub und Gesundheit – Marktchancen für deutsche Heilbäder und Kurorte*. Deutsches Seminar für Fremdenverkehr, Berlin.

Deutsches Seminar für Fremdenverkehr (Hrsg.) (1990) *Tourismus 2000 – Praktiker inszenieren die Zukunft*. Berlin:

Ender, W. (Hrsg.) (1992) *Die Kur – ein Markenartikel*. Institut für Tourismus und Friezeitwirtschaft, Wien.

Fargel, M. (1988a) „Überlegungen für eine gemeinsame Marketingstrategie der deutschen Heilbäder und Kurorte" (Überlegungen), in *Heilbad und Kurort*, 40. Jg., 3, S. 82ff.

Fargel, M. (1988b) „Probleme und Möglichkeiten der Corporate Identity der deutschen Heilbäder", in *Heilbäd und Kurort*, 40. Jg., 4, S. 126.

Forscher, R. (1990) „Die Kur im Kurort der 90er Jahre", in *Heilbäd und Kurort*, 42. Jg., 3.

Freyer, W. und Tödter, N. (1992) *Kurortgesetzgebung in den neuen Bundesländern*, Bonn: Rügen.

Fuchs, W. (1993) „Position deutscher Heilbäder und Kurorte in einem sich öffnenden Europa", in Stadfeld, F. (Hrsg.) *Europäische Kurorte – Fakten und Perspektiven*. Limburgerhof: FBV-medien Verlag, S. 59–65.

Haedrich, G., Kaspar, C. *et al.* (1983) *Tourismus-Management – Tourismus-Marketing und Fremdenverkehrsplanung*. Berlin und New York: Walter de Gruyter.

Hubatka, K. (1992) Ender, W. (Hrsg.) *Die Kur – ein Markenartikel*. Wien, s. 43–79, (siehe Bücher und Sammelbände).

Kaspar, C. (1992) „Strategien und Profilierungsmöglichkeiten der Kurorte", in Ender, W. (Hrsg.) *Die Kur – ein Markenartikel*. Wien, S. 27–42.

Kaspar, C. (1989a) „Von der traditionellen Badekur zu modernen Formen des Gesundheitstourismus, Einführung zum Generalthema des 39. AIEST Kongresses", in AIEST (Hrsg.) *Du thermalisme au tourisme de santé*. St Gallen: St. Gallen, Ed. AIEST, 1989.

Kaspar, C. (1989b) „Was heißt Marketing für Heilbäderkurorte?", in AIEST (Hrsg.) *Du thermalisme au tourisme de santé*. St. Gallen: St Gallen, Ed. AIEST, 1989.

Kirschner, Ch. (1997) „Attraktiver Gesundheitsurlaub – Neue Chancen für unsere Bäder und Kurorte", in *Heilbäd und Kurort* 49. Jg., 5, S. 115.

Klopp, H. und Tödter, N. (1993) „Die Wahl der Rechtsform als unternehmerischer Entscheidungsprozeß im Fremdenverkehrsort", in Stadtfeld, F. (Hrsg.) *Europäische Kurorte – Fakten und Perspektiven*. Limburgerhof, S. 29–45.

Krumscheid, P. (1993) „Das Kurwesen in Zahlen", in Stadtfeld, F. (Hrsg.) *Europäische Kurorte – Fakten und Perspektiven*. Limburgerhof, S. 53–8.

Maschke, J. (1989) „Erfolgreiche und weniger erfolgreiche Angebotsformen im Kurwesen der Bundesrepublik Deutschland", in AIEST (Hrsg.) *Du thermalisme au tourisme de santé*. St. Gallen: S. 124.

Opaschowski, H. und Schoberth, H. (1984) *Verändertes Urlaubsverhalten und neue Kurbedürfnisse*. Hamburg: B.A.T. Forschungsinstitut.

Püttmann, R. (1992) „Der Kurgast 1991", in Deutsches Seminar für Fremdenverkehr (Hrsg.) *Wie erstelle ich eine Fremdenverkehrskonzeption? – Leitfaden mit praktischen Beispielen*. DSF, Berlin: S. 217–27.

Schoberth, H. (1988) *Kurort im Wandel*. Hamburg: Axel Springer Verlag AG.

Schönemann, K. (1991) *Gemeinde und Fremdenverkehr*. Wiesbaden: Kommunal und Schulverlag KGA.

Schreiner, R. (1983) *Die Dienstleistungsmarke – Typus, Rechtsschutz und Funktion*. Koeln: Heymann.

Stadtfeld, F. (Hrsg.) (1993) *Europäische Kurorte – Fakten und Perspektiven*. Limburgerhof.

Wöhler, K. (1993) „Müssen sich die Kurorte umprofilieren?", in Stadtfeld, F. (Hrsg.) *Europäische Kurorte – Fakten und Perspektiven*. Limburgerhof: pp. 13–28.

CHAPTER 10

Nordseeheilbad Westerland, Germany

Hans–Dieter Ganter

Aim
Development of a marketing strategy for a spa, and understanding of spa tourism in Germany.

Keywords
spa; medical treatment; island; nudist beaches

Summary
Sylt is the fourth largest German island. It is located in the North Sea, its area is 100 km^2 and it has a population of 21,000 inhabitants who live in twelve communities. There are about 50,000 beds available to rent to visitors. In 1997 more than 500,000 visitors came to the island, and the number of overnight stays was c. 5 million. Access to the island is easy since there is a railway bridge from the coast to Westerland, the capital of the island. Furthermore, there are ferry links and air links to all major German airports. For tourism medical cures are of major importance and although possible all year round they are concentrated in the spring, autumn and winter. Since the 1960s Sylt has had the image of a high society sea resort and it has succeeded in keeping this particular image in spite of the fact that many prominent people no longer spend their holidays on the island.

Westerland is the capital of the island, located in the centre. Its population is 9,500 inhabitants. It has a long history as a spa, from 1855 to the present. There are numerous facilities for all kinds of sports in the city and a 76 km beach divided into several areas among which some are nudist beaches.

In 1964 a huge indoor pool was built in order to be able to offer all the spa services of a seaside resort independent of the weather. There is also the so-called 'house for the Young Visitor', a facility for children where all kinds of activities are offered. Visitors to Westerland have to pay a visitor's tax of DM 5.50 per day which is used to finance all the facilities and activities necessary for a seaside resort of this kind.

The number of hotels in Westerland is 30, and they offer 3,707 beds. But more important for Westerland both in terms of quantity and quality is the existence of 15,377 beds in holiday flats. The number of visitors in 1997 was nearly 470,000 and that of overnight stays 2.7 million. On average visitors spent 9.8 days on the island. The number of visitors increased by 7.7 per cent from 1996 to 1997, which meant a compensation for the decrease in the year before. There was a slight decrease in the number of overnight stays, however, despite the slightly rising figure of overnight visitors. As to the numbers of guests and overnight stays in terms of months there is a clear peak in the months from May to October with a concentration in July and August. Holiday flats make up 77.5 per cent of all beds and a share of 61.5 per cent of all visitors, while hotels and the like take a 14.7 per cent share of beds, 27.2 per cent of visitors and 18 per cent of overnight stays.

In 1997 only 2,779 visitors came from abroad, which is a share of all visitors of just 1 per cent. From Germany most of the visitors come from adjacent federal states. In terms of age more than 57 per cent are older than 40. The 21–30 age cohort makes up only 8 per cent of visitors, while the share of those visitors older than 70 is nearly as high.

Learning outcomes

After examining this case study, students should be able to do the following:

- identify information on a resort with particular resources and a particular history;
- understand customer structure and customer behaviour;
- identify criteria for an analysis of empirical data;
- draw conclusions for marketing strategy.

Discussion topics

- How can the resort be promoted to other than the current target groups?
- How did the particular customer structure come about?
- What are the problems of interpreting statistics? Which data are missing? How would you gather them?

INTRODUCTION: SYLT, THE SITE AND TOURISTIC CHARACTERISTICS

Sylt is a German island in the North Sea and belongs to the group of the so-called North Frisian Isles, geographically positioned on the West coast of the state of Schleswig-Holstein. With its c. 100 km^2 Sylt is the largest German island in the North Sea and, after Ruegen, Usedom, and Fehmarn, the fourth largest island in Germany. Its total area is about 100 square km with a length of 38 km, and a maximum width of 12 km, however, the narrowest part is only 600 to 800 m wide. There are twelve small towns on the island with a total of c. 21,000 inhabitants, and 50,000 beds available to rent to visitors. In 1997 there were more than 500,000 visitors to Sylt, the number of overnight stays (bednights) was c. 5 million.

Despite its geographical position as an island Sylt is fairly easy to reach. Since 1927 a railway link has existed between Niebuell on the mainland and Westerland on the island, the 'Hindenburgdamm'. It takes about half an hour to get there. Thus, Sylt can be reached from many cities in Germany by train or, by car, via the motorcar transporter from Niebuell. Furthermore, there are numerous ferry links and air links to all major airports in Germany, particularly during the summer. The number of take-offs and landings at the airport of Westerland amounted to *c*. 10,000 with a total of about 80,000 passengers.[1]

Air temperatures are balanced both throughout the day and the year, and together with the constant breezes at the seaside offer special benefits to health. Medical cures are therefore a major part of the tourist activities. Although possible all year round, spring, autumn and winter are especially suited for most of the therapeutic treatments.

For spa tourism in Germany it is crucial for resorts to be officially classified as a spa. There are two categories: 'Badeort' and 'Heilbadeort', with the latter meaning proven therapeutical indications have been documented. There is even the category 'Seebad' or 'Seeheilbad', which means that these categories apply to spas at the seaside. In order to be classified as a 'Seebad' towns have to meet the following conditions:

- its geographical position at the coast or within its near distance (centre of the town or a part of it must not be further than 2 km from the beach);
- constant control of climate (both geographical position and weather) as well as of conditions of air hygiene;
- existence of appropriate spa facilities;
- appropriate nature of a spa.[2]

On Sylt four towns are classified as 'Seebad': List, Kampen, Rantum and Hoernum. Two other towns, Westerland and Wenningstedt, are additionally classified as 'Seeheilbad'. Being acknowledged by the state, therapeutical treatments for the following ailments are found there:

- chronic diseases of the respiratory tract;
- coronary and vascular diseases;
- skin diseases;
- chronic diseases of the locomotor system;
- female diseases;
- children's diseases;
- general faintness.[3]

Since the mid-1960s Sylt has had the image of a high society seaside resort. There were reports about beach parties on nudist beaches given by prominent and famous people. Due to this image more and more visitors showed up following the high society in order to share their fun. The geographical position between the mud flats on the one side and the rough sea on the other accounts for the attractiveness of the island in the first place. Since the beginning of the century this beauty has repeatedly been described by many writers and other artists visiting the island regularly. In the second place, however, it is the holiday cottages and with them prominent people from all parts of the society which add to the attractiveness of Sylt. Altogether, this leads to a proper supply of goods and services, above all in Westerland and Kampen. Thus, most of the producers of high price brands have their boutiques in the main streets of Westerland, furthermore, there are lots of art galleries. The prices are appropriately high. Although many of the high society people nowadays no longer come to Sylt, the image still persists.[4]

WESTERLAND

Westerland is the largest town of the island with about 9,500 inhabitants and is geographically positioned in the centre of it. It has had a long record as a spa ('Seebad'). This was opened in 1855, two years later a shareholder company for the spa was founded and very soon it acquired the image of an elegant spa. At the turn of the century visitor demand was so high that a *Kurhaus* was installed. In 1902, eventually, a family public bath was introduced, which was quite uncommon for those days, since up to then men and women were strictly advised to bathe separately. Nowadays in Westerland there is a beach 7 km long, divided into several areas, among which there are also many nudist beaches. Furthermore, many sports facilities are there so that nearly all kinds of sports can be practised.

In 1964 a huge indoor pool was opened in order to be able to offer all the spa services of a seaside resort regardless of the weather. This pool has been modernized and extended ever since. At present this site called 'Erlebniswelt Sylter Welle' has a water surface of 450 square metres with a water temperature of 28°C. Twice per hour the surf is simulated for ten minutes. Furthermore, there are numerous other opportunities for all kinds of water sports and medical treatments, such as diving courses, sauna, water gymnastics and massages. Additionally, in the pool there is also a parent-and-child area, offering all kinds of activities for children. In 1997 more than 200,000 people visited the 'Sylter Welle', one quarter of which were younger people. Particularly for the care of children the so-called 'House for the Young Visitor' was established, which is open all year. Children can take part in all kinds of activity there.

In Westerland one can also find a casino, cinemas, museums and art galleries. There are daily concerts at the beach promenade from May to October, and there are other concerts and gala nights.[5] About 30 bars are open late at night or until early morning.

Being officially acknowledged as a seaside spa, Westerland is equipped with a health resort centre, the 'Kurmittelhaus'. The range of medical treatment is wide, including baths, massages, inhalations, rest areas, hydrotherapy, and respiratory gymnastics. Medical treatment is offered both in sanatoriums and in the open. One of the specialities is sea water cures offered in the 'Biomaris' health resort at the beach promenade.

Visitors to Westerland have to pay a compulsory visitors' tax, the payment of which is shown by a visitor's pass, the 'Kurkarte'. Currently this tax amounts to DM 5.50 from May 1 to October 31, while it is half that price for the rest of the year. Daily visitors pay DM 6 for a day ticket. For long-term visitors there is a yearly visitor's pass available for DM 154. Proceeds from visitors' taxes are used to fund facilities and activities particularly for visitors, and which exceed the regular budget of a small town like Westerland, for instance, concerts by the spa orchestra, the care of spa facilities and beaches, child care, etc.

The municipal spa office runs a special department for the organization and performance of congresses, conferences and seminars. In 1997 there were 27 events of that kind with a total of *c.* 4,200 participants and 48,000 overnight stays.[6]

At present there are about 30 hotels of all categories in Westerland with a total of 3,707 beds. Furthermore, there are numerous seasonal apartments and flats as well as holiday cottages and villas with 15,377 beds, and 112 beds in guest houses. There are 332 beds in recreation houses, and 682 beds in sanatoria and hospitals. The camping capacity is 1,000 beds. In 1997 Westerland had nearly 470,000 day visitors and 2.7 million overnight stays. The average length of stay in Westerland was 9.8 days in that year.[7]

Let us look closer at the statistic figures for Westerland mentioned above. This will be based on tourism statistics for Westerland and Sylt[8] as well as a visitor survey for Westerland undertaken in 1996.[9] The number of visitors to Westerland increased by 7.7 per cent from 1996 to 1997. This made up for a decrease of 6.1 per cent from 1995 to 1996. The number of overnight visitors, too, increased slightly by 2.7 per cent from 1996 to 1997, while the number of overnight stays decreased by 2.8 per cent in the same period.

If these figures are broken down into months, there is a clear peak in the months from May to October with another clear emphasis on July and August. However, considering the average length of stay of all overnight visitors in single months, there is quite a difference. It is the month of January which is highest with an average length of stay of 20.0 days per visitor while this ratio is fairly balanced throughout the other months of the year between 12.6 and 8.1 days, but for December. One of the reasons for this may be the emphasis on cures in January, which require a longer stay against the other types of accommodation.

As to the ratio of visitors and figures of overnight stay, according to categories of accommodation there is a clear emphasis on seasonal apartments and flats, as well as rooms let by private landlords or landladies. This category has a share of 77.5 per cent of the total number of beds and a share of 61.5 per cent of visitors of the total within this category. These two categories account for 68.6 per cent of the total overnight stays. Regarding hotels and guest houses their shares amount to 14.7 per cent of total number of beds, 27.2 per cent of total visitors, and 18.1 per cent of total overnight stays, respectively.

These figures clearly reflect the structure of tourism both of Sylt as a whole and Westerland in particular. Seasonal apartments and flats are remarkably over-represented and these are owned by people using them as a seasonal residence themselves. This pattern becomes even clearer if one looks at the ratio of overnight visitors as a percentage of inhabitants of German federal states, thus at the market penetration. The neighbouring states of Hamburg (1.21), Schleswig-Holstein (0.95), and Lower Saxony (0.66) are far ahead. This underlines the fact that Sylt is closer as a holiday destination for tourists who do not only stay here for two to three weeks in the summer vacation period but also want to use their residences frequently for weekend trips and other kinds of stays. Furthermore, this pattern also reflects the market position of Sylt for high society, since market entrance barriers both for suppliers and customers are established by its image as a high society resort.

In 1997, only 2,779 visitors (and this is 32 less than the previous year) came from abroad. Their overnight figure was 21,340 (1996: 22,253), which makes an average length of stay of 7.7 days (1996: 7.9 days). The ratio of foreign to total visitors was just 1 per cent. Unlike the high society resorts in countries like France and Switzerland with their respective resorts of St Tropez or St Moritz, for instance, Westerland quite obviously fails to profit from its image outside Germany.

A breakdown of overnight visitors regarding the federal state of their origin shows Northrhine Westphalia ranging first with c. 80,000 visitors, which take a share of 28.9 per cent of the total. Bearing in mind that this is by far the largest state in Germany this is not surprising. Lower Saxony shows a share of 18.4 per cent, and this makes a number of little more than 50,000 visitors. Schleswig-Holstein and Hamburg show a share of 9.3 per cent (25,856 visitors) and 7.4 per cent (20,642). There is also a remarkable share of 8.5 per cent (23,766) coming from Hessen.

In terms of age there is a clear focus on visitors older than 40 who make up nearly 57 per cent of the total number. The age cohort between 21 and 30 shows only 8 per cent and this is clearly under-represented. The share of 71 to 80 year-old visitors is nearly as high, a little more than 7 per cent. Again, these figures underpin both the structure of visitors and the image of Sylt. Younger people normally do not have an income allowing them to take holidays in Sylt without getting into financial problems.

Staff of the Westerland Tourist Office took a visitor survey in December 1996. They asked a sample of 302 people on Sylt, either just visiting it or taking a holiday there. The findings of the survey have to be modified, however, bearing in mind that it was undertaken in December, which is the month with the least frequency of visitors. Therefore the data should not be considered to be representative, rather, they should be regarded as a snapshot. Even more so because the study was performed during the time the 'Surf Cup' was held on Sylt. Having made this reservation, the findings show that recovery and relaxation are the reasons for coming. Some 38.7 per cent visited Westerland because of the beach. Nature was the reason for coming for 35.8 per cent and health for 34.1 per cent. Other reasons mentioned were sports (17.2 per cent), medical treatment (8.8 per cent), and cultural events (4.6 per cent). People were allowed to mention more than one item in this survey.

When asked if they actually use the facilities of the *Kurhaus*, around 50 per cent of visitors said they do not use them at all. Of the other half a little more than one third had medical treatment. The bulk of visitors actually using the facilities of the *Kurhaus* was highly satisfied both with the services offered and the staff.

When asked to assess the indoor pool 'Sylter Welle', 65.5 per cent replied they had never been there; 19.2 per cent had been to the pool several times, 13.25 per cent once. In terms of age structure it was the 36–45 cohort that was strongly represented in going to the pool while the cohort up to 25 was the group having been there several times. Some 57.1 per cent of those who had been to the pool thought the entrance fee was too high, while 41.9 per cent thought it to be appropriate, and 1 per cent said it was too low. A closer look reveals that about 60 per cent of those who had been to the pool several times thought the entrance fee to be too high.[10] Quite obviously the high entrance fee is one of the prime reasons for people not using the pool.

CONCLUSIONS FOR MARKETING

According to the findings of the continuous Travellers Study[11] in Germany the demands of consumers in 1997 have changed compared to previous years. These changes are also reflected in the figures of the visitors' structure and visitors' behaviour in Westerland. The number of holidays taken has decreased by 3.3 million journeys, with most of the reduction occurring for domestic holiday journeys. This is due to the ever growing unemployment rate, increasing uncertainty in financial matters, and net incomes of households going down because of low collective bargaining contract rates as well as rising rates and taxes. This coincided with increasing competitive pressure by cut-price offers for holidays abroad. Taken all this for granted, the conditions of competition in Germany have become stronger. This development particularly applied to Westerland because of its visitor structure. Consumer behaviour in terms of tourism in Germany is characterized by dispensing with second and third holidays, shortening the stay as well as spending less money on holidays according to tendency.

Although Bavaria and Schleswig-Holstein were able to maintain their leading position in recent years according to the Travellers Study, it was the former which faced a strong loss of market share. Obviously the state of Mecklenburg-Vorpommern with its Baltic Sea coast managed to improve its position at the cost of Schleswig-Holstein.

When looking for information sources on holiday destinations Germans tend to rely on the recommendation of friends and relatives, experience of day trips, press reports, information provided by general practitioners, leaflets, TV and radio, according to the Tourism Study. Furthermore, it is travel guides and books that are important in spreading information.

Visitors to Sylt may be divided in categories of holiday makers looking for nature, recovery and relaxation, health or activity, following data provided by the Westerland Tourism Office. And this is also reflected in the preoccupations of the visitors to Westerland, which are above all:

- walking;
- relaxing;
- shopping;
- excursions;
- reading;
- wandering;
- sun-bathing; and
- cycling.

With regard to this development in the tourism market it seems crucial for Westerland to work out marketing objectives and marketing strategies which are able to solve the problems mentioned.

NOTES

1. Kurbetrieb Westerland (1998) *Tourismus-Statistik 1997 – Westerland und Insel Sylt*. Westerland, p. 20.
2. Statistisches Bundesamt (1996) *Tourismus in Zahlen 1995*. Wiesbaden, p. 262.
3. Deutscher Bäderverband e. V. (1979) *Deutscher Bäderkalender*. Bonn, p. 180.
4. For further information see Maak, Niklas (1998) 'Lebenslügen: Sylt', *Süddeutsche Zeitung* 12 August.
5. Kurbetrieb Westerland (1998) *Tourismus-Statistik 1997 – Westerland und Insel Sylt*. Westerland, pp. 18–21.
6. Kurbetrieb Westerland (1998) *Tourismus-Statistik 1997 – Westerland und Insel Sylt*. Westerland, p. 19.
7. Kurbetrieb Westerland (1998) *Tourismus-Statistik 1997 – Westerland und Insel Sylt*. Westerland, p. 2, p. 9.
8. Kurbetrieb Westerland (1998) *Tourismus-Statistik 1997 – Westerland und Insel Sylt*. Westerland.
9. D'Aulnis de Bourouill, A., Mühlbronner, B. and Friedrich, U. (1996/97) *Marktstudie: Gästebefragung in Westerland/Sylt, FH Heilbronn, Hausarbeit zur Vorlesung Tourismusbetriebswirtschaftslehre*. WS 1996/97.
10. D'Aulnis de Bourouill, A., Mühlbronner, B. and Friedrich, U. (1996/97) *Marktstudie: Gästebefragung in Westerland/Sylt, FH Heilbronn, Hausarbeit zur Vorlesung Tourismusbetriebswirtschaftslehre*. WS 1996/97, p. 17.
11. *Reiseanalyse der Forschungsgemeinschaft Urlaub und Reisen e. V.* (1997) Hamburg.

CHAPTER 11

Scheveningen

A successful case of revitalization

Jan Bergsma and Theo de Haan

Aim
To develop an understanding of the problems faced by a tourist resort at a mature stage of its life-cycle and suggest and evaluate possible strategies for regeneration.

Keywords
destination life-cycle; seaside resort development; regeneration strategy; public–private partnership; comprehensive planning; product–market combinations

Summary
The resort of Scheveningen has a long tradition as the most famous seaside resort in The Netherlands. It started early in the nineteenth century as a luxurious bathing place with the well-known 'Kurhaus', attracting aristocrats from all over Europe and deserving its name of 'Pearl of the North Sea'. During the years of growth in visitor numbers Scheveningen also became popular as a destination for lower social classes. Hence other types of facilities emerged and the resort became more oriented towards the domestic Dutch market.

After a slight decrease during the Second World War Scheveningen attracted more and more tourists until 1960 when 1.7 million people visited the resort. However, during the 1960s Scheveningen became a resort in decline. Competition from the Mediterranean resorts was strongly felt in all segments of the market, but also the increase of private car ownership made other resorts along the Dutch coast accessible and attractive and, for some, a good alternative to 'old-fashioned' Scheveningen.

At the end of the 1960s a programme for revitalization was developed, primarily as a result of public sector initiative. In the strategic plan for Scheveningen a comprehensive development approach was taken, which focused not only on the creation of (all-weather) tourist facilities but also on the development of office buildings, commercial centres and housing. Apart from that, new market segments were being targeted. Implementation of the plan was very much guaranteed by creating a consortium in which the public and private sectors co-operated. The local government provided the infrastructure, whereas private banks took care of the necessary investments of DFL 800 million in new entertainment facilities, the restoration of the former 'Kurhaus', office buildings and housing.

After the realization of the plans the number of visitors to Scheveningen increased rapidly during the 1970s and particularly during the 1980s and 1990s to reach the number of 9.1 million in 1996. It is interesting to see that nowadays seasonality is much less pronounced and that the proportion of day visitors is much higher than three decades ago.

In conclusion, one can say that Scheveningen has passed through the traditional stages of growth, stagnation and decline of the 'life-cycle model'. However, it also clearly shows the success of a redevelopment scheme, in which the right strategic choices regarding product and market development were made, and in which a close partnership between public and private sector was pursued.

Learning outcomes

After studying, analysing and discussing this case, students should be able to:

- understand the general factors that underlie the problems faced by a tourist destination at the mature stage of its life-cycle and apply the specific situation of Scheveningen in this context;
- suggest strategies for regeneration, taking into account product as well as markets;
- understand the role and interest of different actors in the planning process;
- evaluate the success of the strategies adopted by Scheveningen.

Exercises

1. Identify the factors that are responsible for the decline in visitor numbers to Scheveningen during the 1960s. Try to find similar patterns in other seaside resorts in Europe and discuss to what extent the problems in Scheveningen are unique as the result of the specific situation of Scheveningen.
2. Suppose you, as a representative of the municipality of Scheveningen, are in charge of producing a plan for regeneration of the resort.
   (a) Which solutions would you propose to the problems in terms of product development and in terms of marketing strategies?
   (b) Which parties should be involved in the implementation of your plan and what would be the different roles and responsibilities of the different players?
3. Suppose you are one of the hotel owners in Scheveningen and you faced the problem of a decline in customers. What action would you take?
4. If you look back to what happened to Scheveningen after the early 1970s, what would you consider being the success factor in the revitalization of the resort?

INTRODUCTION

Scheveningen is a traditional seaside resort in The Netherlands, located very close to the city of The Hague along the North Sea Coast (see Figure 11.1). It was the first and always has been the most famous seaside resort in The Netherlands, not only for the Dutch but also for foreigners.

Scheveningen has a long history, starting in the early nineteenth century as a health resort attracting the 'higher social classes'. Scheveningen flourished early this

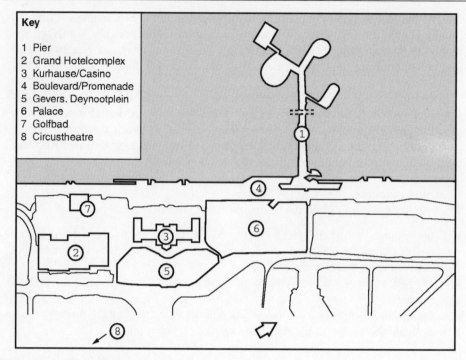

Figure 11.1: Map of Scheveningen seafront.

century but has changed considerably since then. Not only was the traditional 'elite' health tourist replaced by the middle and lower class mass tourist, it also faced – like many other North Sea resorts – a period of stagnation and decrease in visitor numbers and deterioration of its product after the Second World War. In the 1970s measures were taken to revitalize the resort, resulting in considerable growth of visitor numbers.

This chapter will give further details about the historical development of the resort in terms of product and markets as well as in terms of involved private and public sector parties. In conclusion the current situation of Scheveningen will be described and the revitalization strategies evaluated.

HISTORICAL DEVELOPMENT

The period until the Second World War

Scheveningen as a fishing village has existed since the end of the sixteenth century. It became the first Dutch seaside resort in the early nineteenth century with the creation of a luxurious public bath. In 1885 a resort organization was founded and the 'Kurhaus' ('cure house') was built on the site of the former health bath. Since then all kinds of accommodation, entertainments and other facilities have been created (like a permanent circus and the first cinema in Holland). Famous (until today) became the so-called 'Scheveningse Pier', providing a wide range of entertainment.

In the first decade of the twentieth century Scheveningen, with its Grand Hotels (like the Palace Hotel and the Oranjehotel, each with façades stretching over more than 100 metres) was seen as the 'Pearl of the North Sea' and certainly was one of the leading seaside resorts on the continent. Partly this was due to the very good (tramway) connections with the city of The Hague and the further hinterland, containing a considerable number of inhabitants. The visitors mainly were aristocrats; many came from German-speaking countries, who already were familiar with health spas.

Between 1913 and 1940 a steady growth of visitor numbers can be noted (from 75,000 to almost 1 million a year: see Figure 11.2). During the same period, however, the type of visitor changed. Because of the increasing number of 'free days', the shortening of the working day and the availability of cheaper transport possibilities, Scheveningen also became a popular destination for the lower social classes. This was reflected in the diminishing popularity of the Grand Hotels and the emergence of many cheaper forms of accommodation (e.g. campsites, pensions).

Also the proportion of international visitors changed. In 1913 approximately 50 per cent of the visitors were from abroad (mainly Germany); in 1939 this proportion was barely 20 per cent. The traditional 'elite' tourist was more and more attracted by the resorts along the French and Italian riviera, guaranteeing much better climatic conditions.

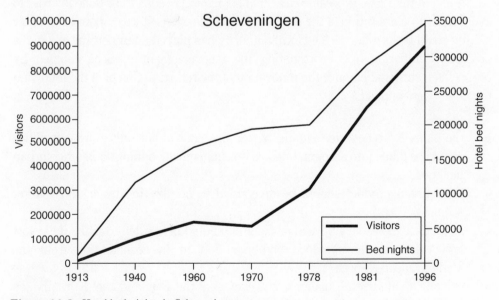

Figure 11.2: Hotel bed nights in Scheveningen.

The 1950s and the 1960s

After the Second World War, in which a lot of damage was done to the tourist facilities, an intensive restoration programme resulted in the 1950s in further growth in visitor numbers. In the 1960s, however, Scheveningen became more and more a resort in decline, which could no longer satisfy the needs of the market. Scheveningen not only completely lost the traditional elite tourist, it now also felt strong competition from the French, Italian and Spanish seaside resorts in the mass market segments. As well as that, the introduction of the private car in many households resulted in the emergence and popularity of many new resorts in The Netherlands and Belgium; traditional resorts like Scheveningen with their stronger orientation on facilities for overnight stays, became less popular. In the summer months the occupancy rates of the accommodations were often too low for a profitable operation. In winter the resort looked completely deserted. The logical result was the deterioration of hotels and other facilities, like the entertainment centre on the Pier, all leading to a decline in visitors numbers. In 1960 Scheveningen still received 1.7 million visitors a year, in 1970 this had dropped to 1.5 million (see Figure 11.2). In particular the hotels lost many clients. Overall spending decreased considerably.

The 1970s: start of the revitalization

At the end of the 1960s it became clear that something needed to be done in order to avoid further deterioration of the resort. Public discussions started about how a new vitality could be introduced. The local authority has played an important role in the process of initiating and coordinating the redevelopment of Scheveningen by producing a strategic plan for the renovation of the resort. In this plan the following principles were applied:

- the plans for renovation should be comprehensive: not only tourist facilities should be taken into account, but also housing, office buildings and other 'urban facilities';
- the tourism product should be diversified to be able to attract new market segments;
- as much as possible, all-weather facilities should be created to make the resort less vulnerable to climatic conditions and to the competition from the Mediterranean resorts;
- existing monumental facilities, however, like the Pier and the 'Kurhaus' (as image-builders) should be maintained and restored.

The main idea behind the redevelopment was that the 'new Scheveningen should be an urban centre for recreation at the seafront, functioning all year round and for everybody'. This meant it should be:

- a seaside resort attractive for the tourist but also with a recreational function for the local population;
- a seaside resort functioning all seasons;
- a seaside resort attracting a wide range of markets;
- a centre representing high recreational value, but also providing high quality conditions for living and working.

Implementation

The local authority encouraged institutional investors and construction firms to form a financial consortium. A number of insurance companies and banks (among others National Nederlanden, Friesch-Groningse Hypotheekbank) and a real estate development company (Brederode) participated. The land which was not already owned by the municipality was acquired by the consortium. This created a development area of 12 hectares and a beachfront of 500 metres.

The financial consortium worked in the form of a public–private partnership closely together with the local government in the realization of the above mentioned projects. Basically, the local government was expected to provide the infrastructure (e.g. roads, electricity), after which the private sector would invest (approximately DFL 800 million) in the extensive (re)building programme, covering approximately 2.5 million square feet.

The actual redevelopment started in 1974 with rebuilding the seafront area (see Figure 11.1):

- the former Grand Hotel area became a quiet living area with some shops and offices;
- the 'Kurhaus' has been completely rebuilt in the same architectural style (costs DFL 86 million). It became a 5-star hotel with over 250 rooms, a casino, first class conference rooms, bars, restaurants and the 'Kurhall', open to the public and at the same time functioning as hotel lounge.
- a new entertainment centre was created in front of the 'Kurhaus' (*Gevers Deynoot-plein*). On the top of this centre 130 terrace apartments were built. Close to it specific facilities for tourists and the regional population have been realized, like an indoor surfpool ('Golfslagbad') with saunas and indoor sports facilities.
- at the location of the former Palace Hotel a shopping and entertainment centre 'The Palace promenade' was created.

It was planned to use the inland Scheveningen area to create office buildings, more housing, parking places and – last but not least – cinemas and a huge theatre on the site of the permanent circus ('Circustheater').

In the early 1980s there was stagnation in the redevelopment activities, due to some problems within the consortium and the city council. In 1987 the insurance company Nationale Nederlanden became the sole owner of the consortium, who agreed with the municipality in 1990 upon the realization of the final phase of the project, particularly aiming at the development of the inland area.

Operation

The city council and the financial consortium together have set up an organization to promote and manage the new facilities: the Scheveningen Resort Board (Stichting Scheveningen Bad.). In this board not only the local government and the private investors are represented, but also employers in Scheveningen, like shop and hotel owners, the local population, Chamber of Commerce and the local tourist board.

CURRENT SITUATION

After starting the redevelopment programme the numbers of visitors rapidly increased. In 1970 approximately 1.5 million visitors came; after realization of the first phase of the redevelopment scheme the total number of visitors already was over 3 million (1978). In the year of the opening of the renovated 'Kurhaus', the 'Golfslagbad' and the entertainment square in 1981 the total number of visitors was 6.5 million. However, the stagnation in the development – particularly of the inland area – in the early 1980s slowed down the growth rate: in 1996 Scheveningen received 9.1 million visitors. The total tourist expenditure in Scheveningen by then was approximately 250 million DFL.

The entire regeneration is almost finished now. The latest developments have been the removal of the casino from the 'Kurhaus' into a new building some 100 yards further inland (1996), the creation of a modern cinema complex (Movie-world) and the opening of a new health centre (*kuurcentrum Vitalizee*). Also the ownership and exploitation structure have slightly been changed. For instance the Scheveningen Pier has been taken over by van der Valk, the biggest motel chain in The Netherlands.

If we compare the characteristics of the visitors of today with those almost three decades ago we also see some interesting developments. For example:

- In the early 1970s, before the redevelopment activities had started roughly 40 per cent of the visitors came to Scheveningen during the high season (July– August). Nowadays the seasonality pattern is less pronounced; there is a much more even spread over the year. The season now runs from April until the end of October (receiving some 80 per cent of all visitors). But also in the winter months a considerable number of people visit the facilities of Scheveningen, like the *Circustheater* which turned out to be one of the most successful and modern theatres in The Netherlands.

- There has been a considerable growth in the proportion of day visitors, mainly coming from the city of The Hague or the surrounding Randstad (including Amsterdam, Rotterdam, Utrecht, in total having approximately 5 million inhabitants). However, the absolute number of holidaymakers (originating mainly from the other parts of Holland and from abroad) and the number of overnight stays, is also increasing, but at a lower rate (see Figure 11.3).

EVALUATION

Although there were some difficulties in the early 1980s, Scheveningen can be considered a successful case of revitalizing a traditional seaside resort. The renovated and newly created facilities made Scheveningen again one of the most popular seaside resorts along the North Sea coast, receiving over 9 million visitors in 1996, which is six times as many as in 1970, the year before the renovation started.

Eventually three main factors appeared to be responsible for the success:

1. The strategy of aiming more at day visitors, realizing that in the overnight segment the competition of Mediterranean resorts was getting stronger and stronger. In terms of product development this underlined the significance of the creation of all-weather facilities to extend the season. Obviously the location of Scheveningen, close to a major conurbation, contributed to the success of this strategy.
2. The principle of guaranteeing a close partnership between the local authority and the private sector in the planning, construction and operational phase of the revitalization project.
3. The comprehensive approach in which the development of tourist facilities went hand in hand with the development of other types of (lucrative!) development like housing and office building.

CHAPTER 12

Santa Claus

The most famous person in the world

Nina Vesterinen

Aim
The main aim for the student is to understand how a chosen theme can be used to create and/or develop a tourist destination. Finnish Lapland and especially Santa Claus Village and SantaPark are introduced.

Keywords
Santa Claus; Lapland; Finland; networking; theme resort; impacts; management

Summary
This case study introduces Finland, Lapland and the Arctic Circle area as a tourist destination. The five different seasons give five different reasons to visit the area. Tourism income in Lapland accounted for up to FIM 5 billion in 1997 and there were 1.45 million registered overnights of which 29 per cent of visitors were foreign.

The main attractions of the Arctic Circle tourist destination are the Santa Claus Village, the geographical Arctic Circle itself, Reindeer Park and SantaPark the Christmas theme park. The area attracts over half a million visitors every year. The various attractions, shops, restaurants and activities of Santa Claus Village are owned mainly by private companies who have established a co-operative society to maintain more professional networking, but the municipality owns some shares as well.

SantaPark theme park is a combination of advanced technology, Lapland and Christmas spirit. It is owned by nine Finnish companies and they expect to receive 150,000 visitors every year. Between these two attractions the Reindeer Park introduces Lappish culture and reindeer pasturing. The Arctic Circle tourist destination is experiencing a time of change and it will be interesting to see how the old and the new attractions begin to work together and how the increasing numbers of visitors are to be managed.

Learning outcomes
After examining this case study, the students will be able to do the following:

- identify the various aspects of theme resort management;
- understand the differences between various types of ownership;

- understand the various economic, socio-cultural and environmental impacts of a resort;
- understand the different expectations of domestic and international visitors.

Discussion topics
- Is it possible for a resort to develop as a successful theme attraction under multi-ownership?
- Identify and critically evaluate the economic, environmental and socio-cultural impacts of tourism at the destination.
- What could be done to lengthen the duration of visits in the area?
- Is it possible to develop a successful summer product around the Christmas theme? If yes, try to develop one.
- What are the advantages and limitations of this resort?

FINLAND: A NATURAL WONDERLAND

Finland is the seventh largest country in Europe in area, 338,000 sq. kilometres, but it is also one of the most sparsely populated countries with a little over 5 million inhabitants. The four different seasons, with light and warm summers and cold and dark winters, as well as the beautiful landscape with almost 200,000 lakes and widespread forest covering 69 per cent of the land, make Finland an interesting tourist destination.

Lapland

The Northern part of Finland, called Lapland, is said to be the last wilderness in Europe. Besides tourism, reindeer breeding is a major means of subsistence for the inhabitants of Lapland. About 6,000 indigenous Lapps still live in Lapland, so their distinctive cultural traditions can be seen and experienced. The average duration of winter is around 200 days which offers good possibilities for winter sport holidays, though during mid-winter the temperature can go down to $-30\text{--}40°C$. In summer the midnight sun (meaning the time the sun does not set at all) lasts for more than two months.

The peak of tourism-related construction in Lapland took place between 1989 and 1991. It has led to the rise of total tourism income, counted today to be FIM 5 billion. In 1998 there were 1.56 million registered overnights in accommodation facilities of which 28 per cent were foreign. Including the unregistered sector (holiday homes) the total number of overnights rises to approximately 5 million. As much as 85 per cent of the total tourism-related demand is domestic overnights. Private and company investments in holiday accommodation have continued to be more than twice the amount of the commercial related investments.

Seasons

In Lapland the year has been divided into five different seasons, which differ from each other by climate and natural conditions, tourist products and a tourist structure. The spring season (February–May) is the most important in Lapland. Tourists, over half a million of which (18 per cent) are foreign, are especially attracted by skiing possibilities, programmed services and Lapland's genuineness. In spring, Lapland's major competitors are the Alps and Canada.

The summer has been problematic throughout the 1990s. Lapland is often a passing through place on the way to the North Cape and visitors stay only for one or two nights. More activities and programmed services should therefore be developed to lengthen stays.

In autumn (September), during the *ruska* when the forests change to autumn colours, Lapland is visited mainly by Finns themselves and by very few foreign tourists. But autumn is very important as an extension to the summer season. Visitors have been quite critical then and more often dissatisfied with such factors as the management of environmental issues, genuineness and information services than during the other seasons.

The most popular reasons for a trip to Lapland during the first snow season (Oct–Nov) are sporting activities and snow conditions. Tourists, mainly young men, often belong to different kinds of sporting groups.

In mid-winter (Dec–Jan) the domestic demand is at a level of 200,000 overnights. Foreign demand has increased its share to 41 per cent of the total number of tourists. About two-thirds of the tourists travel with children and the trip to Lapland is their first trip abroad. Foreign tourists rarely stay overnight during the Christmas season.

ARCTIC CIRCLE TOURIST RESORT

The main attractions of the Arctic Circle tourist resort are the Santa Claus Village, the geographical Arctic Circle itself, Reindeer Park and the new SantaPark Christmas theme park. The area is situated 8 kilometres north of the capital of Finnish Lapland, Rovaniemi. Visitors are welcomed all year around. Santa Claus Village attracts around half of a million visitors every year and it has been estimated that the new SantaPark will increase the figure.

Location

The Arctic Circle tourist resort has an ideal location. It is easily accessible by air, rail and road, for example, most travellers going to the North Cape travel through the Arctic Circle. It is only 2 kilometres to Rovaniemi international airport which receives 40,000 visitors during the Christmas season. The Arctic Circle itself attracts many visitors because of its uniqueness. The short distance between the town and the area has created good possibilities for developing versatile services. Also during the high season the long opening hours tempt the locals to go shopping in the area. The town also offers accommodation facilities for visitors who are taking longer vacations there. The lack of accommodation is one of the weaknesses of the Arctic Circle area as a tourist destination where no accommodation is offered at all.

Santa Claus Village: History

The first landmark of the Arctic Circle, the Cottage, was built in 1950 to honour the visit of Eleanor Roosevelt, the wife of the US president. It then hosted a café, a souvenir shop and a post office. Over the years the number of visitors has increased and the cottage has been extended several times. At the beginning the Arctic Circle Cottage was kept open only during the summer, but around the mid-1960s it was also open during the winter holiday weeks, and in 1970s it began to be open all year around. At the beginning of the 1980s the municipality organized an architectural competition to plan and build an active village with various programmes and shopping possibilities. Santa Claus also had his permanent office built then. More activities such as reindeer rides and a special 'Lapland baptism' were introduced.

The 1990s were a time of reforming and innovation for the Santa Claus Village. The new landmark, the Main Post Office of Santa Claus was built in 1991, which receives over 700,000 letters from all over the world each year. The village was owned by the town and rural municipality of Rovaniemi at first, but in 1993 the shopkeepers began to buy for themselves the locations they were already using.

In autumn 1996 a new building was completed, the Santa Claus Office. The owners are the rural municipality of Rovaniemi and two private companies. Some funding was also received from the Ministry of Trade and Industry as well as from the European Union.

In 1985 the shopkeepers became a merchant association; the main aim was to gain benefits in marketing. In 1997 they considered the area needed more professional networking than before. Some 22 of the 25 entrepreneurs established a co-operative society. In general a co-operative society is established to gain benefits for all the members of the society and to form a network of competence and clients. In Finland a minimum of five persons or companies can legally establish a society. It is not a co-operation of capital because the profit is divided according to the amount of services members have used, not in the proportion of invested money. The members do not have personal liability for the society either. The power of decision-making is not in correlation with the invested amount but the decision-making takes place in meetings of the society. The main aim of the Santa Claus Village co-operative society is to co-ordinate the marketing effectively.

At the end of 1997 the Arctic Circle tourist resort had achieved remarkable results.

The turnover for all 25 businesses was approximately FIM 40 million. It permanently employs 60 people a year and during the high season (June–August and Christmas) as many as 140 people are employed.

Products

The Santa Claus Office (Ltd) offers visitors from all over the world the opportunity to meet Santa Claus in person. The building itself is a typical Finnish round timber cottage. Visitors feel in the Christmas spirit with Christmas decorations, snow sculptures, candles and Christmas carols. At the Office a visitor can privately talk with Santa Claus often in his/her own mother tongue. It is also possible to have a picture taken with him, to order a letter to be sent to a chosen person, or to become a member of Santa Claus Club. One of the member benefits is the opportunity to e-mail Santa Claus. Another product, especially marketed for Japanese is a full wedding service. The Santa Claus Office employs between four and twelve people, according to the season.

The many shops in the Village offer traditional Finnish and Lappish products as well as products related to Christmas and Santa Claus. There are also opportunities for visitors to make traditional products themselves or to see how they are made by locals.

The Arctic Circle – the geographical line – is one of the main attractions of the area. There is a concrete, drawn line in the Village where visitors can cross this magic border, have a photograph taken next to the sign, or receive a diploma for crossing the Arctic Circle.

Many activities are also available such as nature walks and hikes, snowmobile rides and safaris as well as reindeer rides. There are also special events and exhibitions arranged along the common theme. Services include a fully equipped service station and restaurants. Santa Claus Village offers detailed information concerning travel in Lapland. Also fishing permits and maps are for sale there.

The environment

Environmental issues have been recognized in the Village, for example, by organizing recycling points for the use of visitors and entrepreneurs. Many entrepreneurs have personally taken the issues seriously, for example, by choosing the right materials and using recycled paper. But a proper environmental plan does not yet exist that would cover the whole resort.

In the Arctic Circle area most attractions are artificial and built for the tourists. Companies providing safaris and other nature activities, as well as the Arctic Circle recreational areas, are depleting the fragile nature areas.

Most tourists arrive in a motor vehicle. More and more parking facilities have been built over the years. Especially in winter the amount of exhaust gas is high due to the idling of the cars in extreme cold weather. A new parking place further from the exact tourist area has been planned to help the current situation.

SantaPark

It had been a dream for over 40 years to build a Santa Claus land in Finland, the home of Santa Claus. After the dream became true, it still took two years to plan and do back-up work, until in June 1997 nine Finnish companies established a company called Santaworld Finland Ltd to build SantaPark. The shareholders have capital worth of FIM 29 million and they include Finnair Ltd, Finland Post Ltd, Children's Day foundation, Lappset Group Ltd, MTV Ltd, Napapiirin Maja Ltd, Sampo Insurance Company, Tamnova Ltd and Tapsan Tapuli Ltd. The theme park will be caught up in the Christmas spirit at all times of the year. It is a combination of advanced technology, Lapland and Christmas with rides, carousels, rails, shows, adventure, exhibition, games and services such as a shop and a restaurant.

The theme park has been designed by an English company. Many ideas are originally from Finland, but the theme park has some international Christmas influences as well, because half of the visitors will be foreigners. All the other companies taking part in the building process are from Finland.

The Christmas theme park has been built deep inside the Syväsenvaara Fell, which in an emergency situation can be used as a population shelter. The entrance path takes visitors 200 metres to a plaza, that is 11 metres high and 33 metres in diameter, at the heart of the cavern and there is over 40 metres of solid rock above it. From there four corridors lead to the 17 metre wide hall surrounding it, altogether covering an area of 4,000 sq. metres.

The construction and start-up costs together total about FIM 87.5 million, of which the shelter accounts for FIM 46.5 million and SantaPark itself for FIM 41 million. The state funds the actual theme park with FIM 12 million of which FIM 1.5 million comes from the EU. The shareholders have agreed to help children with part of the profit they will make.

SantaPark can host 800 visitors at a time and during the high season it means 4,000 visitors per day. It is expected that 150,000 people, half domestic and the other half foreign, will visit SantaPark every year during the 200 days it is planned to be open. Opening days are scheduled all year round so that during Christmas, summer and other holiday seasons it is open every day, and at other times during the weekends.

Before its opening on 28 December 1998, they had recruited and trained 120 persons. During the high season 45 employees are needed and during the low season 25 at a time. The office staff consists of seven employees.

During the Christmas period Rovaniemi airport receives over 100 charter flights from different parts of the world with 200 passengers on every plane. Many tour operators and hotel chains also have taken a visit to SantaPark as part of their tour programmes.

Reindeer Park

Access to SantaPark begins at the Santa Claus Village. A shuttle service runs between the Village and SantaPark. During the winter if arranged beforehand, visitors can travel either in a sleigh drawn by dogs or reindeer or by snowmobile.

Between these two main attractions a Reindeer Park has been opened. It is owned by the rural municipality of Rovaniemi and Eräsetti Oy Ltd. It is an area covering 30 ha where reindeers will be pastured. It is possible to stop at the Reindeer Park and to enhance one's knowledge of Lapland, the Lappish way of living, nature, reindeer pasturing or just meet a reindeer in its natural surroundings. The rest of the journey can be continued on foot.

CONCLUSION

The Arctic Circle tourist resort is in a time of change. The tourism entrepreneurs are facing new challenges; new attractions need to be opened and old ones to be developed; they have to increase competitiveness, enhance the efficiency of sales, modernize the products, improve quality and find new methods of marketing. Entrepreneurs, developers and financiers of Lapland's tourist industry built up a common tourism strategy for the years 1995–99 to help meet these challenges. Also during spring 1999 a project manager was appointed to implement many ideas for developing Christmas at the resort. The aim in both cases is to increase the tourism capacity and number of visitors. One of the main questions to think about is how the duration of visits could be lengthened.

REFERENCES

Kariniemi, J. (1998) Chairman, Santa Claus Village. Interview, 27 August.

Mölläri, L. (1998). 'Napapiirin matkailualueen kehittyminen', unpublished report. Rovaniemi: University of Lapland.

Santapark News 1/1998. Helsinki: Santaworld Finland Ltd.

Tourism Statistics. (1998) Helsinki: Statistics Finland.

Travel Development Centre (1995) *Rekisteröimätön majoituskapasiteetti ja sen käyttö Lapin läänissä 1994*. SMAK A:68.

Travel Development Centre (1997) *Lapland Export Marketing Study 1995–1997*. Visitor Survey, SMAK E:69.

Viman, T. (1998) Marketing manager, SantaPark Ltd. Interview 27 August.

SUGGESTED READING

internet: www.santapark.com, www.mek.fi

Mathieson, A. and Wall, R. (1982) *Tourism: Economic, Physical and Social Impacts*. Harlow: Longman.

Rogers, H. A. and Slinn, J. A. (1993) *Tourism: Management of Facilities*. Harlow: Longman.

Swarbrooke, J. (1995) *The Development and Management of Visitor Attractions*. Oxford: Butterworth Heinemann.

CHAPTER 13

Tourism management and community participation in York

Tim Bahaire and Martin Elliott-White

Aim

To give students an understanding of how it is possible to develop community participation in a tourist historic city.

This case study aims to make the students aware of the following:

- the types of community participation that have been suggested in the tourism literature;
- the development of both community participation and stakeholder involvement in tourism management in York.

Keywords

community participation; public–private sector partnerships; stakeholders; tourist historic city

Summary

This chapter examines the changing nature of tourism management within the tourist-historic city of York. The socio-economic and environmental impacts associated with tourism in such contexts is well reviewed in the literature together with the need for a more sustainable approach to visitor management. It is argued that community involvement is a key component in the sustainable management of urban tourism. Widening participation in tourism management and policy-making requires the development of appropriate techniques. In the case of York, a number of participation initiatives have been implemented. The tourism partnership in York is particularly active and can be regarded as a model worthy of further evaluation by tourism practitioners and students.

Learning outcomes
To make students

- understand the need for community involvement in tourism planning in urban areas;
- be aware of the need to involve all stakeholders in the tourism policy process in urban areas and in particular the tourist historic city;
- identify the limitations for community participation in tourism management.

Discussion topics

- Why is community participation regarded as being necessary to the success of tourism in urban areas?
- What are the main techniques being used in York to encourage community involvement?
- Who are the main stakeholders in tourism in the tourist historic city of York? Is the community truly represented? Do all stakeholders share the same interests in tourism? Which stakeholders have the power to get things done?
- Identify the benefits of public–private sector partnerships in the tourism management of the tourist historic city of York.
- Suggest the reasons why the full range of community participation techniques are not used in the tourist historic city of York.

INTRODUCTION

A great deal has been written in the tourism literature in recent years on involving the local community in the development and management of tourism destinations. Terms such as community tourism and community participation in tourism have been developed to describe these proposals. The rationale for these suggestions has been that they would make a positive contribution to what has been described in the literature as sustainable tourism.

However, as academics and tourism managers have tried to define what is meant by sustainable tourism, they have found that the concept is ambiguous and is thus capable of many different interpretations. For example, an economically sustainable tourism product may be environmentally unsustainable. To counter these difficulties new terms such as alternative tourism and more recently 'soft' tourism have been developed to describe forms of tourism which are often thought to be in balance with the natural and human environment.

With the exception of some recent work by Brent Ritchie (1993) on Calgary, most of the examples of community tourism and community participation have been in rural or peripheral regions. Other examples have been cited in the developing world where community tourism and community participation have been seen as ways of protecting vulnerable societies. If community tourism and community participation are to have a central position in tourism management and development, then the usefulness of these concepts has to be examined in an urban context in an advanced country.

York is an historic 'gem' city situated in the north of England (see Figure 13.1). Founded in Roman times it has a rich assemblage of buildings, walls and Bars (gateways) representative of its long urban history. The main attractions in the city are the medieval walls and the Shambles, the Minster, the Jorvik Centre, the Castle

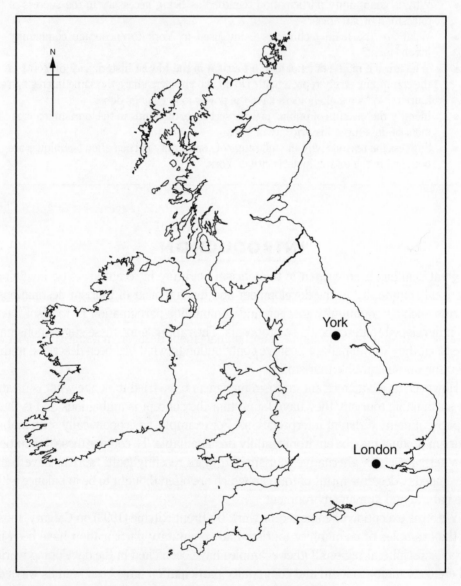

Figure 13.1: Geographical location of York in the north of England.

Museum and the National Railway Museum. This urban fabric has proven attractive to visitors and York, a city with a population of around 100,000 now has around 4 million visitors a year. Tourist historic cities such as York exemplify many of the problems associated with tourism: increased congestion, parking problems, litter, crime, increased commercial rents, the erosion of the historic fabric and a deterioration in the quality of life for residents. Consequently, managers and planners of urban tourism are increasingly turning to community tourism as a means of mitigating against such impacts and maintaining the integrity of the tourism products.

SUGGESTED MANAGEMENT TECHNIQUES FOR THE IMPLEMENTATION OF COMMUNITY TOURISM AND COMMUNITY PARTICIPATION

Community participation seems to have its roots in early 1970s' rural America. Gunn advocated the use of forums to ensure public participation: 'By means of forums with community leaders and constituencies, designers can foster open discussion of the desired goals of tourism development' (Gunn, 1972: 66). Gunn considered that community approaches would contribute to increased quality of life for both residents and visitors. Murphy in a far-reaching work (1985) argued for community tourism. However, despite making the case for community tourism elegantly and designing a model, Murphy did not include a blueprint of how to achieve it in reality.

During the 1980s and 1990s increasing attention was paid to the need to establish techniques for the achievement of community tourism, community participation in tourism planning and development and management decision-making. A number of problems have been highlighted in the literature such as the difficulty of defining community and the unequal power relationships between government and officials, on the one hand, and the community, on the other. The relationship between key stakeholders in the tourism industry and the community is also biased in favour of the industry.

Despite these difficulties a variety of techniques have been mentioned in the tourism literature, which are thought to contribute to the achievement of community tourism and community participation. It is beyond the scope of this chapter to examine the techniques and their application in detail, however, there seems to be a degree of consensus over the techniques which are listed below:

- establish a permanent tourism committee or forum, with the widest possible community (stakeholders) representation which acts in an advisory and consultative capacity to management;

143

- local, regional or national government to give consultative advice and continuous financial support on community issues/initiatives;
- the community to be balloted on key issues in tourism strategy with opportunities to vote for alternatives;
- use of small group processes and/or focus groups to facilitate democratic process;
- the use of regular attitudinal surveys of the community to identify issues and solutions;
- the use of outside speakers and experts to impartially inform the community of the implications of proposals of tourism development and management;
- the provision of educational materials and documentaries, design workshops and visual presentations to inform and educate;
- hold public meetings on key planning issues, introduce measures to improve the quality of work in the tourism industry – training initiatives to raise the career profile of tourism employment;
- organize events, residents weekends, festivals to ensure the widest possible local community participation.

Methodologies such as these vary in their appropriateness according to destination type. The case study of York is indicative of the opportunities and constraints on such initiatives in tourist historic cities.

BACKGROUND TO TOURISM MANAGEMENT IN YORK

In the 1960s the UK government placed increasing emphasis on the conservation of historic townscapes such as that in York. Conservation policies in York became a model for the conservation of other English historic towns, but did not once mention the words tourist or tourism! York at that time had a diverse manufacturing industrial base consisting of engineering, the manufacture of railway rolling stock, and chocolates. The municipal government at this time was not concerned with tourism, but it saw as peripheral to its main preoccupations with modernization and attracting the inward investment of new manufacturing industry.

In the early 1970s the largely Georgian character of the central business district of York only just avoided the sort of redevelopment that was to transform (not always for the better) so many other UK cities. The hands-off nature of York city management towards tourism continued for most of the 1970s. Tourism was seen as contributing to low pay in York and tourists were perceived as a nuisance. During this period it was not unusual in the tourist season, to see York citizens wearing T shirts with the logo 'I'm not a tourist'. For these citizens, in other words, and for many others in the York community, tourism and tourists were seen as making negative contributions to city life.

CONDITIONS LEADING TO CHANGE IN TOURISM MANAGEMENT IN YORK

In the late 1970s and through the 1980s York, as in so many UK cities, saw an acceleration in the loss of jobs in manufacturing employment which accumulatively resulted in fundamental changes in the city's economic base. It began to dawn on city management that the city was becoming largely dependent on the service sector for its income and employment. A new university founded in the 1960s developed a thriving conference trade which helped the economic life of the city. The university's academic community contributed greatly to the initiation and maintenance of the cultural life of the city.

The late 1970s and 1980s also saw the growth of tourism in the world generally for reasons which do not have to be recited here. In particular during this period there was an upsurge of interest in cultural and heritage tourism. In the 1990s as the interest in cultural and heritage tourism has perhaps passed its peak York has benefited from the growth of interest in urban tourism. The result of the changes in the economic life of York has led to a reappraisal of the municipal council's role in tourism management

THE DEVELOPMENT OF TOURISM MANAGEMENT IN YORK

In recent years York city council has worked with predominantly local organizations which seek to enhance the urban environment in the city, for the benefit of residents and visitors. For example, the city council issued a small grant to the association of Voluntary Guides and is supportive of street entertainers and buskers. The city council worked with English Heritage and North Yorkshire County council to refurbish historic buildings through the York Town Scheme. The majority of the city centre is covered by Conservation Area designation. The focus of the city council on visitor management and conservation of the urban environment and a focus on resident and community needs as defined by the council themselves brought them into conflict with the commercial interests of the tourism sector. The private sector established the York Visitor and Conference Bureau (YCVB) now the York Tourism Bureau (YTB) in 1987 to promote the city as a tourist attraction. This consultative body now has a membership of some 200, representative of a broad range of tourist interests in the city. The YTB is somewhat unique for the UK because it was initiated and funded by the private sector.

In the early 1990s the city council commissioned a study by Touche Ross (1994), which, while it identified the strength of York's position in the market, identified a number of weaknesses (lack of reinvestment, poor market intelligence, and failure to exploit synergy between attractions) and threats (absence of monitoring methods, environmental damage/capacity restraints, shopping tourism and the fading appeal of the Jorvik). The Touche Ross study (1994) reinforced the approach the city council had been taking (visitor management) but advocated a stronger liaison with the private sector. Following the Touche Ross report the council, the private sector and key players in the industry established the York Tourism Forum in early 1995. Both the council and the private sector indicated an interest in the community of York. However, while the city council wished to see the views of local residents built into the process, the private sector were keen to emphasize the contribution tourism made to the lives of the local community, as a source of income, in particular. Moreover, the private sector wished to redress what they saw as negative attitudes of residents towards tourism.

The Tourism Forum can be defined as a partnership of the city council, the regional tourist board, York Tourism Bureau, the Chamber of Commerce, the local Training and Enterprise Council, the tourism industry, trade unions and the York Archaeological Trust. Community groups and residents are represented through the council rather than through direct participation.

The Forum have identified a tourism strategy for York (1995) (*First Stop York: Strategy and Action Plan*) with six key goals:

- economic and employment benefits to be maximized;
- the city to be recognized as a high quality tourist destination that is continually being enhanced, both in terms of product and customer service;
- a wide range of quality jobs to be available – with training and career opportunities;
- the potentially negative environmental and social impacts of the tourism industry to be managed so that both the quality of life for residents and the enjoyment of York by visitors will be enhanced;
- local citizens to appreciate the benefits of tourism in York and therefore give it their support;
- those engaged in the industry in York to possess the means to understand and respond to national and international trends in their business.

The elements of the strategy inevitably reflect the interests of different partners but the local community figures quite prominently. However, the input of the local community into the implementation of the strategy is indirect; residents are represented by the city council. The views of local residents on issues in their neighbourhoods are facilitated by neighbourhood forums which are meetings of local residents together with representatives of the city council. Conservationists are represented by the York Archaeological Trust. Employees are represented by the trade unions and non-tourism businesses by the Chamber of Commerce.

Power within the partnership remains unequal: the tourism industry and the local authority remain the main players, though this is hardly surprising as YTB and the city council are the main sources of finance. The city council remains the dominant player within the Forum, though the chair does rotate. The dominance of the council is probably inevitable, owning as it does the City Walls and Bars and a significant proportion of the heritage attractions. The Forum meets once a year and is underpinned by sub-committees/project groups representing the key objectives, including visitor management, market intelligence, product development, bookability, training, events, retailing and residents' support.

Undoubtedly as regards the public in York, the Forum sees itself as largely conducting a public relations exercise on behalf of the tourism industry. However, its attitude is not just a cynical response to perceived negative attitudes to tourism in York. From the semi-structured interviews with members of the Forum it seems that its members are anxious to respond positively to public concerns and not just placate them. One interesting initiative has been the Residents' Weekends where residents receive free admission to a range of York's attractions; Stratford upon Avon runs a similar scheme. This was designed as a 'thank-you' from the industry and a means of informing residents on the doorstep. As part of this development the Yorkshire Tourist Board conducted attitudinal surveys of York residents at each of the attractions. The results seemed to indicate a softening of some of the negative perceptions of tourism held by the citizens of York. So the public relations aspects of the Tourism Forum seems to be working.

SUGGESTED READING

Ashworth, G. J. and Tunbridge, J. E. (1990) *The Tourist Historic City*. London: Belhaven.

Bahaire, T. and Elliott-White, M. (forthcoming) 'Community participation in tourism planning and development in the historic city of York, England', *Current Issues in Tourism* **2** (2–3).

Brent Ritchie, J. R. (1993) 'Crafting a destination vision: putting the concept of resident-responsive tourism into practice', *Tourism Management* **15**(5), 379–89.

First Stop York (various) *Newsletter*. York: Tourism Forum.

Getz, D. and Jamal, T. B. (1994) 'The environment-community symbiosis: a case for collaborative tourism planning', *Journal of Sustainable Tourism* **2**(3), 152–73.

Gunn, C. (1972/1988) *Vacationscape*. New York: Van Nostrand Reinhold.

Gunn, C. (1994) *Tourism Planning*. 3rd edn. London: Taylor & Francis.

Harrison, L. C. and Husbands, W. (1996) *Practising Responsible Tourism*. Chichester: John Wiley.

Meethan. K. (1995) 'York: tourism and the economy', *The Regional Review* **5**(2), 10.

Murphy, P. E. (1985) *Tourism: A Community Approach*. London: Routledge.

Taylor, G. (1995) 'The community approach: does it really work?', *Tourism Management* **16**(7), 487–9.

Touche Ross (1994) *York Tourism Strategy*. London: Touche Ross.

PART 2

LANGUAGE EXERCISES

Introduction

As already indicated in the general introduction, a second main aim of this book focuses on improving foreign language skills. Hence, half of the case-study texts have been complemented by language exercises, in order to meet the following objectives:

1. to help the students widen their lexical knowledge, by encouraging their assimilation and reproduction of specialized and idiomatic vocabulary and expression;
2. to guide the students in practising and developing particular communication skills;
3. to provide them with the opportunity to revise some of the grammar and sentence structure points which commonly cause problems.

A further advantage is that the added attention the students will give to the text while doing the language exercises will in turn ensure a fuller and more long-lasting understanding of the text's subject-matter. Some of the exercises involve role playing and communication which may be used either to practise the language or to deepen the understanding of the issues, or both.

Concerning the methodology, the following points should be clearly taken into account.

1. As this publication is aimed at several learning publics (teacher-led classroom groups, guided self-study, distance learning, etc.), some of the exercises will inevitably appear more or less appropriate according to the user-category concerned.
2. A conscious effort has been made to standardize presentation. However, some variations will be noted, mainly due to the differences in the content and objectives of the case studies themselves.
3. Every effort should be made to do these exercises in accordance with the

151

instructions given in order to achieve maximum effectiveness. However, in a teacher-led context, teachers will feel free to introduce their own personal touch.

4. Even in the exercises dealing basically with grammar/structure points or with communication skills, the technical language aspects are deliberately very much in evidence. Where the exercises require the students to compose their own responses, they are advised to take the same approach, and include as many 'technical' terms and words as possible.

5. Bearing in mind that a teacher will not always be available to provide help with further explanations or with checking answers, the student will find a 'key' to certain exercises. As regards the grammar/structure points practised, the self-help references given, in general, apply to *Practical English Usage*, Michael Swan (1995) new edition, Oxford: Oxford University Press.

6. When completing the exercises, the students are encouraged to constantly refer back to the case study text, in order to obtain maximum assimilation of the technical vocabulary. However, this should not be done for the final 'evaluation' exercise, which is aimed at enabling the students to test just how much of the specialist vocabulary and phrases they have effectively acquired.

A final note concerns the language of the texts. To underline the cross-European dimension of this project, case studies in three languages (English, German and French) are included in this volume – and other languages will be available in volume II.

EXERCISE 1

Concerning case-study 1

Downhill Skiing, Cairngorm Mountains, Scotland

Paul Constable

Learning objectives
- vocabulary: ski resorts, natural environment
- communication skills: advert writing, Internet site page design, public relations work
- grammatical points: figures, comparatives

---

1 COMPREHENSION EXERCISE

1.1 Comprehension

Would you agree that the text is composed of the following parts? If you disagree with any of these suggestions please note down why.

- Part 1 = (Start of text ... to ... 'that are unique within the United Kingdom'): *Characteristics of Scottish skiing areas.*
- Part 2 = (Table 1.2 + commentaries): *Snow conditions.*
- Part 3 = ('Controversy over ski development ... to ... the Royal Society for the Protection of Birds (RSPB)': *Environmental considerations create controversy.*
- Part 4 = (However, the Cairngorm Chairlift company ... to ... end of text): *More money is the answer.*

1.2 Summary

- sum up trends in visitor numbers;
- give five examples of damage caused by the presence of skiing;
- sum up the pros and cons of further investment.

153

2 VOCABULARY EXERCISE

2.1

Note, from the text, ten words or expressions linked to skiing. Divide them into groups of 3 or 4, and make up a sentence incorporating these words or expressions.

2.2

Now do the same exercise for words or expressions linked to environmental issues.

2.3

Fill in the blanks, from words in the text.

(a) The C_____ area is 9 miles east of A_____

(b) The number of tourist a_____ is influenced by the u_____ s_____ and the high winds.

(c) The environmental i_____ include e_____ damage and increased f____ f_____.

(d) The c_____ groups such as the World W_____ F___ for Nature are against plans to extend the ski a___.

(e) The r_____ d_____ p_____ wants tourism to c_____ problems of s_____ employment.

(f) Fauna and flora constitute a k__ consideration, and many s_____ are unique in the United K_____.

2.4

To help you memorize the correct pronunciation of the words you have suggested for the above blanks, check their phonetic spelling in a dictionary.

3 GRAMMAR

3.1 Figures

(a) Write out in letters the figures given in Table 1.1 and Table 1.2 for:
- Cairngorm;
- Glenshee;
- Year 1980/81;
- Year 1994/95.

(b) Is £12,724 million higher or lower than £13 million?

(c) Is £9,254 million higher or lower than £10 million?

(d) How would you say the following dates?
- 1st August 1997
- 22nd June 1995
- June 15th, 1981
- May 23rd, 2002
- 24th January 2121

3.2 Comparisons

Rewrite or repeat these sentences, using the comparative form indicated.

(a) Inferiority
- Tourism provides far more work than any other sector.
- Seasonal unemployment gives much more concern than unpredictable snowfall.

(b) Equality
- Economic benefits are larger than social ones.
- Peak visitation is easier to predict in summer than in winter.

(c) Superiority
- Piste preparation causes as much ecosystem damage as lift installation.
- Littering by visitors disturbs animals less than building ski-hire shops on the mountainside.
- Global warming will have as much effect as opposition from conservation groups.

4 COMMUNICATION SKILLS

4.1 Advert writing

Imagine that the developers mentioned in the final part of the text come to a compromise with the conservation groups, and the interests of both are taken into account. Write the text of a half-page advert to go in a skiing magazine, trying to counteract weak points, and stress positive and new ones.

4.2 Internet site page

Imagine you are part of a conservation group trying to get skiing banned on Cairngorm. Design an Internet page aimed at attracting more supporters to your cause.

4.3 Public relations

Imagine you are one of the directors of the Cairngorm Development Company. Devise a public relations exercise aimed at obtaining financial support from the European Commission for facility upgrading and site improvement.

EVALUATION

1 Definition

What do you call?

(a) the land over which you ski;
(b) something which is difficult to forecast because it is changeable;
(c) a type of bird or vegetation;
(d) the opposite of economic growth;
(e) a well-known Scottish game-bird;
(f) a remote and desolate area;
(g) the physical results of a development on the natural surroundings and life.

2 Re-use

Write the following in words

(a) 1995
(b) 12,043
(c) £9.412 million
(d) 23rd March 2002

3 Remember

(a) What does 70 per cent refer to?
(b) What two factors make this a very marginal ski area?
(c) Draw comparisons between 1987–88 and 1988–89.
(d) Give five negative impacts of skiing on the environment as quoted by conservationalists.
(e) How much subsidy has been obtained, and from whom?

ANSWERS

1.1

Part 1 = Yes
Part 2 = No
Part 3 = Yes
Part 4 = No

2.3

(a) Cairngorm, Aviemore
(b) arrivals, unpredictable snowfall
(c) impacts, ecosystem, flash flooding
(d) conservation, Wildlife Fund, area
(e) regional development policy, counteract, seasonal
(f) key, species, Kingdom

3.1

(a)
- nineteen sixty-one; twelve thousand and forty-three; six hundred and twenty
- nineteen fifty; eighteen thousand five hundred; five hundred
- one/a hundred and eighty-nine thousand; one/a hundred and twenty; one thousand five hundred and seventy-five
- two hundred and eleven thousand; one/a hundred and thirty-two; one thousand five hundred and ninety-eight.

(b) Lower.
(c) Higher.
(d)
- the first of August, nineteen ninety-seven
- the twenty second of June, nineteen ninety-five
- June the fifteenth, nineteen eighty-one
- May the twenty-third, two thousand and two
- the twenty-fourth of January, two thousand one hundred and twenty-one.

3.2

(a) Inferiority
- Tourism provides far less work than any other sector.
- Seasonal unemployment gives much less concern than unpredictable snowfall.

(b) Equality
- Economic benefits are as large as social ones.
- Peak visitation is as easy to predict in summer as in winter.

(c) Superiority
- Piste preparation causes more ecosystem damage than lift installation.
- Littering by visitors disturbs animals more than building ski-hire shops on the mountainside.
- Global warming will have more effect than opposition from conservation groups.

EVALUATION

1 (a) ski area
   (b) unpredictable
   (c) species
   (d) recession
   (e) grouse
   (f) wilderness
   (g) impact
2 (a) nineteen ninety-five
   (b) twelve thousand and forty-three
   (c) nine point four one two million pounds
   (d) the twenty-third of March two thousand and two
3 (a) The part played by tourism in the region's employment
   (b) The high winds and the unpredictable snowfall
   (c) 1987–88 had far more visitors and days skiing than 1988–89. However, 1988–89 had a higher ratio of winter visitors to days skiing.
   (d) See Table 1.3 for a complete list.
   (e) £9.4 million from the Highlands and Islands Enterprise Fund; £2.7 million from the European Commission; altogether this comes to about £12 million from public sources.

Self-help for grammar/structure points

See *Practical English Usage* Michael Swann (1995) Oxford: Oxford University Press.

- dates   part 151, pp. 141–2;
- numbers   part 385, pp. 383–9;
- comparatives   parts 135–9, pp. 118–27.

EXERCISE 2

Concerning case-study 3

Kaunas

Blanca Kraljevic

Learning objectives
- vocabulary
- comprehension
- communication skills
- grammar
- questions for discussion

---

1 VOCABULARY

Explain what the author of the case study means by the following words in the text: monopolistic state organization; transit travellers; inbound; survey; visitor profile; accommodation; feedback; reputation; resort; investment; entrepreneur; service-minded.

2 COMPREHENSION EXERCISE

(a) What are the main differences between the Lithuanian tourism of the Soviet period and nowadays?
(b) How important is the city of Kaunas for Lithuanian tourism?
(c) What can Kaunas offer tourists?
(d) Has Kaunas a tourist information office?
(e) What is the role of tourist information offices?

3 COMMUNICATION SKILLS: INTERVIEWS

(a) Describe interviews which will evaluate the impact of tourism.
(b) Evaluate the Strengths, Weaknesses, Opportunities and Threats (SWOT) of the new Lithuanian economic system.
(c) Write a report analysing the present Lithuanian situation.

4 GRAMMAR

The grammar exercises are based on reported speech. Change the following paragraph from direct to reported speech:

> Information about crossing the Lithuanian frontier has been collected since the middle of 1992. Until 1996, visitors by rail were not registered. Since 1996 information has been presented on a monthly basis, according to means of transport and citizenship, not according to country of residence, which makes it impossible to distinguish transit travellers from same-day visitors and tourists. Registration is not always very precise so statistics can at times be rather confusing.

5 QUESTIONS FOR DISCUSSION

(a) What problems concerning tourism development in Kaunas have you identified in this chapter?

(b) If you were a member of the Lithuanian Tourist Board working for the National Programme of Tourism Development, what would you recommend to improve Kaunas' tourism infrastructure?

Concerning case-study 4

Calvià, Mallorca

Blanca Kraljevic

Learning objectives
- comprehension
- communication skills
- grammar

---

1 COMPREHENSION

1.1 Vocabulary related to the environmental conservation of a beach resort

- Find in the text ten words linked to beach resorts and make up a sentence for each word.
- Find in the text words or expressions linked to sustainable tourism and make up a sentence for each word or expression.

1.2 Summary of the text

- Sum up the problems faced by Calvià.
- Sum up the actions taken by the authorities of Calvià to solve the problems.

1.3 Comprehension questions

Make note of the following in order to discuss them.

- What did you learn about the geographical location of Calvià?
- What did you learn about Calvià as a tourist destination and its influence on Mallorca's economy?

- What did you learn about Calvià's main problems?
- If you were a member of the Balearic Islands' government, which solutions to the problems of Calvià would you suggest?

2 COMMUNICATION SKILLS

2.1 Ideas for negotiating skills

Imagine that you work for an airline with a branch office on the island of Mallorca. Use your negotiating skills in a phone call:

- to a provider
- to a customer
- to your head office

2.2 Ideas for questionnaire skills

Imagine that you work in a beach resort hotel. Design a questionnaire which will evaluate your clients' level of satisfaction.

3 GRAMMAR

3.1

Look for prepositions and phrasal verbs in the text. Look at the following examples of phrasal verbs with their opposite meaning. Give at least one sentence for each verb or phrasal verb in the second column.

1.	go against	favour
2.	bring forward	put back
3.	put on	take off
4.	came on	go off
5.	put on	knock off
6.	put out	collect up
7.	go away	come back
8.	keep to	get off
9.	put up	pull down
10.	put up	take down
11.	put up	bring down
12.	keep up	fall behind
13.	take against	take to
14.	take down	put back
15.	pull ahead	fall behind
16.	take off	land

3.2

The prepositions are missing in the following text. You can find them at the end of the text. Write the numbers and next to the correct number write the missing preposition.

Calvià is a district ___(1)___ the Spanish Balearic island ___(2)___ Mallorca which includes a number ___(3)___ beach resorts including Palma Nova and Magaluf. There is a resident population ___(4)___ 23,000 but ___(5)___ peak times there are 100,000 visitors ___(6)___ a total ___(7)___ ___(8)___ 1.3 million visitors a year. There are 178 hotels ___(9)___ 46,000 beds plus another 60,000 beds ___(10)___ self-catering apartments. There are 15,000 people employed directly ___(11)___ tourism ___(12)___ 99 per cent ___(13)___ the adult population earning ___(14)___ least part ___(15)___ their income ___(16)___ it.

Many ___(17)___ the problems faced ___(18)___ Calvià are typical ___(19)___ those facing Spanish and other established Mediterranean beach resort areas. Uncontrolled development ___(20)___ the 1960s and 1970s had produced resorts where high rise hotels crowded together right ___(21)___ ___(22)___ the beach. The hotels were overdependent ___(23)___ high volume, low yield package tours ___(24)___ the British and German markets but the major tour operators dictated the prices. The accommodation stock was now ___(25)___ need ___(26)___ refurbishment but the low profit margins meant that funds to do so were not available. As a result, the resorts now had a down-market image attracting 'lager louts' whose behaviour deterred the family market. These factors combined ___(27)___ wider market factors had led ___(28)___ declining numbers and the resorts now had surplus capacity.

To counter the problems ___(29)___ a mature tourism destination, the local authorities adopted a number ___(30)___ measures. Planning controls were introduced to control the spread ___(31)___ urbanization. ___(32)___ 1988 Calvià published plans ___(33)___ a Magaluf Renewal Project which included a public esplanade ___(34)___ the beach and other improvements ___(35)___ the public environment and infrastructure. This was the first ___(36)___ a series ___(37)___ projects ___(38)___ all the resorts costing 78 million GBP ___(39)___ Calvià and 180 million GBP ___(40)___ Mallorca as a whole. Legislation was introduced banning external noise ___(41)___ bars and discotheques ___(42)___ midnight. The municipality was given powers to close substandard holiday accommodation and to give grants ___(43)___ the refurbishment or demolition ___(44)___ obsolete buildings. To boost winter visitor numbers, Calvià launched a programme ___(45)___ activities and events ___(46)___ the title ___(47)___ 'Mallorca Calvià Club'.

___(48)___ 1996 Calvià launched a new strategy to ensure a sustainable future ___(49)___ tourism ___(50)___ the banner ___(51)___ Local Agenda 21. The immediate action taken was to modify the Calvià Master Plan, suspending the current zoning ___(52)___ land ___(53)___ development ___(54)___ order to halt urbanization programmes.

Calvià's efforts to tackle the problem ___(55)___ a mature tourist resort have received considerable publicity and this has helped to improve the image ___(56)___ Mallorca as a destination. Visitor numbers ___(57)___ Mallorca have recovered, partly as a result ___(58)___ wider market trends but ___(59)___ the refurbishment the resorts would not have been able to provide the quality holiday experience which tourists ___(60)___ the beginning ___(61)___ the twenty-first century expect.

ANSWERS

1 of	11 in	21 up	31 of	41 from	51 of
2 of	12 with	22 to	32 in	42 after	52 of
3 of	13 of	23 on	33 for	43 for	53 for
4 of	14 at	24 from	34 along	44 of	54 in
5 at	15 of	25 in	35 to	45 of	55 of
6 with	16 from	26 of	36 of	46 under	56 of
7 of	17 of	27 with	37 of	47 of	57 to
8 around	18 by	28 to	38 in	48 in	58 of
9 with	19 of	29 of	39 in	49 for	59 without
10 in	20 in	30 of	40 for	50 under	60 at
					61 of

EXERCISE 4

Concerning case-study 6

Vilamoura

Kate Torkington and Cidalia Correia

Learning objectives
- reading and understanding an academic text in English
- locating specific information
- asking questions
- vocabulary: golf terms and expressions
- writing a press release/summarizing and giving emphasis to information
- conducting an interview

---

1 COMPREHENSION

1.1

Look at section 1 – The Algarve.

(a)   Where is the Algarve?
(b)   What are the main tourist products of the Algarve?

1.2

Look at section 2 – Vilamoura.

(a)   Where is Vilamoura?
(b)   What are the three main focus points of Vilamoura?
(c)   Who is responsible for developing Vilamoura?
(d)   How many beds are currently available in Vilamoura?
(e)   How many rooms in 4 or 5 star hotels are there?
(f)   What is an 'aparthotel'?
(g)   What facilities are available in the marina area for boat owners/crew?

(h) How many golf courses are there in Vilamoura, and how many are planned for the future?

(i) How many beaches are there in Vilamoura?

1.3

Look at section 3 – Vilamoura XXI

(a) What exactly is Vilamoura XXI?

(b) What does it aim to do?

1.4

The numbers below all come from section 1 of the text. What do they refer to?

(a) 3,000

(b) 600

(c) 60 per cent

(d) 45 per cent

(e) 10,390,444

(f) 2,187,265

(g) 3,553,994

2 QUESTION FORMS

2.1

Make questions (based on section 1 of the text) to elicit the numbers given in exercise 1.4. Use *how much* or *how many*.[1]

2.2

Make questions to elicit the answers given below:

(a) ....?

It's a three-hour drive.

(b) ....?

In 1971.

(c) ....?

The golf architect, Frank Pennick

(d) ....?

Yes it is – there's a regular Golf Shuttle bus service.

(e) ....?

Yes – in fact *both* of them have Blue Flags.

2.3

Sometimes, to make a question more polite, we can make it less direct by prefacing it with an expression such as:

- Could you tell me ....?
- Would you mind telling me ....?
- I was wondering ....?
- Have you any idea ....?

Notice the change:

> How many hours of sunshine does the Algarve get per year?
> *Have you any idea* how many hours of sunshine the Algarve gets per year?

When we 'preface' a question in this way, the second clause takes subject-verb word order. If the direct question is a yes/no question, when we preface it we need to add *if* or *whether*.

> *Is it* easy to get from the hotels to the golf courses?
> *I was wondering if/whether it's* easy to get from the hotels to the golf courses.

Now re-write some of the other questions from exercises 2.1 and 2.2, this time adding one of the prefaces above.

3 VOCABULARY

Golf is one of the Algarve's main tourist products. Match the golf expressions from the text with the definitions on the right.

(a)	golf course	1	number of strokes considered necessary for a first-class player to complete the course
(b)	tee	2	sandy hollow from which it is very difficult to hit the ball
(c)	green	3	area with several holes, like a miniature golf course, for practice
(d)	fairway	4	area for playing golf
(e)	par	5	hit the ball using a light stroke, usually on the green
(f)	driving range	6	part of a golf course between the tee and the green
(g)	bunker	7	flat area from which the player strikes the ball at the start of each hole
(h)	putt	8	hit the ball so that it rises steeply into the air before landing a short distance away
(i)	chip	9	a place for practising long-range hitting of the ball
(j)	putting and chipping green	10	area surrounding the hole, with grass cut very short

4 COMMUNICATION ACTIVITIES

4.1 Preparing for an interview

The situation: Lusotur has just received the Green Globe Progress Award for the Vilamoura project. You are a journalist for an English newspaper.

The task: You are going to interview the PR officer of Lusotur to find out more about the Vilamoura project. Prepare the questions you would ask.

4.2 Writing a press release

The situation: Lusotur has just received the Green Globe Progress Award for the Vilamoura project. You are the PR officer for Lusotur.

The task: You have been asked to prepare an international press release in English, describing (in summarized form) the development of the Vilamoura project, and emphasizing its recent concerns with the environment.

4.3 An interview

If you are working with other students, you could role play an interview between the journalist and the PR officer, based on the work you did for exercises 4.1 and 4.2

5 COMPLETE THE STATEMENTS BELOW

(a) Vilamoura is on the .... coast of Portugal.
(b) The first plan for the urbanization of Vilamoura was drawn up in the ....
(c) There are currently 35,000 .... available in Vilamoura.
(d) 1,000 boats can be .... in the marina.
(e) There are 3 golf .... in Vilamoura.
(f) Both of the beaches have been awarded the ....
(g) .... is responsible for the Vilamoura XXI project.
(h) The basic objective of Vilamoura XXI is to establish a .... development programme
(i) .... with nature is the main concept of the project

NOTE

1. See Michael Swann (1995) *Practical English Usage*. Oxford: Oxford University Press, part 254.4, p. 348.

ANSWERS TO THE EXERCISES

1.1

(a) In the south of Portugal
(b) Sun and sea; golf

1.2

(a) In central Algarve
(b) The marina, the beaches, golf
(c) Lusotur
(d) 35,000
(e) 1801 (Table 6.1)
(f) a self-catering complex
(g) a fuelling station, catering/provisions services, electricity/drinking water supplies, rubbish/waste oil collection, laundry, shower blocks, security service, boatyard.
(h) 3 existing courses, a further 27 holes are planned.
(i) 2

1.3

(a) It is the second development phase of Vilamoura
(b) It aims to develop existing and new tourist, residential, sports and leisure facilities in a balanced and coherent way, while respecting the environment. It aims to establish a sustainable development programme for Vilamoura.

1.4

(a) the hours of sunshine per year in the Algarve
(b) the average yearly rainfall in the Algarve in mm
(c) the share of the national gross income from tourism generated in the Algarve
(d) the Algarve's share of the national total of bednights in 1996
(e) the amount of bednights taken by international tourists in the Algarve in 1996
(f) the amount of bednights taken by domestic tourists in 1996 in the Algarve
(g) the number of passengers who used Faro airport in 1996

2.1

(a) How many hours of sun does the Algarve get per year?
(b) How much rainfall is there in the Algarve per year?
(c) How much of the national gross income from tourism is generated in the Algarve?
(d) How many of the national total of bednights were spent in the Algarve?
(e) How many bednights were taken by international tourists to the Algarve in 1996?
(f) How many bednights were taken by domestic tourists in 1996?
(g) How many passengers used Faro airport in 1996?

2.2

(a) How far is Vilamoura from Lisbon?
(b) When was the marina begun?
(c) Who designed the Old Course of Vilamoura?
(d) Is it easy to get from the hotels to the golf courses?
(e) Has either of the beaches got the European Blue Flag?

2.3 (example answers)

(a) Have you any idea how much rainfall there is in the Algarve per year?
(b) Could you tell me how much of the national gross income from tourism is generated in the Algarve?
(c) Could you tell me how far Vilamoura is from Lisbon?
(d) Would you mind telling me who designed the Old Course?
(e) I was wondering whether either of the beaches has got the Blue Flag.

3

(a) 4   (b) 7   (c) 10   (d) 6   (e) 1   (f) 9   (g) 2   (h) 5   (i) 8   (j) 3

5

(a) south   (b) 1960s   (c) beds   (d) moored   (e) courses
(f) European Blue Flag   (g) Lusotur, SA   (h) sustainable   (i) building

Concernant case-study 7

HELLO Tourism

Christine Pratley

Objectifs d'apprentissage
- l'étudiant est capable de lire et comprendre un texte en français;
- l'étudiant développe ses connaissances idiomatiques dans le domaine du tourisme;
- l'étudiant est capable d'utiliser la forme grammaticale du conditionnel;
- l'étudiant est capable d'employer correctement à l'écrit la grammaire de base;
- l'étudiant est conscient de la différence de style entre l'expression orale et écrite;
- l'étudiant est capable de rédiger un rapport en français correct;
- l'étudiant est capable de construire un rapport écrit de façon logique;
- l'étudiant est capable de faire une présentation en français correct;
- l'étudiant est capable de structurer une présentation;
- l'étudiant sait utiliser la communication verbale et non verbale.

Contenu
- expression écrite;
- entraînement au rapport écrit;
- grammaire emploi du conditionnel.

1 COMPRÉHENSION DE TEXTE

1.1

Résumez avec vos propres mots les idées principales du texte.

1.2

Répondez aux questions suivantes.

1. Quel est le sujet du texte?
2. Pour quelle raison le Plan d'Action Communautaire a-t-il développé des actions en faveur du tourisme?

3. Quelle est la structure de l'offre touristique d'un site?

4. Que signifie 'Tf(t) = 100'?

5. Quel est le but du projet 'HELLO Tourism'?

6. Le projet 'HELLO Tourism' contribue à déployer un système de management touristique. Comment veut-on atteindre ce but?

7. En quoi consiste les phases d'action du projet?

8. Quelles sont les différences entre l'île de Milos et la région de Pieria(Dion)?

9. L'achèvement du projet conduit à la production de deux CD-ROM. Qui sont les usagers de ces CD-ROM?

10. Quels sont les critères qui entrent en compte lors du choix des ressources touristiques et qui sont retenus pour élaborer le contenu des CD-ROM?

2 VOCABULAIRE

2.1

Traduisez le vocabulaire suivant dans votre langue maternelle.

acquise	l'hébergement
aigüe	insulaire
la campagne	intégral
les Communautés Européennes	multidimensionnel
la croissance	l'offre touristique
le débarquement	les ordures
décongestionner	l'originalité
l'éclairage	le patrimoine
engendrer	les pays riverains
l'environnement	les ressources touristiques
l'équilibre	le site
la faisabilité	sonore
le flux de visiteurs	les zones littorales
gérer	les zones urbaines

2.2

Choisissez dix expressions dans la liste proposée ci-dessus et faites dix phrases ayant rapport au thème du tourisme. Par exemple: Les touristes aiment *la campagne* pour sa beauté et son charme mais ils provoquent parfois des problèmes.

2.3

Donnez le contraire des expressions suivantes.

simple	encourager
intrinsèque	protéger
la croissance	l'équilibre
diverger	positif
améliorer	la demande

3 GRAMMAIRE

3.1

Dans les phrases suivantes mettez les verbes entre parenthèses au conditionnel.

1. Si les flux de touristes étaient bien contrôlés, les sites touristiques .... (être) plus facile à entretenir.
2. Si les touristes visitaient les sites en hors saison, les sites n'.............. (avoir) pas de problèmes de saturation.
3. Si le projet HELLO Tourism réussissait, les autres pays méditerranéens .... (pouvoir) utiliser ce projet pour leurs destinations touristiques d'accueil.
4. Si un touriste avait conscience des conséquences du tourisme sur l'environnement d'un site, il .... (choisir) sa destination de vacances avec plus de soin.
5. .... (accepter)-vous de participer au projet?
6. Selon les responsables du projet depuis la mise en place de celui-ci l'attitude des touristes .... (avoir) changé.
7. Je .... (vouloir) vous poser quelques questions en ce qui concerne l'influence du tourisme dans votre pays.
8. Vous .... (faire) bien d'informer rapidement les touristes sur les sites non saturés.
9. S'il y a eu un incendie de forêt en Grèce, un groupe de touristes .... (être) blessé.
10. .... (aller)-tu en Grèce si tu savais que les sites touristiques étaient saturés en été?

4 LA COMMUNICATION ÉCRITE

Le cas de management touristique présente le projet HELLO Tourism qui est basé sur la situation de l'île de Milos et la région Pieria en Grèce. Ces sites ont les mêmes conditions de l'offre touristique mais la croissance touristique diverge. 'Celle de l'île de Milos est en voie de développement alors que celle du site de Dion/Pieria est considérée comme déjà acquise, mais caractérisée par une saisonalité aigüe, en juillet et août.' Le projet a pour but de contrôler le flux touristique et de mieux gérer les questions concernant la protection des ressources culturelles et naturelles des sites.

4.1 Cas d'application pour l'expression écrite

Vous êtes étudiant dans une école supérieure de tourisme. Vous devez proposer un projet pour améliorer un aspect du tourisme dans votre propre pays. Inspirez-vous de l'exemple ci-dessus et rédigez un rapport écrit d'environ 1000 mots concernant un projet de management touristique pour une région de votre propre pays.

Ce rapport sera remis à la commission responsable du développement du tourisme en Europe. Cette commission siège à Bruxelles et accorde des subventions pour la réalisation des projets en ce qui concerne le tourisme.

Structure

1. *Introduction*
- Présentez le sujet du rapport.
- Énoncez le problème.
- La longueur de l'introduction dépend de la longueur du rapport.

2. *Développement*
- Définissez le problème.
- Structurez logiquement les différents sujets que vous allez traiter à l'aide de paragraphes et d'alinéas.
- Utiliser les articulateurs pour lier les différentes parties entre elles.

3. *Conclusion*
- Résumez les points importants.
- Donnez les conclusions.
- Donnez les recommandations.

Contenu

Le rapport devra répondre aux questions suivantes:

- Quel est le problème relevant du management touristique?
- Quel est le but du projet?
- Quel est le contenu du projet et pourquoi est-il intéressant?
- Quelles sont les possibilités qu'offre ce projet dans l'avenir? Et que signifie ce projet pour le management touristique?

Sélectionnez les informations et les idées pertinentes en ce qui concerne votre sujet. Posez-vous les questions suivantes:

- Qu'est-ce que je sais sur le tourisme?
- À qui s'adresse mon rapport?
- Quelles sont les informations importantes que je souhaite communiquer dans mon rapport?
- Comment puis-je convaincre mes lecteurs?

Rassemblez vos idées et ordonnez-les de façon logique. Vous pouvez utiliser le modèle suivant basé sur R. WHITE et D. McGOVERN (1994) *Writing English for Academic Study Series*. Prentice-Hall, Hemel Hempstead, pp. 50–1.

Problème	Identifiez le problème à traiter
Situation	Quels sont les problèmes en ce qui concerne le tourisme dans votre pays?
	Quelles sont les caractéristiques de ces problèmes?
	Quelles sont les causes de ces problèmes?
Solution	De quelle manière le problème peut-il être résolu?
	Y a-t-il des solutions alternatives?
	Étudier les avantages et les inconvénients des solutions.
	Quels sont les obstacles possibles aux solutions proposées?
Évaluation	Faites un choix de solutions valables
	Évaluer les résultats

Puis faites lire le rapport à d'autres personnes pour obtenir de nouvelles idées. Enfin, apportez les dernières corrections au rapport.

Faites attention – employez correctement.

- les temps et les conjugaisons des verbes;
- les pronoms personnels;
- accord de l'adjectif avec le nom;
- construction de la phrase (sujet + verbe + complément);
- les articles;
- faites des phrases courtes et claires;
- utilisez la forme impersonnelle, 'il' à la place du 'je'.

5 TEST

5.1

Le test est constitué de questions fermées: Vrai/Faux. L'étudiant doit reconnaître si les mots soulignés sont correctement employés dans les phrases suivantes.

1. Le patrimoine culturel est important pour l'histoire d'un pays.
   Vrai/Faux

2. Le flux de touristes augmente. On constate une certaine croissance.
   Vrai/Faux

3. Les touristes gèrent les revenus du pays où ils passent leurs vacances.
   Vrai/Faux

4. La circulation est décongestionée lorsqu'il y a de nouveaux bouchons.
   Vrai/Faux

5. Les zones urbaines se trouvent à la campagne.
   Vrai/Faux

6. Les zones littorales se trouvent au bord de la mer.
   Vrai/Faux

7. Produire des ordures ménagères est bénéfique pour la sauvegarde du paysage.
   Vrai/Faux

8. La France est un pays insulaire.
   Vrai/Faux

5.2

L'étudiant doit reconnaître si le conditionnel est employé correctement dans les phrases suivantes.

1. Prendriez-vous le train pour aller en vacances s'il était moins cher?
   Vrai/Faux

2. Pourrais-tu m'indiquer où se trouve le site touristique dont tu m'as parlé?
   Vrai/Faux

3. S'il pleuvrait tu prendras tes vacances en Grèce.
   Vrai/Faux

4. S'il réserve son hôtel à l'avance il aurait de la place.
   Vrai/Faux

5. D'après la presse les feux de fôrets auraient cessé.
   Vrai/Faux

6 ÉVALUATION

A la fin du module de français les étudiants peuvent écrire une évaluation dans leur langue maternelle sur ce qu'ils ont appris au niveau de la langue française pendant ce module. L'étudiant pourra inscrire entre *3 et 5 points positifs* dans le domaine des progrès effectués et *3 à 5 points négatifs* en ce qui concerne les points faibles qui doivent être encore améliorés. Ces remarques pourront être utilisées lors d'un prochain module de français langue étrangère.

EXERCISE 6

Concerning case-study 5

Faro – A tourist town?

Kate Torkington

Learning objectives:

- reading and understanding an extensive academic text in English
- taking notes, identifying key points and ideas and summarizing information
- using numbers and figures: saying numbers aloud
- re-writing given information
- grammar: using passive forms to report information and to give opinions
- vocabulary: possible venues for cultural/leisure activities and events
- writing a report

NB As no explanatory grammatical notes are given, references are made where relevant to Swann, M. (1995) *Practical English Usage* (2nd edn) Oxford: Oxford University Press.

---

1 READING

Read the case study carefully. Make notes on the following:

1.1

(a) What do you learn about the geographical location of Faro?
(b) In terms of access (both internal and external), what seem to be the major strengths and weaknesses?
(c) What do you learn about the town centre? (Think about its layout, history, architecture and so on.)
(d) What do you learn about the accommodation available in Faro?

177

(e)   What do you think are the main tourist attractions of Faro?

1.2

If you were responsible for the marketing of Faro as an urban tourism destination, which key aspects of the town would you choose for your promotional campaign?

1.3

What seem to be the main weaknesses of Faro in terms of urban tourism? How could these weaknesses be remedied?

2 NUMBERS[1]

2.1

Say these numbers and figures aloud (the section of the text where you can find them is given in brackets):

34,094	(1.3)
39.3%	(1.3)
72.4%	(1.3)
3,533,994	(1.4.4)
1755	(2)
3,737,058	(3.1)
1.9%	(3.1)
8,000	(3.1.2)

2.2

What do the numbers above refer to? Complete the sentences below, by using and re-writing information from the text:

(a)   34,094 people ....
(b)   39.3% of ....
(c)   72.4% ....
(d)   3,533,994 ....
(e)   In 1755 ....
(f)   Between 1992 and 1996 ....
(g)   Only 1.9 per cent ....
(h)   Around 8,000 ....

3 GRAMMAR – THE PASSIVE VOICE[2]

The text gives many examples of things that *have been done*, things *that are being done*, and things which *will (or may) be done* to improve access to, from and within Faro.

3.1 Access

Using the *present perfect passive*.[3]

What *has been done* recently to improve access?
E.g. New bus routes *have been introduced*.

Now find more examples from the text:

....
....
....
....

3.2 Access

Using the *present progressive passive*.[4]

What *is* currently *being done* to improve access?
E.g. Road access *is being improved*.

Find more examples:

....
....
....
....

3.3 Access

Using the *future passive*, to express *certainty* (will) and *possibility* (may).

What *will/may be done* in the future to improve access?
E.g. The railway line from Faro to Lisbon *will be electrified*.

Find more examples.

....
....
....
....

3.4 Access

What else, in your opinion, *needs doing (needs to be done)*[5] to *improve access*?

What *could be done*[6], or *should be done*[7]?

Give examples:

....

....

....

....

3.5 Conservation and rehabilitation

Now repeat exercises 3.1–3.4, this time thinking about *the conservation and rehabilitation of the town's environmental and cultural heritage*.

4 VOCABULARY

Urban tourism normally involves cultural and leisure activities. For each of the activities below, suggest a venue. (You may find it helpful to look back at Tables 5.6, 5.7 and 5.8 in the case study.)

Activity	Venue
Going to see a film	Cinema
Going to watch a play	i)
Going to a concert	ii)
Going to see an exhibition of paintings by local artists	iii)
Borrowing books on local history	iv)
Watching a football match	v)
Looking at exhibits of local archaeological findings	vi)
Gambling	vii)
Dancing	viii)
Playing squash	ix)

5 COMMUNICATION ACTIVITY

5.1 The situation and the task

- You work for a small British Tour Operator which specialises in tailor-made holidays in southern Europe away from the busy sun and beach resorts. Until now, the holidays offered by your company in the Algarve have been based on rural tourism. Your boss is interested in expanding this to include urban tourism. You have spent a lot of time in the Algarve, and know Faro well.

- Prepare a preliminary report on the suitability of Faro as an urban tourism destination.

6 FINAL ACTIVITY

- Try to do this activity without looking back at the text.
- Fill in each gap with *one* or *two* words.

Faro, the ___(1)___ of the Algarve, lies on the ___(2)___ coast of Portugal. It enjoys a ___(3)___, moderate climate with low ___(4)___. The number of permanent ___(5)___ of the municipality of Faro is around 50,000, although there is also a significant ___(6)___ population connected to tourism and leisure. Most employment in the town is offered by the ___(7)___.

The centre of Faro has a great deal of history – in Roman times it was ___(8)___ as Ossónoba and it was also ___(9)___ by the Moors. Most of the ___(10)___ buildings which can still be seen nowadays in the old walled town were built during the seventeenth and eighteenth centuries. Much of the historical ___(11)___ is currently being restored.

Faro has a busy airport which handles around 3.5 million ___(12)___ per year, most of whom are foreign tourists arriving on ___(13)___. However, a survey ___(14)___ in the departure lounge of the airport in 1995 found that only about 2 per cent of those asked had ___(15)___ in Faro. This is perhaps not surprising when one considers the accommodation available – or rather, the lack of it. Faro's ___(16)___ in the total offer of accommodation in the Algarve in 1990 was only 2.1 per cent.

Indeed, although Faro has several ___(17)___ advantages, such as its southern ___(18)___, good ___(19)___ provided by the international airport and a good ___(20)___ by European standards, it seems that Faro has some way to go before it can consider itself an urban tourism destination.

NOTES

1. See Swann (1995) entry 385, particularly sections 1 and 9.
2. See Swann (1995) entries 407, 408, 409 for general help with the passive voice.
3. See Swann (1995) entries 415.3, 418, 419, 420 for help with using the present perfect tense.
4. See Swann (1995) entry 445 for help with using the present progressive tense.
5. See Swann (1995) sections 293.3 and 357.4.
6. See Swann (1995) section 124.5 for interpersonal use of *could* for making a suggestion.
7. See Swann (1995) sections 495.2 and 496 for use of *should* for expressing obligation/advice.

KEY/SUGGESTED ANSWERS

1.1

(a) In the Algarve – a region in the south of Portugal (capital of this region). On the Atlantic coast, but separated from the sea by the Ria Formosa – a Natural Park (protected area) whose main features are salt-water lagoons, sandbank islands.

(b) Strengths: Access by air – there is a busy international airport. Road access – improving. (Note the Infante D. Henrique motorway – see Table 5.4).

Weaknesses: State railway: slow, out-dated, under-funded. Roads (within the town): congested. Buses: inefficient and insufficient services. Access by sea: extremely limited.

(c) The town centre is divided into three main areas: the *Vila-a-Dentro* (old walled town), the *Ribeira* (waterfront) and the *Baixa* (commercial centre). Town already important in Roman times. Occupied by the Moors. Many historical buildings – mostly from sixteenth, seventeenth and eighteenth centuries; some have been rehabilitated, others are being renovated. Also much modern development – recent proliferation of high-rise buildings.

(d) For example, accommodation insufficient; lack of cultural/leisure facilities; poor road and rail access.

(e) For example: southern location, also central location (in terms of the Algarve); good climate; historical/cultural/built heritage; international airport; proximity to beaches, natural park; good night-life.

2.1

- Thirty-four thousand and ninety-four
- Thirty-nine point three per cent
- Seventy-two point four per cent
- Three million, five hundred and thirty-three thousand, nine hundred and ninety-four
- Seventeen fifty-five
- Three million, seven hundred and thirty-seven thousand and fifty-eight
- One point nine per cent
- Eight thousand

2.2

Suggested answers (others may be possible).

(a) 34,094 people [were living] in Faro in 1991.
              [lived]

(b)   39.3 per cent of the total population of the Algarve live in the municipalities of Faro, Loulé and Olhão.

(c)   72.4 per cent of the total employed population of Faro work in the [service industries]
[tertiary sector].

(d)   3,533,994 passengers passed through Faro International Airport in 1996.

(e)   In 1755
[an earthquake damaged or destroyed many of Faro's buildings]
[many of Faro's buildings were damaged or destroyed by an earthquake].

(f)   Between 1992 and 1996, 3,737,058 people visited the Tourist Information Office in Faro.

(g)   Only 1.9 per cent of the total bednights in the Algarve in 1995 were spent in Faro.

(h)   Around 8,000 students live in Faro, making the nightlife lively and plentiful.

3.1 Access

The bus fleet has been renewed.
A new link road to the airport has been built.
The main Faro–Olhão road has been improved.
Work has been started to extend the airport terminal.

3.2 Access

The airport terminal is being extended.
The development of a railway link from Faro to the airport is being studied.

3.3 Access

The east–west Algarvian railway line will be generally improved.
Faro railway station will be modernised.
The number of check-in desks at the airport will be increased.
An underground railway station may be built at the airport.

3.4 Access

(Many answers possible.)

3.5 Conservation and rehabilitation

3.1 Two former military buildings have been turned into art galleries.
The former seventeenth-century San Francisco monastery has been transformed into a Hospitality & Tourism school.

3.2 The Waterfront Urban Park is being created.
The existing historical heritage is gradually being restored and promoted.

3.3 The old walled town may be totally restored soon.
Two new museums will be opened.

3.4 (Many answers possible.)

4

i)   Theatre
ii)   Theatre, concert hall, night club, stadium
iii)   Art gallery, exhibition centre, museum
iv)   Library
v)   Football stadium, sports ground
vi)   Museum
vii)   Casino
viii)   Night-club, disco
ix)   Sports pavilion (squash court)

6

1. capital
2. south
3. mild
4. rainfall
5. inhabitants/residents
6. floating
7. service industries/tertiary sector
8. known
9. occupied
10. noteworthy/important
11. heritage
12. passengers
13. charter flights
14. carried out/conducted
15. stayed overnight
16. share
17. competitive
18. location
19. access
20. climate

Concerning case-study 10

Nordseeheilbad Westerland, Sylt

Irmela Neu

Lernziele
- Textverständnis
- Kommunikative Kompetenz
- Grammatik

---

1 TEXTVERSTÄNDNIS

1.1 Vokabelteil

1.1.1 Erklären Sie die Bedeutung folgender Begriffe und Fachtermini im Text der Fallstudie:

- Thema: Warum die Touristen in das Nordseeheilbad Westerland fahren

die Nordseeinsel, der Autozug, die Schiffs- und Flugverbindungen, das Seebad, die Kureinrichtungen, der Kurortcharakter

- Thema: Was sie im Nordseebad erwartet

der Badegast, die Sporteinrichtung, die Gesundheitsanwendung, die „Sylter Welle", das Seeheilbad, die Meerwasser-Trinkkuren, die Tageskarte, die Kurabgabe, die Gästezahl, die durchschnittliche Urlaubsdauer, die Gäste- und Übernachtungszahlen, die Beherbergungskategorie, der Wochenend- und Kurzaufenthalt, die Markteintrittsbarrieren, der Ferienaufenthalt, das Einkommen, die Herkunft der Gäste, die Altersstruktur der Gäste, die Befragung der Gäste/die Gästebefragung, die Gästefrequenz, der Wiederholungsbesucher

- Thema: Was untersucht wird

die Marketingmaßnahme, das Gästeverhalten, das Reiseverhalten, das Urlaubsverhalten, das Urlaubs-Ausgabeverhalten, die Gästegruppen

1.1.2 Sortieren Sie das Vokabular

– nach der Wortzusammensetzung, z.B. Wörter, die zwei Substantive enthalten wie „Gästeverhalten".
– nach übergeordneten Aspekten, z.B.: Transportwege: Zug, Autozug, Schiff, Flugzeug, Flugverbindungen etc.

1.1.3 Bilden Sie Sätze mit eigenen Worten, indem Sie die Begriffe und die Information des Textes verwenden.

1.2 Zusammenfassung des Textes

1.2.1 Finden Sie Zwischenüberschriften zu den einzelnen Abschnitten des Textes

1.2.2 Fassen Sie zusammen, was das Nordseeheilbad Westerland bietet

1.2.3 Fassen Sie zusammen, wie sich der Tourismus nach Westerland entwickelt hat

1.3 Fragen zum Textverständnis

- Welches sind die geographischen Merkmale des Nordseeheilbades Westerland/ Sylt?
- Womit ist das Seebad ausgestattet?
- Welche touristische Entwicklung läßt sich feststellen?
- Was hat die Gästebefragung des Jahres 1996 ergeben?
- Welche Marketingmaßnahmen ergeben sich daraus?

2 KOMMUNIKATIVE KOMPETENZ

2.1 Vorschläge für mündliche Kommunikation

- Sie möchten gerne als Gast eine Kur im Nordseeheilbad machen und informieren sich durch ein Telephongespräch über das Angebot für Sie und Ihre Familie.
- Sie sind von der Stadtverwaltung Westerland und möchten gerne einige Zahlen über die touristische Entwicklung erhalten.
- Sie sind Reporter und wollen einen Bericht über Westerland machen. Sie rufen deshalb bei der Presseabteilung an und stellen einige Fragen.

2.2 Vorschläge für Diskussionsrunden

- Stellen Sie sich vor, Sie sollten einen Marketingplan ausarbeiten und diesen der Stadtverwaltung von Westerland vorstellen: wie sieht Ihr Marketingplan aus?
- Entwerfen Sie eine Werbebroschüre für das Nordseeheilbad Westerland und präsentieren Sie die Broschüre vor einem interessierten Publikum.
- Stellen Sie sich vor, daß Sie eine Pressekonferenz über die touristische Entwicklung des Nordseeheilbads Westerland machen. Arbeiten Sie Fragen und mögliche Antworten aus, die Sie mündlich vortragen.

3 GRAMMATIK

3.1 Verben, Substantive und Präpositionen

Lesen Sie den Text noch einmal durch und finden Sie die Sätze, in denen die Verben, Substantive und Präpositionen der nachfolgenden Übungen vorkommen. Die Sätze entsprechen nicht immer ganz genau den Formulierungen des Textes.

3.1.1 Bilden Sie Sätze mit folgenden Verben:

gehören, von Bedeutung sein, einen/den Ruf genießen, als etw. gelten, Sport treiben, verzeichnen, zugute kommen, aufweisen, nutzen, entsprechen, möglich sein, kosten, abhängen, besuchen, seine Stellung behaupten, sich ausdrücken, verändern, Angaben machen, sich verschärfen, eine Rolle spielen, zufrieden sein, schwierig sein, der Grund sein, möglich sein, für angemessen halten, durchführen, ausführen, über etw. verfügen, sich handeln um, mit etw.versehen sein, beurteilen.

3.1.2 Bilden Sie folgende Substantive zu den Verben und umgekehrt:

befragen	die Person	(1)...
	die Sache	(2)...
besuchen	die Person	(3)...
	die Sache	(4)...
verwalten	....	(5)...
betrachten	die Person	(6)...
	die Sache	(7)...
bewegen	....	(8)...
baden	die Person	(9)...
	die Sache	(10)...
übernachten	....	(11)...

die Reise   (12)...

die Anwendung   (13)...

die Einrichtung   (14)...

die Veränderung   (15)...

der Einkauf   (16)...

der Betrag   (17)...

die Frage   (18)...

die Durchführung   (19)...

die Verfügung   (20)...

3.1.3 Bilden Sie das Gegenteil von folgenden Adjektiven, Verben und Substantiven:

möglich   (21)...

wahrscheinlich   (22)...

stark   (23)...

niedrig   (24)...

fallen   (25)...

abnehmen   (26)...

die Bewegung   (27)...

die Gesundheit   (28)...

die Aktivität   (29)...

zu Hause bleiben   (30)...

3.1.4 Ergänzen Sie folgende Präpositionen:

Sylt ist eine deutsche Nordseeinsel, die ___(1)___ sogenannten Nordfriesischen Inselgruppe gehört. Die Lufttemperatur ist ___(2)___ das gesundheitliche Wohlbefinden von besonderer Bedeutung. Mitte der sechziger Jahre wurde ___(3)___ Strandparties berichtet. Die Schönheit der Lage ist ___(4)___ Beginn dieses Jahrhunderts von zahlreichen Schriftstellern und anderen Künstlern immer wieder gerühmt worden. Insbesondere ___(5)___ den Hauptstraßen Westerlands haben nahezu alle Hersteller von Nobelmarken ihre Boutiquen. Es hat als Seebad eine lange Tradition und galt sehr schnell ___(6)___ eleganter Badeort. Heute verfügt Westerland ___(7)___ einen Strand von 7 km Länge. Damit der Kurbetrieb unabhängig ___(8)___ Witterung und Jahreszeit wird, wurde ___(9)___ Jahre 1964 ein Meerwasser-Wellenbad eingerichtet. Inzwischen gibt es zahlreiche Möglichkeiten des Wassersports ___(10)___ verschiedenen Gesundheitsanwendungen. Die Angebotspalette reicht ___(11)___ Wassersport ___(12)___ Liegekuren bis zur Atemgymnastik. Besucher Westerlands sind ___(13)___ Kurabgabe verpflichtet. Westerland verfügt ___(14)___ 30 Hotels aller Kategorien ___(15)___ 3.707 Betten. Die Gästezahlen

Westerlands konnten ___(16)___ 1996 bis 1997 einen Zuwachs___(17)___. 7,7 % verzeichnen. Hinsichtlich des Anteils der Gäste- und Übernachtungszahlen ___(18)___ Beherbergungskategorien zeigt sich ein deutlicher Schwerpunkt ___(19)___ den Ferienappartments und Privatvermietern ___(20)___ einem Gesamtanteil ___(21)___ allen Betten von 77,5 %.

Lösungen

3.1.2:

1. der, die Befragte
2. die Befragung
3. der Besucher, die Besucherin
4. der Besuch
5. die Verwaltung

6. der Betrachter, die Betrachterin
7. die Betrachtung
8. die Bewegung
9. der, die Badende
10. das Bad
11. die Übernachtung

12. reisen
13. anwenden
14. einrichten
15. verändern

16. einkaufen
17. betragen
18. fragen
19. durchführen
20. verfügen

3.1.3:

21. unmöglich
22. unwahrscheinlich
23. schwach
24. hoch
25. steigen

26. zunehmen
27. der Stillstand
28. die Krankheit
29. die Passivität
30. verreisen, weggehen, ausgehen

3.1.4:

1. zur	6. als	11. vom	16. von	21. an
2. für	7. über	12. über	17. um	
3. über	8. von	13. zur	18. nach	
4. zu	9. im	14. über	19. bei	
5. in	10. mit	15. mit	20. mit	

Index

Note: to avoid repetition, while the word tourism/tourist is implied in most of the entries, it is not stated: e.g. capacity limits = tourist capacity; community participation = community participation in tourism.

Only the English language case studies are included. For topics in the French and German versions, refer to the index entries for the parallel English texts.